The Occult Conceit

The Occult Conceit

a new look at astrology, witchcraft & sorcery

Owen S. Rachleff

BELL PUBLISHING COMPANY
NEW YORK

Dedicated to the memory
of my mother

Contents

	Viewing with Alarm	ix
1.	Signs of the Times: Astrology	1
2.	Other "-Ologies" and Delusions: Numerology, Palmistry, Phrenology, Physiognomy, Tarotology, and Omens	41
3.	Magic: Black, White, and Otherwise	69
4.	"Once There Was a Wicked Witch . . ."	97
5.	Above and Beyond: Spiritualism, Precognition, and ESP	123
6.	The High Cost of Humbug	165
7.	A Debunker's Miscellany: From Apparitions to Zombis	177
8.	True Magic: An Epilogue	219
	Bibliography	225
	Index	229

Viewing with Alarm

This is a frankly biased book, as are most books on the occult, with one essential difference—the lion's share of the others are naively enthusiastic and often religiously dedicated to the notions of astrology, witchcraft, and other popular occultic delusions. Not so here. By depending on common sense, and logic, this book denies and then debunks the usual allegations of the occult, both of the past and in the present.

The current craze for the occult suggests, it seems to me, a clear and present danger. This danger is becoming increasingly evident in the widespread proclivity of many immature persons (young and old alike) to govern their lives by the archaic principles of witchcraft and magic, or to conduct their personal affairs and business on the unfounded bases of astrology, numerology, and the Tarot cards.

Further, today there are negativist cults gathering at the feet of so-called prophets, seers, wonder workers, and other sensational types whose credentials are no more valid than the tricks

ix

they employ or the narcotic stimulation they utilize. This current fascination with the occult is happening against a background of continuous social unrest and alienation.

Occultic dependency encompasses another social factor as pernicious as the dependency itself, and that is the violent backlash that it may engender. History has often shown that when witches declare themselves, witchhunters soon arise. Both are equally victims of delusion.

But do these trends, dependencies and backlashes represent a clear and present danger—or any danger at all? Very often those who view such things with alarm are taken to be merely alarmists. What danger can there be in a harmless scan of one's daily horoscope or in a cutting of the Tarot cards? Are the approximately 400 witch covens in the United States malicious and incipient movements of a potentially parapolitical nature, or are they merely a form of useful group therapy interwoven with a little free love and flagellation? Why should anyone view with alarm the thought of communicating with the dead, forecasting the future, or seeking the aid and guidance of psychic seers?

Briefly, the danger lies in ignorance, and the hazard is manifested in the influence of that ignorance on a turbulent society. The harm is propagated further in the impediments that may develop on the road of scientific progress if, in fact, a whole generation, nourished on superstitious fallacy, can grow to maturity despising science and denying its need of advancement. The danger is likewise in mental attitudes that abandon a reasoned philosophy of life in favor of a set of astrologic marching orders that seem to offer all the answers—past, present, and future. There is political and social jeopardy as well in the establishment of the occult as a central force in a so-called counter-culture. Founded on fear, superstition, eccentricity, and irrational evidence, such a force owes no fidelity to the rational laws, morals, or ambitions of traditional society.

Rooted in the superstition that man can achieve godhood by magic, such philosophies are inherently the seedbed of tyrants. And where the endemic fascination for mischief is embraced as a way of life, such a force may, at its worst, promote another barbaric scourge such as that of the Nazi cult; or it may fracture into coteries, communes, or one-man crusades to rid the world of "evil" by the "righteous" grace of homicide.

The craze for altered states of consciousness, the emphasis on intense eroticism and anti-social behavior, and the secrecy and elitism characteristic of occultists throughout recorded time could also become a vibrant and attractive ideology for the disaffected; a potentially unifying force among disjointed and alienated segments of society; the positive philosophy of the negative ambition; the religion of the revolutionary; the creative aspect of anarchical plunder.

To be sure, those who accept astrology as religion, who view witchcraft as a beautiful, meaningful human experience, who devour the prophecies, the nostrums, and the magic of the modern seer may not regard themselves as irrational, immoral, or destructive members of society, and, indeed, in most cases they are not. But in the crunch of facing up to the agonizing choices that a cultural breakdown so often demands, could those who merely consider themselves dabblers truly resist the blandishments of occult persuasion? If forced to choose between Establishment science (cold, inhuman, insensitive) and the benevolence of magic, in which they've always cherished a yearning belief, could such people detach themselves from slavish adherence to a cult leader, a master who promises what they've always revered: love, beauty, and transcendental power through witchcraft, magic, and sorcery? And if this witchcraft, magic, and sorcery eventually entailed regression, sacrilege, self-abuse, perversion and, above all, ritual plunder and homicide, could the susceptible individual cut himself loose from the new crusade once it had started, or would it be too late?

The Occultniks

Early in 1970 a young man boarded an airliner bound for Boston, and in the course of his attempt to hijack the plane, he killed one pilot and seriously wounded another. This man was no Cuban exile or political extremist. He was simply a spook-ridden individual intoxicated by the occult and drawn into his murderous adventure by the influence, he said, of the moon and the stars on human destiny.

Known as "the Professor," the young man had for years amused and fascinated his friends and neighbors with his eccentric appearance (top-hat, cape, and silver-headed cane) and by his apparently innocuous astrological mumbo jumbo and prophecies.

Sirhan Sirhan, the assassin of Robert F. Kennedy, was similarly deep into theosophy and a member of the mystic Rosicrucian cult of San Jose, California. (When taken to prison, he insisted that the few dollars found on his person should be forwarded to the Rosicrucians for payment of his dues.) Neither theosophy nor Rosicrucianism can be held directly responsible for Sirhan's heinous crime, but, even so, the peculiar motivation of occult philosophy, the adverse influence of quasi-mystical ideologies on eccentric individuals is of formidable significance.

The examples of these influences are many: witchery and Satanism in the Manson cult; Tarot card imagery used as a signature of a murderer who said his cause was to free the world of materialism and pollution; the antics of WITCH (Women's International Terrorists Corps for Hell). These factions and others like them are the extreme, the glaring cases, but they are symptomatic of a growing tendency of individuals to become what may be called occultists, or, in the modern idiom, *occultniks*. Occultniks are those who, in one form or another, are "hung up on" or "into" the notions of the occult or who favor an occultic view of the world and of moral motivation. This characterization includes the extreme examples just cited, but it also involves the coven witches of New York, Los Angeles, Boston, and Detroit; the precogs and seers seen on television talk shows; the myriad astrologers, from the pseudo-scientific types to the countless "readers and advisors"; the members of the Satanist Church of San Francisco and the Spiritualist Church of New York; the psychics and the psychic investigators; those who buy and sell amulets, charms, and Tarot cards for divination; buyers and sellers of horoscopes, hand charts, crystal balls, and phrenology guides; those who attend seances and those who see ghosts; those who venerate ESP and magnify parapsychology; the discarnates, the reincarnates, and others. Today there are millions of them—occultniks all—practitioners and followers. They will not tell you: "I *believe,*" or "I have faith" in the veracity of astrology, witchcraft, magic, or any other aspect of the occult. Instead they emphatically state: "I *know* it works; it is a fact, a provable, repeatable truth for now and all times. It has always been true. Science is error. Mystery is reality. *We* have the great enlightenment; *we* have proof. Simply because there are no explanations doesn't mean that occultism is not true. To be sure, the very fact that there are no explanations is the surest sign of truth. Only science seeks explanation, in its usual bungling, destructive fashion. Occultism is beyond explanation, beyond discovery: this is its definition, its truth, its appeal!"

"It would be a bold man who would attempt to find a blanket explanation for all apparitions and all physical phenomena of a paranormal nature," says British occultist Douglas Hunt in *Innerspace Magazine* (November, 1970). Does he mean that such attempts are not to be dared? Parapsychologists often work under the principle that no explanation is the real explanation, that proof consists of random incidents and anecdotes drawn together by their inexplicable elements, all the more valid because they do not yield to natural analysis. Science is scorned because it seeks the matrix, the core and mechanism of the evidence. On the other hand, if a scientist cannot at first find the answer, he does not eagerly relegate the problem to the sacrosanct regions of the occult (beyond all human understanding); he labels the phenomenon temporarily unsolved, but he assiduously continues to probe the possibilities.

The occultist/occultnik piles anecdote upon incident, stamps them all "unexplained," which for him is explanation enough, and offers them as evidence of his philosophy. Such evidence forms the overwhelming bulk of most essays, treatises, and books concerning the occult experience. Hardly one in ten of these "proofs" can be trusted for veracity. By and large they are hearsay stories or unwitnessed subjective testimony, unrelated in any way to the practices of controlled testing or the principles of judicial evidence.

A typical story from the past—still offered as proof—concerns the Greek dramatist Aeschylus. Warned by a soothsayer that he would die in a certain month as a result of something falling on his head, the poet cautiously went alone to the wheat fields of Sicily to wait out the ill-fated period and thus, he hoped, to escape his fate. Alas, one day while dozing under the open sky, Aeschylus was struck on the skull by a turtle that had fallen from the beak of a bird. The bird, wishing to dine on its prey, had dropped the turtle on what it thought to be a stone but what, in fact, was Aeschylus' bald pate! The great Greek poet thus died as was predicted.

Despite the apocryphal nature of this cunning tale, one nagging question persists: if Aeschylus was alone in the wheat field when he was struck by the falling turtle, how do we know so many details? How can we regard this story as proof of anything, whether it seeks to prove the ineluctable course of fate or the precision of precognition? And though it is an absurd story, its structure is nonetheless identical to the structure of the stories recounted by modern occultniks concerning premonitionary visions, apparitions, poltergeists, and the validity of precognition and astrologic prophecy. Because such "evidence" is so highly suspect and apocryphal, this analysis will not even try to deal with each and every "proof" that is offered by the experts on occult. Rather, it will concentrate on the key principles of the various delusions, the occultic systems, and their inherent fallacies and contradictions, for if a system is fundamentally false, if it is based on misconceptions and errors, all its essential parts must likewise be false. Should there be a few cases, or even several, where there appears to be resounding proof or conclusive fact associated with the basic error, these instances must be regarded not as proof, but as coincidence, potentially yielding to scientific explanation. If a man is given the wrong instructions about finding a certain address and yet, by some luck or chance, he comes upon that address, this does not mean that everyone seeking that same address should resort to the same faulty instructions.

The Specific Fallacies

The basic error of the popular pastime of astrology is revealed in the definition that astrologists themselves have concocted. For if as they say, astrology is a system in which celestial bodies influence human affairs, one may logically ask why this influence radiates only from twelve constellations, eight planets (Earth is not influential in this schema), the sun and the moon, but *not* from the billions of other celestial bodies, known and unknown, in our galaxy.

In fact, astrology adheres to the twelve constellations and the other known bodies of the solar system (but not even all of *them*) simply because the ancients, in their limited view of the universe, utilized these factors. As a result, modern astrologers and their clients are restricted to a primitive cosmology founded more on antique metaphor than on practical function. If this logic were extended, astrologers might be expected to accept the corresponding principles of medicine, law, and property formulated by the ancient Egyptians and Chaldeans over three thousand years ago.

The underlying astronomic, metaphoric, and sophomoric fallacies of astrology are discussed in Chapter 1; the fallacies connected with numerology, palmistry, Tarot, and others are covered in Chapter 2. From these it will be seen that wordplay, not magic, is the essential and dominant inspiration in these fields.

The overall fallacy of magic (or sorcery) is almost self-evident. If indeed it is the force it is supposed to be, why has it exerted such little influence in human history? It seems likely that a magician or sorcerer, empowered as he allegedly is with the ability to raise the dead, to transmute lead into gold, to curse enemies unto death, or to fulfill the sweetest dreams of love, power, and wealth, would surely have played in the past and would continue to play a dominant role in society. But that is not the case. The world still belongs to the politicians, the generals, the magnates of industry and finance, and to those who, by dint of their talent and perspiration, earn themselves a place in the sun. Occultniks will tell you that many of these people are, in fact, magicians, and that they have achieved their goals not by the usual methods but with the methods of the occult, described in Chapter 3.

The fundamental problem of witchcraft explored here is its alleged beneficence and modern renovation from a historically traceable Satan cult to an ethereal form of ethical culture. The fallacy of this metamorphosis—as well as the magical basis of witchcraft—will be shown in Chapter 4.

The area of psychical research that encompasses ESP, precognition, and spiritualism, with its testing and pretensions, still lies buried in the supernatural. Psychical researchers insist on relegating their findings to the occult, where there is no explanation according to the usual scientific laws. J. B. Rhine, the mentor of parapsychology, described prophecy in the *American Weekly* (March, 1952): "In transcending the limits of time . . . [prophecy] shows a power of mind to act outside the confines of material law." It is this *outside confine* upon which psychical research is based; therein lie its fallacy and impediment (see Chapter 5).

The high cost and criminality of much occult delusion is probed in Chapter 6. The problem here is one of law enforcement and public vigilance.

Specific notions of occultniks will be investigated in the miscellany of Chapter 7. Each will be accompanied by its inherent fallacy and similarly inherent scientific explanation. A brief epilogue about true magic concludes these pages. This is the "magic" of science—provable, workable magic that promises to accomplish and, indeed has already accomplished, much of what sorcerers, witches, astrologers, and seers are still blindly attempting to achieve.

Debunking the occult—as this book attempts to do—is, as already noted, a fairly serious task, considering the social implications involved. At the same time, it may be hoped that this effort will be entertaining and informative, especially for those countless thousands who maintain a healthy curiosity about a fascinating subject. To them, to the committed occultist, to the skeptic as well, this work is addressed.

Though founded in the most primitive reaches of human fear and nurtured in the darkest ages of human history, the occult is nonetheless the stuff of our times—a snake oil for the twentieth century. It deserves our investigation.

The Occult Conceit

1

Signs of the Times: Astrology

THE astrology delusion runs so deep in modern times that many individuals responding to the question "When were you born?" pipe up not with the month and date of their birth but with their alleged zodiac sign. An equally popular symptom of the stargazing craze is the earnest game of "spotting signs," which one can see played at cocktail parties any day of the week.

"Oh, I'll bet you're a Gemini," coos the young receptionist to the ad exec in his Cardin copy. "You're so witty and multifaceted; *but,* like every other Geminian," she adds, "ever so slightly fickle and dogmatic."

In another corner of the room, an over-thirty bachelorette breathlessly asks a physicist, "What's your sign? Pisces! How wonderful. I'm Aquarian—very compatible you know; in fact, ideal!"

Had the physicist been a Scorpio, our bachelorette would have been obliged to seek a new companion because, according to her astrologist, her astro-psychologist, solar biologist, astrologue, or any of the other types who have assumed pretentious titles, Scorpios and Aquarians just do not click.

Of course, the woman in question need not have bothered with a human astrologer; she could have obtained the services of Astroflash, the computer in New York's Grand Central Station that dishes up a personality portrait and a six-month forecast in ten minutes flat at $5 a customer.

Five dollars is only a scintilla of the amount expended for manifestations of astrology. It is estimated that $200 million was recently spent on horoscopes, readings (both the computer and human varieties), zodiac jewelry, astrological food, records, wearing apparel, and so forth. In fact, the astrology delusion has become a full-fledged industry. In 1969, approximately forty million Americans consulted an estimated ten thousand professional astrologers. For those folks who stayed at home, there were in the same year more than two thousand newspapers that carried regular horoscope columns and astrological advice. There were, in addition, at least twenty high-priced pulp magazines devoted entirely to the subject of astrology. The facts and statistics about astrology—like those concerning air pollution—are constantly changing for the worse. The United States (and much of Western Europe) seems determined to cover itself, like a frightened child, with the tattered and generally discredited security blanket of astrology and other occultic frauds.

Where It All Began

Astrology is perhaps the oldest divinatory art. Prehistoric man, as soon as he could stand upright, turned his head to the skies to learn the everlasting "truth" about the universe and about the meaning of his own existence. Eventually, stargazing evolved into a rudimentary form of religion, which the Babylonians (or Chaldeans) later codified into a national faith. Nightly, with the naked eye alone, the ancient Chaldean priest could quite efficiently perceive the transmuting nature of the heavenly bodies. To him the glowing planets, like the unpredictable gods, seemed to frolic in the darkness, changing their places from night to night, passing back and forth among the constellations with divine abandon. Quite naturally the Babylonians named the planets after their gods, a tradition that eventually spread throughout most cultures, especially to those of Greece and Rome.

The smaller bodies were likewise named and catalogued. More than two thousand years ago, the Greeks coined the names of the constellations in the zodiac, the broad band of heavenly bodies lying just north and south of the ecliptic. The Greeks thought that the area of the zodiac was the playground of the gods. Like the Babylonians, the Greeks named their constellations after legendary creatures and heroes of mythology: the Ram Aries, with its golden fleece; the Bull Taurus, who was really Zeus on an adventure; Castor and Pollux, the Twins; and the Centaur Sagittarius. Because these creatures possessed mythical and magical influences, it was felt that these same influences extended to human destiny in a series of vibrations or influxes emanating from the stars to the man at the moment of birth. Thus a Gemini, for one, must be "witty, multi-faceted, and at times fickle," because in Greek and Roman mythology, the Gemini were Castor and Pollux, the clever sons of Zeus (witty), the Twins (multi-faceted), the Two (two-faced or fickle), and so forth ad absurdum.

The Scapegoat Sky

When the Babylonians formulated their quasi-scientific cosmology, interrelating human destiny with the stars, they relegated the sky to a scapegoat status, in that the vicissitudes of life and the upheavals of history were conveniently attributed to the relative positions of the heavenly bodies. For several thousand years the sky played a central role in man's religion and philosophy. The heavens were holy, the living quarters of the gods; they served as the backdrop against which the Earth grandly loomed as the center of all the universe. This egocentric —or geocentric—view of the cosmos was eventually rejected as a result of scientific revelations of Copernicus and Kepler in the sixteenth and seventeenth centuries. As astronomy disproved the geocentric system of the universe, astrology became a science based on discredited hypotheses.

Galileo's telescope (1609) confirmed the Copernican theory of the universe and revealed a plethora of constellations never imagined by the ancients and therefore never included in their systems of influence upon human destiny. Today eighty-eight visible constellations have been identified by the International Astronomical Union; those in the zodiac compose roughly one-seventh the total. The Greeks knew only forty-eight constellations, but most of these, they believed, had no influence on human destiny because the gods (the planets) avoided them and chose to pass through only the zodiac area. That is why such star clusters as Ursa Major, Ursa Minor (the Big and Little Bears), Cetus (the Whale), Lupus (the Wolf), and Orion (the Hunter) play no part in modern horoscopes, even though many of them are "adjacent" to the more influential constellations.

Similarly, the planets Uranus, Neptune, and Pluto did not figure in the original astrological formulas of the Babylonians or the Greeks simply because they were unknown at that time; in fact, Pluto was discovered only as recently as 1930. Astrologists have managed to incorporate these latest discoveries conveniently into their schemes just as they have tried to finesse the age-old problem of precession, explained later.

In the Middle Ages—roughly from the fifth to the fifteenth centuries—astrologers continued the classic cosmology, compounding what Franz Cumont called, in his *Astrology and Religion Among the Greeks and Romans* (1912), "that desperate error on which the intellectual powers of countless generations were spent." That error unfortunately persists in our own time.

In a little manifesto entitled *Foretell the Future* (1968), for instance, we are told the exact reverse of the Copernican proofs, namely, that the sun, moon, and planets *circle the earth,* an idea apparently accepted by the well-known television personality Sybil Leek, who reports, in her *Diary of a Witch,* that the *sun moves westward* toward Los Angeles, where it "dies" every day. A paperback called *Astrology for Everyday Living* (1966) informs us that the stars are fixed in their positions and cannot be altered, nor can their influence change. This is said despite the fact that stars are known to have a beginning and a termination and that the equinoxes progressively shift.

A publication issued by Zodiac International, which is responsible for individual yearly horoscopes by sign, discusses the problem of "planetary influence" with all the logic of a Neanderthal shaman. Planets, we are told by these modern diviners, are composed of the same cosmic materials that make up human beings; ergo, the cosmic force contained in the planets must naturally exert an influence over us. If this is so, then why don't we—as bodies of cosmic materials—exert the same sort of cosmic influence over each other?

Not only are we led away from the errors of astronomy in this paperback pronunciamento, we are also liberated from the shackles of psychology and sociology. People born under the same sign, it avers, basically have "the same approach to life." Indeed, this theory continues, persons born at the same moment in the same hospital will live practically a carbon copy of each other's life.

Now it may not seem fair to pick on these admittedly low-brow exercises in popular astrology. You may ask why I do not grapple with the more studious and somewhat esoteric tomes that have been written on the serious side of the subject. The answer is twofold: first, the serious stuff sounds serious, but it is no more valid than *Foretell the Future,* at fifty cents a copy; second, the paperbacks are the primers that the public gobbles up, the propaganda that feeds the philosophy and shapes the attitudes of those who believe in astrology. Paperbacks are the chief offenders—the chief sources of bunk and, consequently, the logical targets for debunking.

How It's Supposed to Work

According to basic astrology, at the moment a newborn baby draws his first breath, a tiny but influential portion of the cosmic influx, or influence, flows into his being—body and soul. This influx thereafter determines the whole pattern of his personality and his destiny on earth. This is not a surprising idea, if one believes that this influx is a composite of universal magnetic forces, or vibrations, radiating through space from the planets, the moon, the sun, and the zodiac (and only zodiac) constellations. This cosmic influx supposedly alters our own internal influx just as a magnet attracts or repels metal particles. Furthermore, as the popular astrologist sees it—despite Copernicus—Earth stands at the center of the solar system, and around it the heavenly bodies "rise and fall" in varying degrees. The relationship of the zodiac constellations to one another and their height on the imaginary map of the skies are the chief factors that magnetize or determine practically everything about our lives. Indeed they are as important, some would say, as our genetic composition.

The chart of one's natal debut is popularly known as the horoscope. It is, like a navigator's map, full of astronomical verities because, ironically, modern astrology relies for its horoscopes upon a series of *astronomical* charts known as the Ephemerides. Since the late seventeenth century, these charts have been kept in order to record the day-by-day "profile" of the sky from any given vantage point on earth for the benefit of navigators.

A complicated, pseudo-scientific formula has been developed by astrologists over the years for the purpose of determining the various aspects or relative positions of the heavenly bodies, which in turn determine the varieties of man's personality and fate.

Among the most essential of the relationships is the position of the planets at the moment of parturition. Planetary influence is determined by such profundities as how fast a given planet moves, how bright or dim it is, and what color it is. Fast-moving Mercury, for instance, is responsible for one's intellectual acuity, or lack of it, and also for such activities as travel and social progress. Venus, because of its association with the Roman love goddess (and before that, with the Greek Aphrodite and the Babylonian Ishtar) dominates one's love life and artistic inclinations. Red-colored Mars, long presumed to be the symbol of the Roman war god, gives us our courage, our aggressiveness, or—if Mars is not in the right position—our timidity and blandness. The king of the Roman gods was Jupiter and his is therefore the biggest planet; accordingly, Jupiter affects wealth, success, and social status. Mysterious and ominous Saturn governs the troubles and upsets of life, but when conditions are favorable, Saturn offers security. Uranus is connected with change, revolution, and originality presumably because Uranus was the "original" god of Greek mythology, the "grandfather," so to speak, of Zeus. Watery Neptune is the planet of dreams, ideals, and impressions (watery things are constantly changing their shape). After 1930 Pluto was included in the astrologer's system—but what to do with it? Some savants ignore it as a Johnny-come-lately; others relate it to Uranus; still others rely on the fact that the planet was named for the Roman ruler of the underworld and regard it as a sinister and sorrowful influence. As we will see again and again, linguistics and puns play a major role in the formulation of the astrologic creed.

To these orbiting planets astrologers add the star we call the sun and Earth's satellite known as the moon; however, the moons of the other planets are ignored (the ancients never heard of them). Despite the fact that the sun is a star and the moon, a satellite, they too are allotted distinctive influences as are the planets. The sun has a very significant influence on life, growth, health, and one's vitality and will; in short, when favorable, it produces a "sunny" disposition. Those most influenced by the sun (Solarians) are, according to a popular manual of the 1930s, "of medium height, well made, of lemon coloring, mixed with red, with oval faces, full beards, auburn or golden hair . . . large mouths and thick lips . . . a body running more to muscle than to fat." In addition, Solarians are seduced by beauty, they love decorations, dread death by fire, and when ill-fated, often bear ungrateful children.

Moon-influenced people, known as Selenians after Selene, the moon goddess of Greece, are moony, dreamy, romantic (in short, the June-moon-spoon variety) and, according to the aforementioned manual, "are nervous, and inclined to paralysis and strabismus." Despite these afflictions, Selenians often turn into poets, sailors, musicians, and authors of fanciful novels. One must dutifully add that they are also among the worst drunkards, liars, and egotists, and "very few become orators."

The moon is a favorite item of astrology because it allegedly possesses powers that prove, scientifically, the fantastic claims of celestial influx. Take, for example, the tangible business of tides; isn't this proof enough of how the heavenly bodies affect our lives?

The fact is that the phenomenon of tides is a purely gratuitous incident of nature. If the tides did not exist, there would be no tidal disasters and less confusion among mariners and fishermen. The moon does have a physical influence upon the earth—specifically a magnetic pull. And of course there is a psychological effect, which no one denies. A full, bright moon apparently floating against a sable sky does present a compelling sight, especially to romantic individuals, but the anticipated effect is produced entirely in the mind of the beholder.

Naturally for those who view the moon as a body capable of waxing and waning or rising and falling—as astrologers do—anything is possible. Sensible observers know that the moon itself never changes its form and that it is a continuously orbiting satellite of the earth. Why a full moon, 'upon which no shadow of the earth is visible, has any more effect than the same body darkened by the earth's interference, is purely a question of symbolical and mythical cant.

The cumulative influence of the planets—great as it is—pales next to the influx of the particular constellation "through which the sun is passing" at the moment of one's birth (the Sun Sign). It is almost unnecessary to outline the characteristics of the Sun Signs since they have become shibboleths of our time, showing up on cocktail napkins, scarves, towels, plates, and toilet tissue. It is also rather difficult to choose from the myriad astrological opinions found in the popular literature concerning the most obvious features of any given sign. In one account, for instance, we may read that Capricorn is practical, ambitious and patient —three generalities that could just as well apply to Taurus. In another, Capricorn is skillful but restless, which are sometimes Virgoan attributes. And so rather than dwell on the plethora of vague and meaningless adjectives that many modern astrologers associate with each birth sign, it may be more amusing, and revealing, to focus on a work called *The Encyclopedia of Occult Sciences,* first offered in 1939 but updated in 1968. In large part it sounds like a tome of the seventeenth century.

A Tour of the Zodiac

According to *The Encyclopedia of Occult Sciences,* beginning with the first day of spring (the astrological new year), or the cardinal point, we find Aries, the Ram (March 21–April 20), sometimes shown as a sea ram with a fish's tail. Besides their basic attributes of aggressiveness, leadership, and generosity, Ariens have "few or no children, many enemies and jealousies." Like the ram who appears in their constellation, they will "batter their heads up against the adverse forces of life," for example, Charlie Chaplin as the tramp (he is an Arien).

From April 21 to May 21 come the calves of the constellation Taurus the Bull. They are "bull-necked," stubborn people, self-opinionated, but with an inquiring mind and an affectionate nature. Taurians, according to the encyclopedia, will live good long lives "if the subject itself does not shorten it." "Self-indulgent," Taurians are quick to point out that Shakespeare, Kant, and Richard Wagner were born under their sign. But they will rarely mention Adolf Hitler.

Gemini, the sign of the Twins, runs from May 22 through June 21. It produces admirers of art and science, eloquent and witty speakers, but fickle lovers beset by "worries, troubles, and long unions." In their careers, Geminians excel at dentistry, sewing, and other dexterous skills such as telling jokes, like Bob Hope, Beatrice Lillie, and, of course, Jean-Paul Sartre.

The summer is ushered in with Cancer, the Crab, on June 22; it influences birth through July 23. Cancerians have banded together in mass objection to the ominous nomenclature of their sign, and in many places the name of the dread disease has given way to the euphemism "moon children" because, according to astrology, the moon is associated with this constellation. This name change was necessary because Cancerians are terribly sensitive and impressionable folks, imaginative and "never lucky until late in life." Ignoring this last prophecy, Cancerian John D. Rockefeller was a multi-millionaire by age forty.

Leo, the Lion, dominates births from July 24 to August 23. Lion-hearted, leonine, and full of mane, the cubs of Leo are particularly ambitious and therefore somewhat heavy-handed (or thick-pawed). They have "unpleasant brothers and sisters, suffer long illnesses, and discover that their fortunes suddenly rise and fall," just as did the fortunes of Caesar, Napoleon, and Mussolini, three well-known Leos. But how Leo-born Mae West fits into this fluctuation is not clear.

From August 24 to September 23, meticulous Virgo stars in the zodiac. "She comes crowned with corn and rules the womb, the intestines, and the genital organs," but very chastely and with all the virtue and caution suitable to a maiden. Frequent journeys are in store for Virgos, and a "fight for independence will be faced." Virgo women are fussbudgets, but their male counterparts, we are told, find it no problem to "panel a den or install a new floor." Imagine Virgo F. Scott Fitzgerald installing a floor!

The autumn begins with Libra, ruling from September 24 to October 23. The symbol of Libra seems out of place among all the mythical animals and fantastic creatures of the zodiac since it is represented by a simple pair of scales. Because of this imagery, Librans are either well-balanced or ill-balanced individuals. An artistic sign, it is nonetheless plagued by frivolity (the ups and downs of the scales) and an aversion to dirt. According to one sage, Librans are very aesthetic souls, adoring flowers, music, elegant gems, and garments. Is it any surprise that Oscar Wilde (October 16) was a Libran? How about Mahatma Gandhi?

Scorpio, the Scorpion, slithers between October 24 and November 22. Whereas Virgo is the chaste and virtuous guardian of the genitals, Scorpio is a stinger (or swinger) when it comes to love. Passionate yet gracious, diplomatic yet quarrelsome (stinging), Scorpians are given to "dueling, mountain climbing, and playing checkers." There are lots of athletes among Scorpios, both the baseball and the bedroom varieties and there are, of course, several other professional types: preachers—Billy Graham; cowboys—Roy Rogers and future kings—Prince Charles. Their activities seem to be most salubrious since, according to one epic on the subject, Scorpios are among the longest-lived people in astrology.

The Centaur, who is also an archer, Sagittarius, governs November 23 through December 22. Sagittarians adore horses and hunting and are "victims of relentless slander," perhaps because of their suspicious breeding. Withal they are a clever lot, and they provide the world with its largest share of bachelors—although Sagittarian Frank Sinatra is not usually among them.

Winter comes in with Capricorn, which reigns from December 23 to January 20. "Its type," we are told, "are mournful, thin-faced, impassive"; in short they resemble goats, the animal that symbolizes their sign. This is not to say that they are unpleasant people; Capricornians often have a fine sense of humor and "good eyesight." In addition, they make excellent bookkeepers and politicians. Capricornians Richard M. Nixon and Barry Goldwater are examples of the winner and loser aspects of this sign.

January 21 to February 19 is governed by Aquarius, the water carrier, whose followers are a very unusual group, the result of a magical mixture of air and water. It is the astrologer's sign, we are told, perhaps because astrologers like to be associated with such worthy Aquarians as Abraham Lincoln, Franklin D. Roosevelt, Douglas MacArthur, and Thomas A. Edison—not to mention Clark Gable, Lana Turner, and Eddie Cantor.

Despite their originality, leadership qualities, and resourcefulness, Aquarians have "weak calves and ankles and are advised not to travel by sea."

The menagerie finally comes full circle with Pisces, the sign that rules February 20 through March 21. The ancients imagined two fishes swimming towards each other when they plotted the imagery of this constellation. The indecisive motion of these relentless swimmers gives Pisceans a somewhat unsettled destiny, as well as ulcers and arthritis. A "maleficent star," it nevertheless bestows a measure of mystery upon its adherents and gives them insight that others lack. Although an insensitive astrologer calls this sign "the hell of the zodiac," a more generous seer advises Pisceans not to despair of their uneasy lives, for their characters have many subtleties that others will soon perceive and cherish. After all, Washington, Einstein, and Michelangelo were all Pisceans, and they eventually found their places in the *Who's Who* of history.

Combinations of Things

Mention should be made, in connection with the Sun Signs, to the concept of *cusps.* If you were born, so the astrologers say, anywhere from five to seven days at the beginning or end of your constellational period (the cusps), it is then to be expected that you will bear in your personality and in your destiny certain traits and configurations of the sign immediately preceding or following your own, depending on whether you are on an early cusp or on a late one.

Thus a versatile, witty Geminian (May 21–June 20) born on May 22 or 23 will possess many of the preceding Taurus traits, and his wit may therefore be somewhat plodding or bullish. Should a Geminian be born on June 18, 19, or even 20, he may find that his usual sparkle has become somewhat altered by the romantic influences of Cancer, the following sign.

By this constrained but useful stratagem, astrologists believe they can handle the myriad persons who do not and will not fit neatly into their zodiac categories. Often the trick works, since the gullible individual naturally welcomes any idea that expands his predetermined personality and predestined fate. On closer inspection, however, the cusp concept is really more of an embarrassment to astrology than a face-saving device. Because of the cusp factor, almost two full weeks of each zodiac period are, in effect, not fully pertinent to the usual descriptions of that period. No one, unless he is born squarely in the middle of his sign, can consider himself absolutely Gemini, Leo, Virgo, or any other sign.

Another factor employed by astrologers to explain the inevitable variations among members of the same sign is the *ascendant,* the constellation rising over the eastern border at the hour of one's birth. Because it seems to accompany the sun as it rises, the ascendant allegedly influences personality, destiny, and even physical appearance with as much force as the Sun Sign itself. Thus a person born at noon with the sun in Aquarius will have Taurus in the eastern horizon, or Taurus ascending. The water carrier's mysterious traits will therefore be blended with the practical stubbornness of the bull.

Physical characteristics are likewise determined by the ascendant sign. An ebullient Gemini may turn out to be horse-faced if Sagittarius, the Centaur, is his ascendant—or fish-faced, if Pisces rises on the east. Any of the twelve signs may similarly influence the Sun Sign, so that the permutations are quite extensive. As a result one may find swinging Scorpios inclined to be virtuous because Virgo is the ascendant, or Capricorns who abandon thrift because moony Cancer is on the eastern horizon.

According to astrologers, the location of the various planets in the constellations at the moment of one's birth also significantly shapes and varies the basic Sun Sign influence. Quickwitted Mercury "passing through" Gemini, for instance, heightens the quick-wittedness and restlessness of two-faced Geminians. Stubborn, thick-necked Taurians, when dominated by Venus, turn out to be not boors but pacifists, or any other permutation that may result when one crosses a bull with a love goddess.

Similarly influential are the four basic elements of the universe as outlined by ancient decree: fire, water, air and earth (meaning soil). Each of the twelve constellations falls into one of these four subdivisions. Fire signs are Aries, Leo, and Sagittarius; one can expect fiery temperaments from individuals born in these signs, especially from Aries, who is ruled by warlike Mars. Earth types are Taurus, Virgo, and Capricorn—the "earthy," or practical, people. Gemini, Libra, and Aquarius are air signs, and they are naturally airy, breezy, and, in some cases, blowhards. The mysterious qualities of water are left to Cancer, Scorpio, and Pisces (the Crab, the Scorpion, and the Fish). It can be seen once again how essential word association is in assigning the various constellations to the elements. It would be hard to imagine Pisces, the Fish, for instance, as an earth sign, although some daring imagists might like to think of a "fiery" bull as opposed to an earthy bull or a watery Aquarius.

There follows a veritable Pandora's box of other variations on the theme completing the profiles of the various signs. Each, for instance, is associated with a day of the week, based on the ruling planets (for example, the sun equals Sunday); each has its own color, plant, metal, and scent (Aries is garlic); and each rules a specific organ or area of the body, a concept reaching back to the practice of medicine in ancient Babylon.

The ancients reasoned that if the universe (the macrocosm) was ruled by the stars, it may be true that man, the microcosm, is ruled in the same way. And if man and his parts are thus governed, perhaps one could establish a link between the ailment as predestined by astrology and the herbs and natural medicines similarly influenced by the stars. It is possible, by this reasoning, to see how extract of crab apple could counteract the crabby stomach of a Cancerian, or the pulverized horns of a goat might soothe a skin disease suffered by a Capricornian.

From this ingenious and ingenuous system of medicine, modern astrologers continue to prescribe their own medical nostrums and diagnoses to gullible devotees, prudently protecting their prescriptions with italicized warnings that astrological indications are "not meant to take the place of competent medical advice." But while one is waiting for the doctor, there's no harm in finding out that Ariens often suffer from dental problems and lockjaw (Aries rules the head and face); that Taurians may expect stiff necks and laryngitis (Taurus rules the throat and neck); that fickle Geminians will suffer with problems in their limbs (the limbs are ruled by Gemini); and that Cancerians are doomed to rumbling stomachs (not only because Cancer the Crab governs the stomach, the breasts, and lungs, but also because Cancerians love sweets, pastries, and starches).

Fiery Leos can expect heart attacks, bilious livers, and aching backs, but they are nevertheless "bright-eyed and rosy-cheeked"; Virgoans are rarely ill, but that is of little comfort since they are likely to be desperate hypochondriacs. The nerves, kidneys, and bladder are ruled by Libra, and although Librans "appear to be healthy," they are natural victims of sciatica, rheumatism, and enuresis. Robust Scorpios have long lives, if they do not fall victim to overeating, immoderate drinking, or sexual excess (Scorpio rules the groin). The half-man, half-horse, Sagittarius is very well balanced in most respects, but he must guard against overwork, creaky joints, injured hips, and ailments that afflict the thighs, which are ruled by Sagittarius. Capricorn takes over at the knees, with skin diseases in evidence (but who can find fault with the complexion of Capricornian Marlene Dietrich?). Weak-ankled Aquarians are told by one astrological seer to avoid smoking, presumably because smoking is bad for ankles, calves, and lower legs. Down at the feet are Pisceans, and naturally "Oh, my aching feet" is their universal complaint. Perhaps because of this podiatric agony Pisceans are more inclined to use pep pills, liquor, and caffeine than are people under any other sign.

One can imagine the possible dangers in the foregoing information, especially when dealing with highly impressionable people who are devoted to astrology. Consider the subtle but long-lasting effects that a Scorpio might suffer from reading, as he can in *The Encyclopedia of Occult Sciences,* that "heart trouble due to a cruel loss by death" awaits him. In the same volume, Cancerians are warned that they "incline to cancer and tuberculosis" (as well as to rumbling tummies). It is no wonder that they changed their name.

Such ominous twaddle is not restricted to physical aspects. A popular nineteenth-century seer, Madame de Thebes, has drawn up a chart of planetary types according to their moral dispositions. Natives of Mars in her scheme are described as "loose livers"; moon children are weak willed; and Mercurians (Geminians) are "unscrupulous." To the faithful, such insinuations have their effects, and that is why the Aquarian woman mentioned earlier would flee from the sight of a Scorpio. Loyal and constant Aquarius, it seems, must suffer an almost fatal poisoning from the ardent sting of the lusty Scorpio. Thus, what might be a perfect match is, alas, taboo according to astrology.

Astrologers employ further complex influences: descending bodies, as opposed to the ascendant; planetary cycles; specific aspects known as conjunction, opposition, trines, squares, and sextiles (all of which refer to the various degree groups assigned to each celestial element on the horoscope); and definitions of the decani—three groups of ten days each per zodiac sign, each ruled in turn by its "Lord," or planet. These items encompass most of the impressive but pseudo-scientific jargon connected with astrology for the last three hundred years. Trying to place them in proper rational perspective is very much like offering a sensible and scientific explanation of a Rube Goldberg machine.

The Houses of the Sky
The Houses of the sky, like the planets and the constellations, are supposed to have great influence over life, death, health, wealth, happiness, and sorrow. These Houses are a clever invention used by astrologers who have long attempted to cope with the fact that because of precession—the subtle shift in the direction of the earth's axis of rotation—the constellations are no longer where they should be according to the nearly two-thousand-year-old schema of the Egyptian astronomer Ptolemy. In his *Tetrabiblos* (c. 130 A.D.) we learn that on March 21 the sun is "passing through Aries." In fact, however, the modern sky reveals that the sun is actually in the path of the constellation *Pisces* on the first day of spring. The shocking truth is that in the years since Ptolemy, each sign in relation to the earth has moved westward by 30° and therefore lies due west of the constellation that still bears its ancient name. Astronomers are constantly correcting their findings on the basis of precession, but astrologers, being less disciplined, have fab-

ricated the concept of Houses in order to finesse the embarrassment of precession. Recognizing the enormous influence of the nomenclature of these constellations—Sagittarians like to hunt, Taurians are bull-necked, and so forth—one can imagine the dismay that would occur if the names of the constellations were shifted one sign westward in imitation of the true course of the universe.

Reluctant to bother with the true course of anything, astrologers offer the notion that the twelve constellations were "born" in twelve separate solar houses, represented by twelve huge divisions of the sky near the equator. Although the constellations may have slipped 30° westward out of their Houses over the last eighteen hundred years, much of their original influence remains locked with great vitality within each House. Consequently, it is unimportant where the specific constellation Aries may be, since its original House remains at the March 21 vantage point. It is fixed there by the gods and consequently corresponds exactly to the old Ptolemaic zodiac. Thus, House I stands where Aries was before it slipped 30° westward; House II, with Taurus; House III, with Gemini; House IV, with Cancer; and so forth. It should be noted that astrologers do not call these Houses by the names of their former occupants, for example, the "House of Aries," but prefer to label them with the Roman numerals I to XII; perhaps they will expose their ruse if they use the constellational names. The subtle implication is made that the solar Houses are not simply identical to, but are ramifications of the essential influences of the constellations in the horoscope.

House I, in which Aries was "born," supposedly influences personality and appearance, and, after all, Aries is the aggressive "personality" type. House II (Taurus) has charge of money and income, two areas that would please the practical, solid Taurian. House III indicates travel, intelligence, and manual dexterity (the Gemini-Mercury traits); similarly, the traits of Cancer show up in House IV: love of home, environment, and family. House V, the Leo House, influences one's love life, talent, and children—Leos are libidinous and often go on the stage. The sixth House (analogous to Virgo) is guardian of health and labor—likely areas for the meticulous Virgoan. House VII is the marriage House, controller of partnerships, original home of the romantic Libra. Ominous House VIII rules death and legacies; excessive Scorpio, with "a knack for acquiring wealth," lived there. House IX is the domicile of religion, philosophy, and dreams; Sagittarius, ruled by Jupiter, fled there, leaving behind the religious fervor of the king of the gods. House X rules careers, status, and motherhood—there skillful Capricorn lived. House XI, associated with friendly Aquarians, influences choice of friends, social ambitions, and hope. The last House, standing just west of the first, is the Piscean abode, a mysterious place that controls "enemies, secrets, the unconscious mind, and its limitations."

Astrologers, adhering to this ancient scheme—as they must unless they want an astrological revolution—are really trying to say that the original two-thousand-year-old positions of the constellations still convey their alleged influences, by way of the solar Houses, despite the fact that natural precession has taken place. This is like saying that a person can get drunk by drinking water poured from a bottle that once contained whiskey.

As if the problem of precession is not enough, the modern astrologer has to cope with the startling news that the constellations, which Ptolemy and others studied many thousands of years ago, were in fact largely delusions. It takes approximately 4.3 years of our time for the light of the nearest star—excluding the sun—to reach our eyes. Thus, if tonight we look up and find that Alpha Centauri, the nearest star to the earth, has apparently vanished from space, it would really mean that it had actually exploded and disintegrated 4.3 years ago. Similarly, if it exploded tomorrow night, it would still take another 4.3 years for us to know about it. Considering the enormous distances of "light years" and the uncanny illusions of time and space they encompass, and adding to that the faulty perception of the human eye, how can anyone take seriously the influx of a constellation?

Problems of Logic

Any astronomer so inclined can tear to shreds the premises of astrology. Few would waste the time—and who can blame them? But there are considerations other than astronomical in the debunking of this popular delusion. Logic itself, the arsenal of common sense, is enough to support an effective crusade. Four logical categories lend themselves to this perusal: the semantic or wordplay problem in astrology; the inconsistencies and ambiguities of astrologers; the fallacy of drawing parallels between horoscope types; and the ludicrous extensions of astrology into daily life.

Semantics

References have been made to the wordplay dependencies of astrology, past and present. Bull-headed Taurians, two-faced Geminis, and well-balanced Libras are obvious examples of this inclination. Astrologers have always drawn great meaning from the nomenclature inherited from antiquity, as if the gods themselves had bestowed these names as clues to their elaborate schemes. Thus it was no accident, they feel, that the planet named for Venus controlled one's love life and romance; in fact, even the Chaldeans had identified this planet with their love goddess Ishtar—more proof of divine predestination. Logic will show, however, that the Greeks and Romans simply followed the Chaldeans in planetary nomenclature; thus the planet named for the Chaldean warrior god Marduk was similarly named for the Greco-Roman warrior god Mars. And once this was done, the name itself stimulated further characteristics: war-like, hostile, and belligerent. Seigneur of Salerno, a typical seventeenth-century astrologer, bases many of his evaluations on the interplay of names and words. The astrological conjunction of the moon and Mars in a given horoscope, he opines, "brings accidents such as sword stroke and bullet wounds" (the effects of the inconstant or dangerous moon blended with the warlike propensities of Mars). Similarly, the conjunction of amorous Venus with the same unpredictable moon, according to Salerno, "causes women of quality to become enamored of menservants." Salerno's methodology is as popular with modern seers as it was in the seventeenth century. Indeed, without the ramifications of various synonyms, antonyms, homonyms, and puns, one might safely say that astrology could not exist as we know it: Geminians would not be two-faced; Leos might be sheepish, not leonine; the air signs would not be airy; and the fire signs could conceivably be as cold as ice. It is only as a result of simple puns that Aries (the Ram) is aggressive, like a battering ram; Taurians are considered bullheaded and stubborn because of Taurus, the Bull; Cancer (the Crab) is a sign of tenacity, as in the claw of a crab; Leo (the Lion) is as proud as the king of beasts; Virgo, the Virgin, is chaste; Libra is changeable (or unchangeable) like the Scales; a Scorpio is secretive, as is the burrowing and ominous scorpion; a Sagittarian, the archer, is a straight shooter; a person under the sign of Capricorn, the Goat, is as thrifty as a goat, who wastes nothing; an Aquarian is as resourceful as a reservoir; and someone born under the sign of Pisces (the Fish) is as evasive as a slippery salmon.

Semantics play a similarly important role in Chinese astrology, which antedates even the Babylonian system. Instead of being governed by the stars, however, the ancient Chinese placed their destinies at the mercy of the moon. To them the lunar year, not the month, of one's birth was of particular significance.

Our months are ruled by the images of the constellations, but the Chinese year is dominated by the figure of a simple barnyard animal: one may be born in the year of the Rabbit, the Dog, the Pig, the Ox, and so forth. Naturally, as might be guessed, persons born in the year of the Dog (1970 was such a year) are loyal, clever, and enjoy the company of human beings—in a phrase: man's best friend. Ox people, however, are patient, speak little, and work hard—sort of oriental Taurians. For some inscrutable reason, Rat folks are charming, though fussy.

Further elucidation of the wordplay weakness in astrology is offered by the Chinese system. In ancient China the planet Venus was known as the "Metal Star," a cosmic body that purportedly governed such earthly pursuits as the buying of metal goods, the grinding of knives, and the minting of coins; it was not in any way related to lovemaking or the other usual Venusian attributes, simply because it was called "Metal Star," not Venus.

Inconsistencies and Ambiguities

The illusion of consistency is created in most horoscopes by means of vague generalities and ambiguous adjectives. Describing the personalities of Cancerians (moon children), one manual states that they are shy, timid, and introspective; another pegs them as serene, composed, and tender; still a third says that they are easily wounded, generous, and sympathetic. All three descriptions convey the traditional concept of sensitivity, which is the code word for Cancerians (presumably they are soft-shell crabs).

But a generality is a generality. The following descriptions, taken from a few current manuals, do not pertain to Cancer and yet, in line with the above, they just as easily could. The first is extracted from the evaluation of Pisces: "You have a considerable store of *emotions*," it says; the next is Virgo: "You like doing favors for others. . . . you are *generous* and *kind*"; finally a Libran—not a Cancerian—is described: "Despite your many accomplishments you can be remarkably *modest*." In other words, emotional, generous, timid Cancerians are interchangeable in these areas with Pisceans, Virgoans, and Librans.

Consistency in such evaluations is as much a question of

semantics as the wordplay problem previously discussed, and for this reason astrology is obliged to grind out ambiguous platitudes and intangibles. Even in a "personalized" horoscope provided in a private session with an astrologer or via the computer, the specifics are few and far between. Often the precise interpretation of what one may read or hear is left entirely to the individual's own imagination. How else but subjectively could one handle such pronouncements as this from a computerized Aquarian horoscope: the subject, it says, will live in "an aura of icy independence and [there will be] a vacuum where your heart lies." Does this bolster the Garbo complex, or endanger gregarious aspirations? It's up to the individual.

What does one do with the scientific truth of the statement "Lady Luck will smile on you"? The next time you win a two-bit poker game, will you assume that your destiny has been fulfilled?

Modern astrologers tend to be generous, cautious and pseudo-psychiatric in their evaluations, even while they are submerging them in purple prose. An example is this consensus from Astroflash, the computer: "Life is a dream," it says to a Cancerian, "populated with shadows and will-o-the-wisps [in which] a wearied soul floats where its visions and chimeras lead it."

Fifty years earlier, clients of astrology were not quite so pampered. Then one could read dire and specific predictions of "danger of wounds . . . falls and rises (in fortunes) and expensive removals" for Aquarians. Ely Star, a popular astrologer of another generation, minced no words with Ariens; she said that they will know only variable luck, conjugal differences, broken friendships, few or no children, situations not easily settled, and many enemies and jealousies.

Having skittered through the pages of Freud, a modern seer named Janet Harris views Ariens in a different way, commensurate with the 1960s. Ariens are, according to her, unable to catch all the nuances of other people's personalities and thus may seem superficial and aloof; but deep down, of course, they want to be liked despite their brilliant and often irritating egos. An Arien is "likely to have a large family." How about conjugal differences? Once Ariens have sown their wild oats, they settle down to "lasting matches." Ely Star might have read the wrong signs about Aries, or it is possible that Janet Harris' information is incorrect; it is necessarily true that at least one of them is wrong and obvious that both descriptions are simply balderdash, based on wordplay and metaphor.

Astrologers of the Middle Ages, of the Renaissance, and even of the seventeenth century did not hesitate to pinpoint the very day, hour, and manner of death for infants whose horoscopes they were asked to draw. Unfortunately we have little extant proof to show the accuracy of such findings. King Louis XIV of France had such a horoscope drawn by a highly respected practitioner of the day, Jean Baptiste Morin de Villefranche, but it judiciously omitted the mention of death. First published in 1661, when the "Sun King" was 23 years old, it does tell, however, of a wonderful life, full of riches, grandeur and prestige—likely predictions for a king. Louis' greatest achievement, the fact that his reign lasted seventy-two years, one of the longest reigns in history, is never hinted at. This omission may not be faulted as an inconsistency, but nevertheless it exemplifies the kind of necessary evasion endemic to past and present astrology.

Inconsistency as a major fault or flaw of astrology is analyzed best with reference to a specific horoscope—namely, the author's own from Astroflash. Not only is this particular document replete with ambiguities and generalities (not to mention misinformation), it is also self-contradictory and specifically disagrees in many areas with other readings pertinent to the same sign, Cancer. The astrologers who created this document attempt from the first to escape such criticism in their opening "caveat," which advises that one cannot get a correct interpretation of the material offered unless he is sure to adapt it to his "mode of existence, standard of living, and development." In addition, the six-month forecast available at additional cost is useful, we are told, only when one takes into consideration his "present situation and environment." Thus a terminal patient in a hospital, reading of a long journey out of the country and remembering to adapt this prediction to his "present situation," might logically conclude that he's about to die (presumably, he will be duly impressed with the prediction). Why the horoscope itself specifically fails to recognize the rather significant eventuality of this patient's death is obvious: it simply cannot deal in specifics. Even the disclaimer that the stars influence but do not dictate one's future, that "man, having free will, largely determines his own fate," does not satisfy that discrepancy. A man's death has very little to do with his exercise of free will, and if the stars have any influence at all on human destiny, they surely should reveal specifically that a man is expected to die on a given day, not simply that he will take a long trip as a result of the fact that Mercury is in his birth sign.

Further analysis of the author's IBM horoscope is revealing in this area. After establishing that this Cancerian possesses a "pronounced double nature" (he is materialistic and spiritualistic at the same time), the horoscope goes on to speak of the subject's innate recognition of his own values, a worthy trait, but one which "may cause the appearance of arrogance." So far so good, but on the very next page the same subject is warned about his tendency toward "complete self effacement," which may cause him to mistrust himself and to appear "listless, apprehensive, and retiring"—no longer arrogant, apparently no longer aware of his "innate values." This inconsistency is repeated when this same formerly arrogant subject is told that, career-wise, his modesty, the "by-product of a kind of timidity," will sometimes cause him to be overlooked.

Two other areas of apparent contradiction are perceptible in the welter of words which makes up the subject's horoscope.

Concerning love (the Venus influence), first he is told that his heart, avid for novelty, compels him to become "enamored of everything" (or everyone) at once. In the same paragraph, however, it is "feared" that the subject *may* suffer (the subjunctive verb is always used in horoscopes) from a "relative inability to love."

Ambition is another hazy topic in this horoscope. "You sin more from lack of ambition than anything else," it announces. "You are tempted to be content with little, or at least to depend more on luck than on yourself." But is this the same person who is told, in the same horoscope, that progress may seem delayed because "your social, philosophical, and religious goals *are so high* . . . "? How is it that in one place he is told that he tends to depend more on luck than on himself, but in another place he is assured that "success will be achieved by *your own strength*," because of "your quality of enthusiasm, willingness to fight, and combative spirit that will bring on this success."

Some may argue that it is perfectly possible for a person to lack ambition, depend on luck, and nonetheless achieve success by his own strength—or for that matter to become enamored of everything all at once and yet be unable to love—especially if such a person possesses a "pronounced double nature." All this is very true, but we hardly need a horoscope to tell us what any amateur psychologist can deduce, nor should we be expected to accept these "truths" as heavenly pronouncements radiated in an inalterable and persistent influx from the constellations, the moon, the sun, and the planets.

The ambiguity deception in astrology is as artfully evasive as the clever puns and word games noted before. One persistent method of evasion concerns the alternate variables. "You will take a long trip," predicts the astrologer, "*or* you will venture into some higher plane of thought, some high-flown speculation far from your routine existence." This two-faced revelation shrewdly enables the horoscope to cover the widest range of common possibilities. Should the subject actually take a trip (even if it's only to his mother-in-law's house) he will remember that the stars predicted it. If there are no actual trips anywhere at all, the faithful follower will assume that a venture to some higher plane of thought (like reading a poem) was, in fact, the predicted trip. Similar trick phrases permeate all horoscopes. Someone is told that his "hopes" for romance will soar during a certain season. Anyone's hopes may soar anywhere at any time; what most people crave are specific predictions—the proverbial "tall, dark stranger" and so forth. Nevertheless, where the horoscope cleverly uses "hopes," the gullible usually substitutes "opportunities."

The ambiguities afforded by these tricky and catch-all phrases, combined with enough sheer old fashioned coincidence, create some semblance of authority even in the most vague and discrepant trash. Padding the trash with good sound advice, which every horoscope contains, also adds a certain quality of respectability to the whole delusion. Who can argue with something that warns you to "reread all the fine print in any contract you may have to sign"?

There is a noticeable tendency in most horoscopes toward caution and conservatism. Specific, unauthorized advice on money matters, medical treatments, and unlawful practices is —in many places—illegal. We are therefore always told by law-abiding astrologers to hold on to our present jobs until better ones come along, to seek medical and legal advice whenever necessary (in preference to witch doctors and sorcerers, we presume), and to be discreet in our personal conduct, "as there is a danger of unfavorable gossip . . ." An underground newspaper, being less restrained, printed dubious horoscopes advocating, wherever possible, sex changes, family desertions, and drug use.

Before leaving the question of inconsistency within and among horoscopes, we should analyze one of the most popular and appealing areas of any horoscope—the area of compatibility and marriage. Two popular manuals were compared to the author's computerized horoscope to see what, if anything, would emerge. The results: inconsistency triumphs again. Libra and Aquarius are considered excellent mates for Cancer by IBM. But *Zodiac International Compatibility Guide* calls Libra "a little difficult to get along with, especially in close association" and regards Aquarius with indifference. Something entitled *Pick-a-Partner* sees difficulties with Libra but doesn't mention Aquarius at all. The computerscope warns the Cancerian of difficult relations with Aries and Virgo. On Aries everyone agrees, but *Zodiac International* offers Virgo as the "most compatible" (along with Taurus, Scorpio, and Pisces), with which *Pick-a-Partner* complies. Cancer, the subject's own sign, is called "best bet" by the computered horoscope, but it goes unmentioned by *Pick-a-Partner* and is declared not unfavorable, but "lacking in energy and interest" by the *Zodiac International Compatibility Guide.* In short, as far as this subject is concerned, tossing a coin to find a mate seems far more reliable.

Odious Comparisons

A very seductive means by which horoscopes lure their readers is the constant comparisons made between the subject and some celebrity who shares his sign and thus his traits. In modern horoscopes these celebrities are usually Hollywood or television personalities or the most enviable members of the Jet Set. People such as Shakespeare, Napoleon, and Lincoln are sprinkled in among the others to give a historical tone.

Clearly, assassins, gangsters, or ill-fated *has-beens* are generally omitted lest they cast a pall of turpitude on one's own future and destiny. The usual association is intended to excite all sorts of fantasy associations. What Aquarian can resist the tingle of satisfaction that darts into his life when he reads that among those born together with him—sharing his characteristics, his fate, his experiences—are such enviables as Clark Gable, Tallulah Bankhead, Lana Turner, John Barrymore, Lord Byron, Edgar Allan Poe, and Mozart!

To be sure, every sign has its star performers, and Aquarius is not the only Hollywood-heavy constellation; Leos, it seems, practically fill the ranks of the motion picture industry (Lucille Ball, Robert Taylor, Eddie Fisher, et al.); and bull-headed Taurians, oddly enough, seem to spawn excellent crooners and jazz musicians (Al Jolson, Bing Crosby, Duke Ellington, Ella Fitzgerald).

The coincidence—and it is only coincidence—of finding Jolson, Crosby, and Ella Fitzgerald together in Taurus is evidence for one of the more common arguments used to justify the significance of horoscopes. Astrologers have spent a lot of time fitting famous personalities into their schemes in order to prove beyond much doubt that the system is valid and dependable.

They try to justify the variations within Sun Signs by reminding us that there are several "types," negative and positive, for examples, among descendants of the same sign. Thus, they aver, while Oscar Wilde represented the most obvious and in the long run the most unfortunate Libran traits, Mahatma Gandhi reflected the most positive and admirable of such distinctions. Libra is, after all, the sign of clergymen, diplomats, artists, and poets, so, according to the cant, it is perfectly possible for Wilde and Gandhi to coexist in the same sign. This sort of justification, indicating that there are negative and positive Librans or successful and unsuccessful Aquarians, is so transparent that it is insulting. What group of ten people picked at random in the street irrespective of their horoscopes wouldn't also cover the same broad possibilities of achievement and variety? And every sign (according to astrologers themselves) is replete with clergymen, diplomats, and artists. Adlai Stevenson was certainly a diplomat, but not a Libran (an Aquarian, in fact), and the aforementioned Lord Byron, though an Aquarian, would have given Oscar Wilde quite a bit of competition in aesthetics, decadence, and off-beat inclinations had the two of them been of the same generation.

Those born in Gemini are supposed to be sparkling, versatile, dexterous, and eloquent. The most celebrated world figure in Gemini is no doubt the late John F. Kennedy. He seemed admirably to fit the eloquent witty designation of Gemini, but he is just as easily remembered for Scorpio's graciousness, the sincerity of Aries, and the ambition of Leo.

The "crooner sign" Taurus, however, may appear to some as proof of the consistency of horoscopes regarding celebrities and their similar careers. But though it is true that Jolson and Crosby were born in the April 21-May 21 period, astrology doesn't explain how crooner Frank Sinatra can show up in Sagittarius, nor does it explain how Karl Marx gets to be a Taurian. On top of which, singing and crooning are never given as the usual Taurian traits in popular horoscopes.

Frequently offered as conclusive proof of parallelism among members of the same sign is the case of Leo. It greatly impresses astrologers and their followers that Alexander the Great, Julius Caesar, Napoleon, Mussolini, and Fidel Castro were all born between July 24 and August 23. Apparently Leo favors power and tyranny. Most descriptions about Leo do in fact include some reference to regality, dominance, and a showmanship-type of success. However, like all other signs, Leo is replete with every type of mentionable and unmentionable individual in the human scope. Yet the fact that Caesar, Napoleon, and Mussolini were all ill-fated Leo tyrants of Latin descent may indeed give the shrewdest skeptic pause.

No trustworthy historian would assert that Caesar, Napoleon, and Mussolini were—as one example—coequal in the quality and scope of their achievements or the impact of their lives. Caesar was, for his time, a benevolent despot who quite literally refused to be crowned emperor even when the crown was offered him. Napoleon, although an egalitarian, did not refuse the imperial crown—and Mussolini, though uncrowned, was neither benevolent nor in any way egalitarian.

Caesar was a reformer who was venerated for his reforms even after his death. Napoleon undertook great social reforms but undid his effect by grandiose military schemes that nearly depleted the population of Europe. Mussolini, it is alleged, caused the trains of Italy to run on schedule, but beyond this no one ever speaks of Il Duce's reforms.

Both Caesar and Napoleon were great strategists and historians—but Caesar was, in the long run, a winner; Napoleon failed in the ultimate test. Needless to say Mussolini is not even in the same league. All three dictators seem to have come to the same end: Caesar assassinated, Napoleon exiled, and Mussolini shot down and humiliated in death. But this apparent bond also breaks down under careful scrutiny. Caesar's death did not diminish his glory *or* his power—in fact his heir and grand-nephew Augustus became emperor soon after him and, in honor of his uncle, assumed the title Caesar—which word has lived on into modern times as "Kaiser" and "Czar."

Napoleon's final exile put an end to his influence; the Bonapartes ruled only once again (though they are still available). His dreary exile to St. Helena lasted almost a decade. Then, riddled with cancer, Napoleon died in bed. His demise was neither sudden nor spectacular as was that of Caesar, nor was it humiliating as in the case of Mussolini. Il Duce was not technically assassinated, rather executed "kangaroo style" by the partisans. After death, his body was ingloriously exposed to the jeering crowds, who, along with history, now remember him as a malevolent clown.

The only career that even nearly parallels Mussolini's, although tenfold as terrible, is that of Adolf Hitler, who is astrology's greatest embarrassment because he was astrology's greatest devotee and plotted out many of his ruinous schemes on the basis of daily horoscopes especially drawn for him by a staff of official astrologers. But the valid comparison between Il

Duce and Der Führer has no bearing on astrology, since Hitler was not a Leo, but rather a "practical, gentle, stubborn" Taurian.

Try as it may, astrology is still unable to draw any conclusive meaning from the fact that Warren G. Harding and Marie Antoinette were both born on the second day of November, when the sun was in Scorpio. This purely coincidental and meaningless detail has absolutely no effect or influence on what may seem to be parallels in their lives and personalities. Only a desperate mind would attempt to prove the validity of the stars by saying that both Harding and the Queen of France were after all rulers of their respective countries and that neither exactly lived up to the highest standards of excellence in office. Such tortuous parallels could be found between any two persons born on any day of any year. The differences are far more telling and bespeak the individuality of man. Even the famous Siamese twins, Chang and Eng, who shared not only the same horoscope but the same bloodstream, were as different as two people under such circumstances could be. According to those who knew them, one had a restless nature, and the other was passive. Often they quarreled about whether to get up and go somewhere or to lie around the house.

Astrology in Daily Life

The extensions of astrology above and beyond the personal horoscope are worth noting, if only for their outrageousness. For instance, there is something called horary astrology which characterizes the "horoscope" of each hour and day of the year. It is this application which affords us the dubious benefits of the astrology columns in most newspapers and magazines. By horary reckoning, December 13, for instance, has its own celestial configurations just as does the individual born on December 13. Astrologers combine the personal horoscope with the horary readings in order to determine how this particular day—or any day—will affect the reader even if he were born in July or August.

For some it may be a "variable day," one in which to bide your time and avoid "unusual experiences in matters of affection." Or it may be a disturbing day, in which "much tact will be necessary with your associates, especially superiors, who are not likely to favor you." The very same day for someone else may be difficult, full of arguments with your mate, if you have one, or it may be a good solid day in which "financial affairs show some improvement." The range of horary possibilities has at least 365 variations, and the details characterizing each day may also range in scope from vague and cautious ("today is a fairly good day for dealing with superiors") to downright fussy ("this is a fine day for any artistic or creative project . . . do favors for children").

It doesn't take too much imagination to see how potentially dangerous horary astrology can become when pursued by credulous and gullible individuals, those who need both the discipline of daily marching orders and the ostensible comfort of knowing that their destinies are all plotted out and predesigned. Uneasy with the problems of gullibility, most daily astrology columns and even popular books devoted to the subject refrain from outright and specific instructions and advice. This they do in deference to the law and to their own obvious limitations. However, their caution does not prevent a highly imaginative devotee from forming his own misinterpretations. Upon reading that "financial concerns are likely to need care," coupled with the prognosis that today will be "disquieting," the anxious devotee may rush down to his savings bank, withdraw all his money, and hide it under his mattress. If, on the following day someone burgles his apartment and makes off with his savings, he is left as much a victim of astrology as of the crime wave.

Imagine the impact on a neurotic housewife when she reads that on April 18 "marital problems are likely to arise." The cautious use of "likely" makes little impression on her anxious mind, so, no matter what happens that day, she will be expecting marital problems at every turn. As a result, she is likely to misinterpret every remark, to misread every gesture. Her susceptible mind may soon become a warehouse of insults, hurts, and suspicions. Neither her anxieties nor her suspicions will be allayed until she can read in her faithful Astrology Guide that at long last "domestic difficulties will probably ease . . ." Of course by this time her harried husband may have picked up and left her—unless he, too, is a devotee and restrains himself because of the fact that "today, impulses should be checked—and no trips taken."

An event recently reported in the French press points up the extent of mass hysteria that an astrologic reading can produce in gullible minds. Mme. Soleil, a very popular astrologer of Paris, reportedly predicted in 1971 that according to the stars an administrative building somewhere in the southwest of France would collapse in the month of April. A newly constructed post office in Bordeaux (still standing) seemed to fit, exactly, Madame's prognosis, and, as a result, panic spread among the postal workers therein.

Even though Mme. Soleil denied making such a forecast, the French newspaper *Le Monde* reported on April 22 that "so Delphic is her reputation that a number of post office workers have prudently gone on holiday." A slowdown in mail delivery for the citizens of Bordeaux was thus not the result of a labor dispute, but rather the impact of astrology on suggestible minds.

Psychologists, psychoanalysts, and others concerned with human behavior are very well aware of the so-called power of suggestion as it applies not only to advertising and to political propaganda, but also to astrology and prediction of the future. More often than not, the gullible person fulfills not his actual destiny but the destiny he has talked himself into. "It would be impossible," says the psychologist Gordon W. Allport of Harvard, "to estimate how large a portion of anyone's personality is acquired through the instrumentality of suggestion, but it must be a very sizable part . . ." So sizable a part, in fact, that there are some impressionable types who can actually become pale and wan when they are told that "they look peaked and drawn." It is of course true that the same impressionable mind may react in a wholly positive way when he learns, if he is a Leo, for instance, that he is a "dynamic, natural leader of men." Unfortunately, most susceptible human beings tend to be pessimists; they will dismiss a positive prognosis but will wallow in the sheerest hint of trouble or disaster.

The problems of suggestibility in the "sciences" of the occult, especially in astrology, are not without larger social implications. Men of influence and power are sometimes devotees of the astrologers' arts. Everyone has heard reports of bankers, investors, and politicians who guide themselves (and their clients or constituents) by the influx of the stars. Hitler, who kept a staff of astrologers at his side throughout his disastrous career, never exceeded twenty miles per hour in his car, owing to a prediction concerning his death in a speeding automobile. Less eccentric, perhaps, are the numerous Hollywood-type celebrities who are always eager, especially on television, to reveal their addiction to horoscope readings and zodiac charms. They may not have the power of Der Führer, but they certainly help to compound the glittering popularity of the delusion by virtue of their own glitter and fame. Whatever the real influence of these individuals—powerful or merely popular—the message they convey is that somehow, in a totally unscientific but nevertheless valid procedure, the celestial bodies direct the course of our lives, the choice of our mates, our fortunes, careers, health, and abilities. In addition to these rather life-and-death considerations, horary astrology is available should we want to know when to buy or sell a given stock; where to go on a trip (or if we should go at all); whether a particular day will be positive, negative or neutral; whether it will be a backdrop for a rousing family feud, for a passionate night of lovemaking, or for some indeterminable event that the susceptible mind fashions for itself.

Just as each man and each day have their own astrology, it should come as no surprise that various nations and sovereign states are likewise ruled by the stars and beholden to the skies. The United States is a Cancer because it "drew its first breath of life" on July 4, 1776 at 3 o'clock in the afternoon. The popular astrologer of the 1930s, Evangeline Adams, went so far as to draw up a horoscope for the United States, with some interesting results. On July 4, 1776, Miss Adams discovered that Gemini was ascending; as a result, America is a restless, inventive country, multi-faceted and fickle when necessary. Combined with these resounding truths are the influences of Cancer itself—the home loving (patriotic), sensitive, generous qualities so abundant in the "good old USA." All is not rosy and harmonious, according to Miss Adams' reading. Because of the conjunction in 1860 of Gemini and Mars, plus Saturn, the Civil War broke out. Owing to a similarly malevolent conjunction of Uranus and Mars in 1942, she predicted another war. With the Civil War, Miss Adams had the luxury of hindsight, but her prognosis about war in 1942 was made from the vantage point of the 1930s—a good reading, one may say. Actually war broke out for the United States on December 7, 1941, 24 days before the onset of 1942. But why quibble? Clever astrologers do have their share of good guesses and fortuitous coincidences—Miss Adams more than most. She also shared the confidence of influential men such as J. P. Morgan, who no doubt gave her, inadvertently or otherwise, valuable pieces of information that she was clever enough to turn into prophecies. This possibility notwithstanding, the basic guide to astrology that Evangeline Adams wrote in 1930 remains one of the most popular books ever circulated by the 42nd Street Public Library in New York.

How does one determine when a country is born? The United States poses some problems in this regard. Technically, the Declaration of Independence was voted and resolved by the founding fathers not on July 4, 1776, but two days earlier on

July 2. It was made public on July 4. One might compare this to the birth and baptism of a baby—in so doing, the birthday becomes July 2, and Miss Adams' calculations fall through. Even July 2 may be rushing things, and it is possible that the birthday of the United States should be considered October 17, 1781, the date of the British surrender at Yorktown—or perhaps it should be April 30, 1789, when George Washington became the first president of the new republic. Nit-pickers, on the other hand, may insist on October 12, 1492, the landing of Columbus (not in the United States but in San Salvador), or on the date of the Pilgrims' landing in New England, or the English landing in Jamestown. There are countless possibilities.

If a nation may have a "horoscope," why not a whole epoch of history, an age, a millennium? Accordingly, astrologers have dissected human history into various ages of two thousand years each, all ruled by the zodiac in almost the same fashion as it rules our individual lives. By such reckoning, astrologers tell us that the period 6,000–4,000 B.C. was the Age of Gemini because at the point of the vernal equinox on March 21, 6,000 B.C., the sun was in Gemini. This explains why the art of writing developed during this period; Geminians, you may remember, are ambidextrous, inventive, and versatile. Two thousand years ago, more or less at the vantage point of 1 A.D., the Age of Pisces dawned—a supposedly troubled age, full of war, plague, misery, upheaval, and confusion. It was also a time of great music, art, literature, philosophy, admirable periods of peace, prosperity, enlightment, progress, and scientific achievement. In short, to the historian, the Age of Pisces (and indeed any age) encompasses just about *everything.* The astrologer is less expansive in his view: this age was defined not by Shakespeare, Michelangelo, Beethoven or Picasso, but by Napoleon, Hitler, Stalin, and company. The progress of medical science and the arts is to astrologers a weak pulse compared to the preponderance of wars and pestilence in this period—as though any period, especially one of 2,000 years duration, is free of war or peace.

The highly vaunted Age of Aquarius is, according to popular cant, due to begin on March 21, 2000 and with it we may expect the "dawning" of a remarkably communicative, orderly, peaceful, and romantic 2,000 years. Aquarius, the Water Carrier, is resourceful, friendly, and humane, *but* it is also unpredictable, excitable, and oversensitive. Incidentally, astronomers at the Hayden Planetarium have poured cold water over the imminence of the Aquarian millennium. According to their quite conclusive calculations, the so-called Age of Aquarius will not dawn until around A.D. 2570. The popular American astrologer Carroll Righter—whose column appears in over 300 newspapers—declared that the Age of Aquarius began in 1904; apparently it's off to a very slow start.

There is almost no area of human or earthly concern into which the delusion of astrology has not been extended. Often it is bestowed in tandem with other fancies of the occult—card reading, palm reading, or the Cabala. The ramifications are endless, just as are the methods and contradictions of astrologers themselves. Some venerate the zodiac, others actually drag in extraneous constellations, and some ignore constellations and dwell on "Houses" and planetary aspects. Interpretation is the real name of the game (or hoax), and for this reason, it is very likely that two astrologers will come up with two different readings on the same horoscope. Even so, they will both seem close to the mark simply because the ill-defined and all-encompassing semantics they use serve to protect and enhance the delusion.

Recently, in this context, an experiment was tried in which the identical horoscope was mailed to over 100 persons who had submitted their natal information to a post office box number. Each person was told that the horoscope pertained to him alone. Although all twelve birth periods were represented by the recipients, with varieties as opposite as Leo and Cancer, almost everyone who received this alleged "personalized" reading accepted it as such, and many admired its pertinence and exactitude. A Libran may be duly impressed by the way a generalized horoscope for Libra seems to fit his personality; but if he read a Gemini chart labelled Libra, he would probably have the same reaction.

As the Stars Fade . . .

Mass susceptibility to the primitive delusion of astrology reveals some of the anxieties and insecurities of our times. Many people are seeking a panacea for their problems, no matter how fictitious the cures may be. Science seems to appall these people, but the mumbo-jumbo of Merlin the Magician does not.

A sensitive view of this condition was offered in *McCall's* by its editor Shana Alexander. "All forms and systems of astrology," she wrote, "are based on a single assumption: that there is a relationship between the stars and human beings. On the surface, how preposterous! Yet if one can accept the premise, how beautiful and ordered and serene the world becomes . . .

"Astrology is the perfect panacea, the universal antidote for everything that ails our modern world. It replenishes our nearly empty cup of mystery and feeds our hankering for harmony at the same time. Paradoxically, it is a shield against both clarity and chaos. It relieves us of responsibility to know: if astrology is true, why bother with anything else?"

Miss Alexander echoes a query raised nearly two thousand years ago by a Roman philosopher named Arellius Fuscus. "If the pretentions of astrology are genuine," he wrote, "why do not men of every age devote themselves to this study? Why from our infancy do we not fix our eyes on nature and on the gods, seeing that the stars unveil themselves for us, and that we can live in the midst of the gods? Why exhaust ourselves in efforts to acquire eloquence, or devote ourselves to the professions of arms?"

Why not indeed, if all is determined from the outset by the

stars—even if the stars only impel, not *compel* (as most astrologers are quick to aver), why not rule our lives with horoscopes and astrological delineations? To some the answer is: yes, why not? After all, is it not a comfort to know that those of us born in the sign of Gemini will be two-faced but versatile, that the Taurians among us are stubborn as bulls yet gentle as calves, or that some Cancerians will live lives "populated with shadows and will-o-wisps [in which] a weary soul floats where its visions and chimeras lead it"?

2

Other "-Ologies" and Delusions: Numerology, Palmistry, Phrenology, Physiognomy, Tarotology, and Omens

Numerology

Because of the cosmic conformity of numbers, some mystics assert that numerology, not astrology or any other ology, is the only valid and dependable occultic system of divination and prophecy. Numerologists acknowledge their debts to the ancient astrologers and are quick to incorporate into their own system astrological cant, specifically when celestial numbers are concerned. Even so, for the numerologist it does not greatly matter what month or sign a subject was born under, but rather what Birth Number and Name Number he represents. Just as there are Librans and Leos and Pisceans in astrology, there are Number Two people and Number Five people, and so forth up to Nine in the pseudo-science of Numbers.

The Background

Man's fascination with numbers, like his veneration of the sky, is derived from antiquity. The Bible, as one ancient example, is replete with numerical connotations, a condition upon which much of the Cabala is based. There are the Ten Commandments, the Twelve Tribes, the Forty Days and Nights, the Seven Seals, and the Fourteen Stations of the Cross.

Medieval Hebrew Talmudists, like the Cabalists, fashioned an involved biblical code system called *gematria*. In it, every significant word of the Scriptures was given its numerical equivalent so that alleged mysteries and puzzles buried in the holy text become at once explicit and resolved, at least to the gematriast. Proof that Moses actually wrote the Farewell Song ascribed to him in Deut. 23;1-6 is evident when read according to this code. The first six Hebrew letters of the first six sentences of this Song, states gematria, have the numerical equivalence of 345. The number values of Moses' own name (in Hebrew) equal the same—345. Thus a form of anagram was apparently worked into the text by the ancient scribes as a message to future generations.

The Greeks, under the impetus of the philosopher Pythagoras (sixth century B.C.), adored the mechanics of numbers and extended their permutations to encompass a *weltanschauung* in which the chaotic elements of nature were finally drawn together by the exactitude of numerical conceptions.

According to the Pythagoreans, a fixed system of magic—and therefore of divination—evidently lay at the basis of numerical philosophy, since everywhere and always one plus two equal three, three plus four are seven, ad infinitum. Medievalists and modern men have revelled in the fascination of "sacred numbers," which presumably do mathematical tricks and therefore are magical. The number 142857, for example, is a well-remembered sacred number that has remained unshaken throughout the centuries. It is obtained by dividing the eternal number 1,000,000 (one, or God, plus six symbols of endlessness) by the mystical number 7. Attach as many zeros as you like to the eternal number, and the results will always be 142857. We must now add up the sacred number in a column in order to understand the true wonder of this ancient revelation. The sum of such addition is 27. But double digits are not pure enough in numerology, so 2 and 7 themselves are added, resulting in 9. Beginning with 1 (God) and numerous zeros (the infinite), numerologists divided by the mystic 7 and eventually ended up with the ultimate digit 9. The numbers from 1 to 9 are the foundation of numerology, and upon these nine digits "all materialistic or human calculations can be built."

A clue to the fallacy of the so-called magic numbers may already be evident in the mumbo jumbo offered above. Numerologists, as opposed to mathematicians, are apparently amazed by the simple and mechanical procedures of arithmetic. What makes 142857 so sacred to them is the fact that it is produced with the aid of the God number 1, the sacred number 7 (though why 7 is sacred is questionable) and that in the long run it reduces to the ultimate digit 9.

221-1570 also reduces to 9, and it is merely a typical American telephone number. Of course a numerologist will explain that it is probably not so typical as the unenlightened may think, for if the party answering the phone is also a Number 9 (born on the 9th, 18th or 27th of any month) and if the date is also either the 9th, 18th or 27th, surely, according to numerological lore, something of importance is likely to result—a big business deal or even a romantic assignation. After all, according to one numerologist, numbers are not human creations, but they "have an independent existence of their own and are merely observed by sufficiently intelligent mortals."

How It Works

There are two major systems of numerical equivalency, two keys to the occult meaning of one's name. One is simple, obvious, and direct. The nine digits are set out in a row and the alphabet is lined up under them. Thus A to I are 1 to 9; J to R are 1 to 9; and S to Z are 1 to 8, omitting the third 9 simply because there are no more letters available in our alphabet. By this method the name Lincoln, for example, reduces to the double digit 34 and further reduces to 7 (3 + 4 = 7).

The more highly regarded equivalency system supposedly evolved from Hebrew, with a dash of Chaldean and Greek influence. Ancient and obscure as it is, it is naturally favored by modern mystics. In this system the digit 9 is omitted since, to quote the reasoning of Cheiro, the celebrated seer of the 1920s and 1930s, "the ancient masters of Occultism knew that in the 'Highest Sphere' the Number 9 represents the nine-lettered name of God and for this reason no single letter was ascribed to it." This doesn't mean that a name cannot reduce to a 9—in fact, Lincoln's name, by this old system, does exactly that—but only 1 to 8 are equivocated.

The Traditional Code
A, I, Q, J, Y = 1; B, K, R = 2; C, G, L, S = 3; D, M, T = 4; E, H, N = 5; U, V, W, X = 6; O, Z = 7; F, P = 8.

By using this key in relation to one's most commonly used name, the so-called Name Number is achieved—9 in Lincoln's case. This is only one of the various numerical factors that each of us represents.

Of primary importance is the Birth Number. In Lincoln's case it is 12 (February). Again reducing it to a single digit we arrive at 3. Already the observant will notice that Lincoln's Name Number and Birth Number are not in harmony. Even using Lincoln's first name does not bring him into numerical unity; this, according to the experts, bodes ill.

Cheiro's system of numbers, that is, the traditional code, along with his analysis of palmistry, is generally regarded as definitive among devotees of numerology. Whatever method is used, it should be clear by now that the Birth Number in conjunction with the Name Number resembles one's horoscope —to wit, the key to one's true personality and fate.

Other numerical factors are derived by some practitioners from the vowels of the name (the Heart Number, which reveals one's inner nature and deepest goals) and from the consonants (the Personality Number—one's outward characteristics). Some others like to play around with the subject's address, telephone number, or in the United States, his social security number. But these are merely variations on the same theme.

Numerical Metaphors

Once the Name Number and Birth Number are calculated, we are faced with trying to understand what these numbers imply. On the surface they all seem to be sterile and ordinary items. Does it matter, one may ask, that Lincoln's Name Number is 9, and his Birth Number is 3; isn't a number just a number? Some hint has already been given of how numerologists view the nine digits in metaphoric terms. To them 1 is the singularity of God, 7 is mystic, 9 is elevated to the "Highest Sphere" (presumably of the Cabala). Working out the traditional qualities and mystic meanings of the nine digits involves a procedure almost identical to the semantical associations of the astrologic signs. To believe in this system one must simply accept the fundamental metaphors set out for each number, just as in astrology one accepts the planet name "Venus" and therefore the Venusian illusions that automatically follow.

The digit 1 in this context is associated, logically, with unity, singleness, and ultimately with God. It is also related to the sun, because the sun (since Copernicus) is the singular center of the solar system—ergo, Sunday is the first day of the week in many Western countries. The sun is also the source of life, heat, light, a great and indispensable positive force. Number 1 people, those born on the 1st, 10th, 19th, or 28th of any month, plus those whose names add up to 1 (although the birth date is still the more important designation) are creative, original, and dynamic (or aggressive) individuals. Sunny types, they are also noted for singlemindedness and monomania. The religious innovator Martin Luther was a 1 (November 10), and so was the individualistic Woodrow Wilson (December 28). Less sunny but nonetheless inventive were Chopin (March 1) and Edgar Allan Poe (January 19).

The singularity and unity of 1 is halved to make 2. This dualistic blow coupled with the fact that the moon is a 2 "planet" (the second most relevant celestial body) cause Number 2 people—those born on the 2nd, 11th, 20th, or 29th of any month—to be somewhat second-raters, weaklings whose energy has been halved; number 2 people are also gentle, romantic and artistic souls, often ill-fated or forced to play "second fiddle" in life. Marie Antoinette (November 2) seems to fit this bill. But Thomas Edison (February 11) looks like a glaring exception to the rule, and from what we know of him should have been a 1—unless of course he secretly "second guessed" the many inventions usually credited to him.

Resuming the dynamic, creative, and anti-dualistic force of 1 is Number 3, the digit of Jupiter and the symbol of the male generative force (the three parts: one phallus and two testicles). Number 3s (born on the 3rd, 12th, 21st, or 30th) are accordingly dominant and energetic individuals, given to leadership, great success, and scintillation. Winston Churchill (November 30), Voltaire (November 21), and the aforementioned Lincoln do seem to fit this delineation—overlooking, of course, Lincoln's tragic end and the long road to greatness which Churchill plowed, finally becoming prime minister of England when past 60 years of age.

If 2 is a weak, passive number because of its dualistic construction, then 4 is twice as disjointed. Accordingly, Number 4 people (4th, 13th, 22nd, 31st) are described by one numerologist as being "solid, practical, uninspired and uninspiring." They "lack any creative spark . . ." and are grim, plodding, and envious drudges, the stepchildren of the numerical creed. Cheiro and other more lenient numerologists try to obviate these gloomy traits by interpreting Number 4s as dependable, salt-of-the-earth types, given to despondence but "inclined to be attracted to social questions and reforms," apparently owing to the creative influence of Uranus, the 4 planet. Some of the born losers among the 4s were George Washington (February 22), also a Piscean, which is the stepchild of the zodiac according to some opinions; Sarah Bernhardt (October 22); Richard Wagner (May 22); and the "solid, practical, uninspired, and grim" Lord Byron (January 22).

The odd number 5, like 1 or 3, is a bright, positive, and dashing pigeonhole. Associated with the planet Mercury, Number 5s (born 5th, 14th, 23rd of any month) "live on their nerves and appear to crave change and excitement." Gamblers, lovers, adventurers, their "lucky stone," according to Cheiro, is appropriately enough a diamond, which sparkles like their personalities. Who can think of a more appropriate Number 5 than Louis XVI (August 23), the stupid King of France, beheaded during the Revolution?

Though 6 is an even number like the enervated 2 and 4, it is nonetheless a strong force, for it comprises two threes—a double dynamism. The fortuitous combination of being a feministic even number and an aggressive odd number gives Number 6 people (born on the 6th, 15th, 24th of any month) the qualities of harmony, equanimity, and cheerfulness. Owing to the lure of their planet Venus, they are sensuous, artistic, and generous. When negatively inclined they become smug, gossipy, and conceited. Celebrities among sixers include Joan of Arc (January 6), Napoleon (August 15), Rembrandt (July 15) and the ill-fated Maximilian, Emperor of Mexico (July 6).

Because it is the sabbath number, and for other vague reasons, the ancients thought 7 to be a holy number, invested with mystery. Seven people (born on the 7th, 16th, 25th of any month) are accordingly mystics, scholars, occultists, somewhat secretive and aloof from the world. They are also, because of Neptune's influence, given to travel and sensitive poetry. Oscar Wilde was a 7 (October 16) whose secrets were brutally revealed. No mystic but certainly a scholar was Newton (December 25), and Elizabeth I of England (September 7) is reported to have held herself continuously aloof, especially from marriage.

The compound of 4 is 8—double trouble, as it were, and ruled by the powerful planet Saturn. This allegedly constructive planetary influence saves Number 8s from complete ruination, when it *does* save them, for as Cheiro reports, "Number 8 people are either great successes or great failures," with no happy medium in their lives. A less forbidding evaluation appraises them as determined, self-confident, and generous souls who often gather great riches to themselves. Or, if unlucky, they will plug away at losing battles until they drop. In addition to this precarious existence, Number 8 people (born on the 8th, 17th, 26th of any month) are often victims of fate who ultimately "lay bare the tragedy of their souls before Divine Justice." Mary Queen of Scots (December 8) was such a loser, but J. P. Morgan (April 17) and John D. Rockefeller (July 8) could hardly be called victims.

Finally there is 9, the Mars number, a masterful digit reserved for great minds, high achievers, and eccentrics. The aforementioned association of 9 with the secret name of God, the fact that gestation usually lasts nine months, that there are nine known planets, and that 9 when multiplied by any other digit produces a number that always adds up to nine ($3 \times 9 = 27 = 9$; $5 \times 9 = 45 = 9$; etc.) contribute to the occult reverence for this, the last factor in the numerical alphabet. Number 9 names from history (born on the 9th, 18th, 27th of any month) include Kaiser Wilhelm of Germany (January 27), Ulysses S. Grant (April 27), Nicholas II, last Czar of Russia (May 18) and Teddy Roosevelt (October 27)—a mixed bag if ever one existed.

In addition to the basic nine digits and their extrapolations, some numerologists emphasize the value of compound numbers. The identical twins 11, 22, 33, and so forth are especially important and favorable, even 22, the double dualist whose sum is the unfortunate 4. Non-identical compounds such as 10, 12, 13, 14, and so on are investigated in order to find the inner and secret meanings of life. Cheiro, for one, relates these entities to the images on Tarot cards, soon to be discussed.

The Name Number is studied to determine one's personal fate. Cheiro attempts to demonstrate this axiom in the case of Napoleon Bonaparte. "The great Napoleon," he says, "originally wrote his name as Napoleon Buonaparte. Later on in his life he changed it to Napoleon Bonaparte. This change had a curious significance," to wit: NAPOLEON = 5, a strong, successful, positive number. Fortunately, the old name Buonaparte also equals 5. Ignorant of numerology, the Emperor of France carelessly decided to frenchify his last name, thus changing the numerical value of that name to 8, which, according to Cheiro, represents "revolution, anarchy, waywardness, conflict with human justice, and generally a tragic ending to life." Worse yet, the total of Napoleon (5) and Bonaparte (8) equals 13, which reduces to the unfortunate 4.

Now at last, historians will understand why the aggressive Corsican failed to solidify his vaunting dreams. The reason: somewhere along the line he dropped the u in his surname. Defeat was inevitable.

This diverting but ridiculous demonstration highlights some of the grand rules of numerology. Above all, the key numbers in one's life must be harmonious or complementary. The Birth Number and the Name Number should be identical for the best results, but failing that—as at least eighty percent of all cases do—one must try to equivocate them at least ostensibly. If the Birth Number is weak (2, 4, 8), try to strengthen the name number by adding a middle initial or revising the spelling of a surname, so long as it doesn't become Bonaparte. Dropping Richard for Dick, for example, may help.

The birth date of course is less susceptible to such alterations. However, the accommodating numerologists can finesse even this problem by adding the month and year numbers to an otherwise lackadaisical date.

To further elucidate: if one is stuck with a 4 name and an 8 birth date and he doesn't wish to change his name, there are nevertheless many possibilities, we are told, by which he may eschew the harsher strictures of his fate. Number 8 people (born on the 8th, 17th, 26th) should avoid living in houses whose addresses add up to 4 (such as 22, 130, 400, etc.). The same is true for number fours; they must avoid number 8 addresses. Avoiding such addresses, they also avoid "sorrow, misfortune, and strange fatalities."

Someone born a 1 whose name equals 2 can evade the 2 influence by changing his address and telephone number, especially if they equal 2; and he should avoid using the 2 in all transactions, agreements, and love affairs. If you are a 1, numerologists advise, get married on 1 days, or equally strong 5 days. According to traditional numerology, it's up to the individual to juggle his numerical schema until the smoothest harmony is achieved. After a while, of course, it may become a compulsion such as not stepping on the cracks in the pavement, as the faithful slave of numerology adds, subtracts, and multiplies every possible combination of numbers in his life before setting out each day on to the battlefields of existence.

1, 2, 3—You're Out!

The fallacies of numerology are similar to those of astrology, for numerology, too, is a system tied to metaphor and philology, dependent on sheer coincidence and shrewd or vague interpretation. Take the case of Napoleon again. Born on the 15th, he was therefore a 6, supposedly the number of harmony, sensuousness, and ambition. His name was, at first, a 1 (5 + 5 = 10 = 1), the number of unity, leadership, singlemindedness. As we know, the Emperor clouded up his future by changing the spelling of his surname. Retrospectively, any clever numerologist can and does explain that the harmonious 6 of Napoleon's Birth Number, spurred on by his dynamic Name Number (1), brought him to great power and fame. The brilliant number 5 (ruled by Mercury) dominated the name Napoleon, by which the Emperor was widely known. This explains his military career, his political good fortune, and his success. Finally, say the numerologists, he befouled his destiny by dropping the fatal letter u in B*u*onaparte—and the results are a matter of history.

This kind of *a posteriori* prophecy is obviously an intellectual fraud. Any historical figure can be fitted into the Procrustean bed of numerology (or astrology) by merely stretching his 1s, 5s, or 9s at the headboard and amputating his 2s, 4s, and 8s at the foot.

When the outcome is unknown, the results may not be so fortuitous, as in the case of Herbert Hoover, who was President of the United States when Cheiro decided to draw up Hoover's numerological configuration.

Born on August 10, 1874, Hoover was a number 1. His name, including the middle name Clark, ultimately added up to 5. As noted, 1 and 5 are vigorous, positive numbers. Somewhere along the line Mr. Hoover dropped Clark from his usual appellation, but even so he remained strong, positive, and well-favored as a 3. In addition to the positive powers of his name and birth date, Hoover was dominated by the beneficent qualities of the sun, for as Cheiro explained, August 10—Hoover's birthday—falls in the period known as the House of the Sun (July 21–August 28). The President's success seemed assured by these reckonings. But was it?

"I most deeply regret," reports Cheiro in 1931, "that, in considering the numbers influencing President Hoover's life, I must conclude by saying the indications are that, unless great precautions are taken before he finishes his presidential term, he will face considerable danger of death from fire, explosion, or attempts on his life by fanatics or anarchists."

Evidently great precautions were taken. As everyone knows, Herbert Hoover outlived his presidency by 30 years and died in bed at the age of 90.

Palmistry

Cheiro derived his name from the Greek word for hand, Χειρο *chiro*. Besides being the "world's greatest seer" as well as numerologist, he was the author of a system of palmistry, or chiromancy, highly regarded by mystics even today. In this most tactile of the popular occult arts, one is expected to find the key to personality and fate in the lines, bumps, lumps, crevices, and other characteristics of the hands. Only phrenology—head bump reading—allows the seer such a personal contact with the secrets of life. Yet despite these ordinary anatomical aspects, chiromancy is thought to embody all the mystical splendor of a Hindu cult.

Like numerologists, palm readers also resort to astrological conceptualization in order to complement and amplify their art. Cheiro laced numbers and stars in and among the lines and bumps of the hands he examined. He also analyzed the quality and color of the skin, the hair, and the nails on the hand (presumably hangnails and calluses were also involved in the reading of the hand).

Palmists are proud of the fact that police throughout the world regard fingerprints as a sine qua non of crime detection. The swirls and whorls on the tips of each finger are, say the palmists, part and parcel of the overall fate pattern. Of course, Scotland Yard and the FBI are completely unconcerned about the *meaning* of such fingerprint convolutions; the singularity is what interests them, since no two sets of fingerprints have ever been found to be identical, even in cases of identical twins. Crediting palmistry with scientific authority simply because police labs utilize fingerprints is like authenticating astrology because mariners and astronauts guide their vessels by means of celestial maps.

Background

Alexander the Great reportedly received one of the first treatises on palmistry in recorded history. It was lettered in gold so that the emperor might more easily pursue what was called "a study worthy of the attention of an elevated enquiring mind." Other elevated minds devoted to palmistry in ancient times allegedly include Aristotle, Pliny, Paracelsus, Albertus Magnus, and Augustus Caesar. But the delusion is not confined to the ancient West. Scanning the lines of the palm is a popular pastime of Orientals and a favorite occultism in India today.

Palmistry first became a popular fad probably around 1475, when a book entitled *Die Kunst Ciromantia (The Art of Chiromancy)* was published in Augsburg, Germany. The Church at the time had no use for what it termed this pagan and heathenistic preoccupation. Quite naturally it associated chiromancy with witches, gypsies, vagrants, itinerants, and pickpockets—with good reason. While telling the gullible subject that he would soon gain great riches in this world, a palmreader would make off, unnoticed, with his customer's purse. We have heard about crossing the reader's palm with silver *before* the reading begins; it should be obvious why this was done. When the reading was ended, very often, the subject had no silver to dispense.

Today most sensible people regard palmistry as a carnival amusement. Even aficionados of the occult seem to have rele-. gated the art of palmistry to the status of a minor divination, a mere codicil to astrology and numerology. Even so, in the great "leap forward" recently experienced in all occultic fields, chiromancy seems to be gaining new adherents. After all, they say, while one must share his horoscope with hundreds of thousands and his numerical patterns with millions throughout the world, the uniquely individualistic configurations of the palm assure the subject of a truly personalized reading. As Cheiro reminds us, the greatest study of mankind is man. Does it not follow that man's two hands are logical, perhaps indispensable, sources of this studious investigation? Of course, the irreverent might ask why the soles of the feet, replete as they are with lines, lumps, bumps and swirls, do not play an equal part in the grand detection of fate. Though surely less elegant than palm reading, foot reading could in the current intellectual climate become a new occultic art—a veritable *footnote* to the other magic sciences. Those concerned might wish to call it *Podology*.

How It Works

To appreciate chiromancy one must accept the following deduction: as man is a microcosm of the universe, so is man's hand a microcosm of man. Therein lies his story. On the left palm, destiny is etched in unalterable patterns like the orbits of the planets. The right palm, however, changes and develops even as life itself develops. Cheiro expresses it this way: "the left (hand) shows the inherited tendencies; the right, the developed or cultivated qualities."

First with the left hand, then the right, several lines and attributes are studied by serious palmists. Running from the ball of the palm beneath the thumb to a point somewhere under the first three fingers is the so-called line of fortune or destiny, which governs man's fate. Swinging down like a bow from under the index finger to somewhere under the smallest finger is the heart line—one's emotional indicator. Parallel to this bow-like line at a distance usually one-half inch or so down toward the thumb is the head line, thought to govern man's intellectual powers. This curve usually is connected to the semi-circular life line that fences off the ball of the thumb and runs downward toward the wrist. The fate, heart, head, and life lines are the major etched designs. To them one must add the more sculptural mounds and bumps and the minor lines, which fall into various geometric configurations: the bracelets, for instance, which ring the wrist; the marriage and progeny creases, found alongside the ball of the little finger; the line of intuition or imagination running downward from the pinkie; and the health line or Hepatic line, racing at a sharp diagonal from the pinkie base to the base of the thumb. Concerning the mounds we enter the astrological aspect of palmistry, for each of the major mounds is identified with planets and naturally, therefore, each planetary metaphor follows suit, to wit: the mound of Venus—the large fleshy extension of the thumb—is associated with love and passion, as usual. Just above it, at the fold of the thumb, is the *positive* area of Mars (courage, vitality), while the negative mound of Mars is directly opposite; it governs belligerence and brutality. Mercury's mound is under the little finger. It refers to mentality and quick wit (just as Mercury always does). Under the ring finger is the sun mound, and here one looks to find the extent or lack of success. The middle finger rises above the mound of Saturn, which controls one's more intense and personal moods. And under the index finger is Jupiter's mound—storehouse of ambition and power. The romantic moon fills out the palm under the negative mound of Mars, just above the wrist opposite the thumb. Here one may seek and find indications of imagination, talent, and other moon-June-spoon emotions. Search as he will, the palmist will not find a mound of Neptune, Uranus, or Pluto. These Johnny-come-lately planets were unknown to the ancients who dreamed up the basic elements of palmistry. Certain French and German seers of the 17th century, however, have added zodiac attributes to the various bulges of the fingers. Thus Aries rules the upper section of the index finger, while Virgo can be found on the lowest third of the middle finger. Although Cheiro avoids these confusing zodiac distinctions, being more concerned with lines than with bumps, older chiromancers have gone so far as to cover the palm and fingers with every human inclination from religious devotion (upper section, index finger) to logic (second section, thumb) to one's capacity for deception (lowest third, pinkie).

Can there be a set formula for reading these lines, bumps, and curves in face of the facts that no two hands are alike, and that some people may have a clearly defined health line while others have none at all? Despite the odds, palmists have managed to come up with a pseudoscientific (and quasi-intelligent) set of formulas based not on logic and scientific truth, but on metaphor and analogy, as is the case with astrology and numerology.

A fleshy, dominant mound of Venus, for instance, indicates—as one might guess—a fleshy, dominant love life, while a flat uninspired Venus mound points, alas, to a love life of the same dimensions. And so it follows that a deeply incised health line bodes well for a solid, healthy life, and a long, sharply defined life line naturally foretells a long, sharply defined life. If the head line of the subject joins the life line at the wide arc over the thumb, he is surely a man whose life is governed by his head; and if his heart line plunges toward the mound of the moon (the imagination mound), he will, of course, be possessed by a fantasy-ridden emotional life.

Three creases of marriage may mean three marriages. Or perhaps they indicate three phases of one marriage (the palm reader must be careful not to offend a monogamous customer). Even a bachelor may have marriage lines, especially on his destiny hand, for this will indicate the marriages he might have made but avoided. On the bachelor's right hand three marriage lines indicate three opportunities in the offing or three phases of a single opportunity, and so on.

Practitioners of the Past

Whereas Cheiro is frequently plodding and mechanical in his descriptions and instructions—thereby presumably giving his system the illusion of accuracy—the more flamboyant chiromancers of the seventeenth and eighteenth centuries tend to startle and jolt with their theatrical elaborations. Witness the celebrated reading offered by the soothsayer Mlle. Le Normand, who, in the early nineteenth century, drew up a complicated palm chart of Napoleon Bonaparte—the favorite subject of all occultic divination. Le Normand's conclusions about Bonaparte's fate and personality, based on his palm, were published in 1827, six years after the emperor's death. The original reading, however, was drawn up in 1807, two years prior to Napoleon's divorce from Josephine (another client of Le Normand). The palmist's prophecy about the separation so deeply impressed the emperor that in December, 1809, he secretly had Mlle. Le Normand arrested and detained for about two weeks until his divorce was finalized. A little investigation into Le Normand's prophecies shows that she was apparently more of a shrewd guesser than a mystic seer. Her 1827 published reading of Napoleon's palm is apparently an exercise in *a posteriori* proof in which she justifies his fall from fame because Saturn was "placed just below two stars (on the extreme tip of the second finger) . . . a disastrous omen for him." The divorce prediction, which was based on a reading predating the actual event, is also nothing more than *retrospective* "clairvoyance." That Bonaparte wanted to get rid of Josephine was not exactly a secret, even in 1807. Many a seer, even today, simply forecasts rumors which he or she has gleaned in private, hoping that these rumors materialize as facts. When they do, everyone is duly amazed.

More amazing is how anyone can put the slightest faith in such an obvious and transparent system as palmistry. It abounds even more than astrology and numerology in silly inferences, all the more silly because they are based on the most commonplace varieties of anatomy. Here is a random excerpt from a popular manual that clearly exemplifies the wordplay essence of the palm reader's delusion. "Imperfect lines," it states, "confused, twisted, denote a bizarre being, lacunae, dangers . . . Fine and numerous [lines] mean nervousness, activity. Broad, not very deep, not very numerous, they show calm and power of resistance. Broken, cut, they mean stops, changes, dangers, restless fate. Regular and numerous they indicate a noble life, intellect, sensitivity."

May one add in this vein that dirty lines—those filled with grime—indicate labor, hard work, messiness . . . ?

Fortunately there is some humor in all this gibberish as long as one does not take the guidelines seriously. According to the manual just quoted, if a lady's head line is forked, her mound of Venus high and broad, and if her line of adultery is found rising toward Mercury and the Sun, she is undoubtedly "a woman born to deceive men." Similarly, there are adulterous men deceiving women; for proof, one needs only to note their heart lines joining their life lines and forming a cross on Jupiter (under the index finger).

Another weighty tome on chiromancy warns of two parallel lines moving from the ball of the palm to the mound of Saturn. The possessor of this configuration shall "dwell in many places and be poor at the end of his days." Supposedly the double lines show waywardness, and Saturn is, after all, a melancholy mound. How much happier the subject would be if his double line ran into the Solar bump; if so "many offices of honor and great lordship and great rewards shall be given him . . ." Such folderol was concocted in the sixteenth century by a certain André Corvo, but how far in tone is it from Cheiro's twentieth century treatise that advises: "When the line of Fate rises from the wrist and goes straight up the center of the palm to the mound of Saturn . . . luck, brilliance and success will attend Destiny, and extreme good fortune may be anticipated." Note that Cheiro speaks of a *single* line, not to be confused with Corvo's double-trouble design.

As mentioned earlier, palm readers are greatly concerned with the shape of hands and quality of nails. Naturally, continuing the eternal metaphor, they say that spatulate hands belong to artists and creative men such as Rembrandt, Rubens, and Napoleon III. Square hands belong to "squares"; pointed ones to men (and women) who make a point of things, such as Robespierre, Milton, Shakespeare, and George Sand—at least so we are informed by nineteenth-century French palmist Henri Rem. It is a fascinating puzzle to ponder how he knows the shape of Shakespeare's hand. No doubt it came to him supernaturally, as did all his other insights.

The movement of the hand, its posture, and its deportment are also studied by chiromancers. Caressing and lasting handshakes indicate a voluptuous personality, while a handshake "caressing with pleasure bespeaks carnal desire." Corvo relates this astounding axiom: "When you see a man keeping his hand shut, meaning the thumb hidden within the fingers, then that man is a miser who will manage to survive by hook or crook."

The lines, mounds, and other elements that are part of the human hand are clearly functional and not mystical by nature. If one watches his palm as he slowly closes his fist, he will observe that the presence of lines and creases quite mechanically enables the skin of the palm to fold and turn, for each line assists in the natural movement of the fingers and thumb without torturing the skin. As for the mounds, they usually develop in relation to the type of work that the hand pursues. Texture of skin, hair, and nails (presuming that the nails are unbitten) indicates not one's personality, but possibly the state of one's health, since peeling or cracking nails suggest a vitamin deficiency but not necessarily an inclination to feeblemindedness.

There are lines to be found at the inner crevices of the elbow, on the soles of the feet, on the eyelids, and in several other less prominent parts of the human anatomy. Are these also mystical indicators of fate or merely functional folds and creases? Whatever the case, most sages ignore them, although a "science" called metoposcopy (facial lines) used to be studied in eighteenth century France. In this belabored scheme, the creases of the forehead relate to the planets, and the zodiac is represented all over the face; the lines of Libra, for example, are found near the upper lip, while Virgo occupies the area generally harassed by the "crow's feet" of middle age.

The Magic Anatomy

Before leaving the magical aura of the hand and face, we should mention a few other anatomical systems of divination that, while relatively obscure, are nonetheless sought and studied by certain occultists even today.

Physiognomy is the overall title for those methods of divination and prophecy which utilize body parts and somatotypes.

Facial morphology is one of the favorite digressions. It requires no great fuss since all the magician needs to do is to study the subject's mien, even from afar. The metaphoric extensions of this system are so patently obvious that one imagines a ten-year-old child as its author, to wit: light blue eyes indicate gentleness and kindness; yellowish eyes, murder and deviation. As to the nose: well-shaped, it means a lofty mind; a hooked nose implies greed; wide nostrils, expansiveness. Furthermore, the brave man has "keen eyes, well arched brows, pointed chin, muscular neck, broad and well built body." But, beware the "irregular pale face with narrow ears, thin lips, slanting eyes . . . legs thin and badly shaped," for this depicts a "man of evil disposition."

Perhaps, some may say, this system lacks precision—is there no more precise physiognomic method on which to base one's philosophy of life? To be sure, occultists depend on phrenology when all else fails. This is, of course, the system of head bump reading, allegedly developed in 1758 by German anatomist Franz Josef Gall. Studying head types and skulls, Gall reached the conclusion that the various protuberances and valleys of the cranium revealed the shape of the brain and, therefore, personality traits and possibly the fate of the entire corpus. Gall and his disciples divided the cranium into over forty areas, each describing a human asset or tendency. If the area is large and protruding, it naturally (or supernaturally) follows that the trait associated with this bump will also be pronounced. On the other hand, depressed areas signify a depressed emotion, tendency, or what have you.

According to Gall the amative nature is supposedly located at the base of the brain. If the area is large, strong, and protruding, one can assume that he is examining an amorous subject (the subject should not be caressed too affectionately, lest he become aroused). The dome of the skull relates to man's religious and benevolent senses. A ridge there suggests a greedy, irreverent soul, but a bulging forehead indicates good learning abilities, memory, and "resistance," presumably—when well developed—the ability to withstand distraction.

The pseudoscience of phrenology, with its random identification of bumps, assumes that the human skull is a fixed or predetermined part of the body, as are the fingerprints. Actually the newborn cranium is extremely malleable and assumes its form very gradually, for months or possibly years after birth. In addition, the shape of one's head may be quite markedly affected by the process of birth, such as whether or not the doctor used forceps at delivery or merely grasped the emerging head with his hands.

Gall's idea that the formation of the cranium indicates the shape of the brain and, by extension, the intellectual and emotional qualities of the individual is unfounded in science. Even post-mortem analysis of the brain itself has not revealed any meaningful association between *brain shape,* or convolutions, and mental abilities.

Thus, at best, a visit to a phrenologist may afford the subject a pleasant scalp massage.

Tarotology

Perhaps the only redeeming quality about the delusion of tarotology (or cartomancy)—divination by cards—is the fact that some very beautiful and artistic decks have come down to us from the past. Especially fascinating are the various Tarot decks often reproduced in books and in modern facsimiles, such as the handpainted deck of King Charles VI of France, dating from 1392, one of the oldest and most elaborate extant. These cards were fashioned, it is said, for the purpose of distracting Charles during the early days of his madness. As a result, the popularity of telling fortunes and uncovering secrets by the cards soon spread like wildfire through the French court of the day. Before long, several noblemen and their wives became rather alarmed that their frequent infidelities and other transgressions would be revealed to the light of day by this apparently faultless form of divination. Pretending that the card playing craze threatened to bankrupt the aristocracy (since gambling was part of the game), influential figures at court passed an edict forbidding Tarot and other forms of cartomancy. Naturally the practice at once went underground. "Speakeasies" devoted to card reading became endemic in France, and the craze continued to spread.

There are two distinct but related aspects of cartomancy. One uses the common deck we know today, with fifty-two cards (no joker) of four suits, ten digits, and the royal house. With these ordinary bits of laminated paper, usually reserved for bridge and canasta, one can supposedly uncover all manner of truths. The do-it-yourself cartomancer lays out a fixed number of cards, usually conforming to the number of the day selected for the reading, and he studies them for messages that appear alone or in tandem with other cards. An ace of hearts by itself may thus indicate "receipt of money or a gift . . . ," but coupled with the queen of diamonds, the ace takes on added detail and fascination, since the queen represents a woman of beneficence who can be of great assistance—presumably in collecting the money promised by the ace of hearts. Should the jack, or knave, of spades crop up between the ace of hearts and the queen of diamonds, one may expect a young, deceitful person to intrude in the beneficial proceeding. One old manual warns the reader to "look after the servants" if the jack of spades appears near the jack of diamonds.

The more elaborate and occultic aspect of cartomancy involves the ever-popular Tarot deck. These cards are in fact intended solely for divination, although a few parlor games such as "Old Maid" have derived from Tarot.

Invested with an ancient past and with many legends of prophetic success, the Tarots are increasingly sought after as a guide in love and fortune and a revelation of fate. Among the college crowd today, Tarot and the Chinese prophetic system *I Ching* have surprising popularity. One may find a Tarot pack incongruously lying on top of a copy of Einstein's theory or next to a sophomore algebra textbook.

A Brief Survey of Tarot

In Tarot, once again the metaphor rides high and wordplay is inevitable. According to an allegedly definitive tract, the Juggler card of the Tarot represents "a change of position" (or juggling). The Hermit card (depicting an old wanderer) means digression, waywardness, possibly getting lost on a trip; the Hanged Man is self-explanatory, it sometimes portends a capital execution; but it can also mean sacrifice or simple trouble leading to doom. Most glaring in its metaphoric fault is the Sun card, which we are told implies "everything is clearing up—a happy or sunny omen."

Occultists like to believe that the mystical Tarot cards originated in ancient Egypt (a favorite source of arcana) and were brought into Europe by the descendants of the pharaohs, who were called by the sobriquet "gypsies," from Egyptians—a linguistic connection which applies only in English.

The actual source of the Tarot is probably Arabic. The usual tie-in with the Cabala often found in Tarot favors this mid-Eastern origin, and it is said that the entire pack of cards was conceived and designed by a committee of Cabalists in Morocco around A.D. 1200. From there the cards traveled to Europe, probably in the saddle bags of merchants and emirs. The deck created for Charles VI was traditionally believed to be of Saracen origin; this fact supports the Arabian source theory. An Italian Renaissance game *tarrochini* was probably of the same origin.

A modern Tarot deck consists, with some variations, of two series: the major arcana, numbering twenty-two cards, and the minor arcana, which has fifty-five or fifty-six cards and closely resembles a modern gin rummy deck. The major arcana is what diviners used to tell fortunes and personality traits. All sorts of medieval ruling figures and symbols appear in the twenty-two different images. There is a King and a Queen (or Empress and Emperor), a Pope and High Priestess (sometimes called the Lady Pope in deference to the pagan earth goddess), as well as a Devil, a Juggler, a Hermit, a Pair of Lovers and ominous Death, with his sickle.

For pure unfigurative symbolism there is the Wheel of Fortune, the Falling Tower (possibly a phallic derivation), the Day of Judgment (Gabriel blowing his horn) and other oddities, including Temperance—a sort of fifteenth century Carrie Nation—and Strength, which in one case is depicted by a woman pulling apart the jaws of a lion.

Countless interpretations have naturally accrued to each card of the major arcana over the last five hundred years, and few systems are identical in their methodology of divination. However, metaphor ties all loose ends together; even someone unschooled in the jargon of Tarot can guess that the Pope represents wisdom, piety and glory; the Lovers, love; the Wheel of Fortune, "the conception of spiritual duration . . . (or) the rising and fall of hopes," and so forth. Of greatest importance are the relationship of one card to another and, in some systems, the relationship of the cards to the obtuse and contorted layers of the mystic Cabala.

Whatever the method, the results are reportedly the same. As the gullible and superstitious person might say: "It's in the cards." A sample reading of a single Tarot card may suggest some of the contortions that Tarot readers are expected to surmount in order to come to grips with the "divine secrets of Tarotology."

The Emperor is represented in traditional decks by a bearded prince seated in profile on a throne, with an eagle on his shield. His legs are crossed, his head is covered by an iron helmet, and in his hand he holds the scepter, symbol of generation. "Look at him well," we are advised by *The Encyclopedia of Occult Sciences,* "and you will see that his attitude reproduces the 4 which is the hieroglyph of Jupiter and the star of the fourth leaf is, in truth, Jupiter." (This bit of mumbo jumbo refers to the fact that the Emperor card is numbered fourth in the deck and that the Arabic number 4 resembles the astronomical sign of Jupiter, ♃ . There are no coincidences in the occult.) "This number 4," we are further informed, "denotes the universal quaternary (the four elements). The card's letter value, based on the Hebrew alphabet [because Hebrew is the original basis of the Cabala], is *daleth,* which means thorax. A better translation, however, is breast, nourishing breast." In short, the meaning of the Emperor card is "fulfillment."

One of the most popular and dreaded cards of the Tarot is the Hanged Man (number 12). As mentioned, it signifies sacrifice and death, but like everything else in the occult, this is open to interpretation and metaphoric chicanery. A seventeenth century tarotologist, Count de Gebelin, rejects the whole conceptualization and figuration of the Hanged Man, whom he calls Prudence. The dreadful error in naming this card, Gebelin believes, resulted from the misinterpretation of some "wretched presumptuous card maker, who, understanding nothing of the beauty of the allegory concealed in this picture, has taken upon himself to correct it, and in doing so to disfigure it entirely." A man hanging upside down on a gibbet—the traditional pose of this card—should actually be represented by a "prudent man" with his foot suspended in the air, cautiously looking for a "spot on which he can plant it securely." The wretched card maker referred to above apparently could not translate Latin properly, and when he read *pede suspenso* (suspended foot), he turned the man upside down and carelessly *suspended* him *by* the *foot*—hence the "Hanged Man." If the Count is correct in his indignant analysis, number 12 in the modern Tarot pack is completely erroneous, not only in its own meaning but also in its relationship to other cards. The modern French occultist, de Givry, dismisses the Count's revolutionary analysis and points to the Hanged Man in the famous deck painted for Charles VI. This he assumes is infallible. But even here, the Hanged Man hardly looks hanged at all; instead he appears to have been snared by a lasso and turned upside down. Without the rope and the topsy-turvy position, he might very well resemble de Gebelin's concept of Prudence.

Does it really matter if number 12 is a Hanged Man or Prudence? It does to the occultist, since to believe in Tarot is to accept the unfailing symbolism of each card and to believe that the laying out of these cards is predestined by some supernatural force or power. Astrology and numerology are implausible enough, but at least there one is dealing with celestial bodies and respectable permutations of arithmetic. In tarotology we are asked to venerate a pack of paper cards adorned with primitive designs.

Divination Delusions Deluxe

At this point one might enjoy plunging headlong into a few other forms of divination venerated by man since ancient times. Both fortune and future, for example, can be read by means of nephelomancy (cloud formations), or capnomancy (reading patterns of smoke). If these are not authoritative enough, there is always ornithomancy (interpreting the songs of birds) or the unfailing science of pegomancy (reading the splashes and bubbles in a fountain).

In Austria on New Year's Eve, celebrants drop spoonfuls of hot wax into ice water, and, by interpreting the forms produced, they hope to foresee what the new year will bring. When hot lead is used, this high science is called molybdomancy. But for absolute precision in such things, one must look to kephalonomancy, a simple and unfailing method of divination in which the "reader" studies the boiled head of an ass, which, like examining the entrails of a bull (engastrimancy), was one of the favorite prophetic practices of the ancient Greeks.

Should birds be unavailable for ornithomancy, the air pollution too confusing for capnomancy, or if you are too fastidious for kephalonomancy, even the most ordinary objects and events may be used for successful divination. As any occultist will tell you, omens are everywhere. To read them, however, one must be observant. Three areas ought to be studied: what is seen, what is received as a gift, and what is done. The black cat crossing the road is a well-known omen in the "what is seen" category. Since cats were thought to be the friends of witches, and black cats considered to be demons incarnate, this omen was and is believed to portend trouble, even death. But a donkey rolling in the dust signals fine weather, and a spider spinning its web indicates that someone is plotting against you. Spilled ink means trouble in business (especially if it's red ink, I presume); a shoelace coming undone equals interesting news; and, naturally, a falling or shooting star is a sine qua non of good fortune—unless, of course, a piece of it lands on your head.

If you receive a black cat as a present, the previous ominous association changes to good—the same good news applies to gifts of roses, mirrors, birds, and pennies with holes in them. Beware a gift of sapphires or knives (they cut friendship), and never accept a pair of Turkish slippers.

When you are sated with reading omens from what is seen and what is received, you can firm up your prophecies by evaluating what is done, to wit: if you drop an egg, give bread to the poor, sneeze, or rub a humpback, good luck will befall you. But should you step on a ladybug, break a mirror, sing on Friday, or pretend to be lame, you may be assured of impending trouble.

The reason, origin, and basis of these and countless other omens and superstitions twist back in time to the earliest rough-edged workings of the human imagination. Most of them, however, can be easily comprehended in the perspective of common sense. Again metaphor and wordplay association underlie the so-called mystic procedures. Here, for example, are some glaring symbols in the omen category and with them their painfully obvious interpretations: an open window—possible robbery; a

serpent—calumny or deceit; a chain—harmony or love; a dog
—friendship; a lion—triumph.

In reading tea leaves or coffee grounds, if you see a circle
containing dots, a baby will soon be born; a well-made triangle
means unexpected good fortune; a truncated triangle, in-
security. A period at the end of this sentence means that this
chapter is ended.

3

Magic: Black, White, and Otherwise

IN June, 1970, the *New York Times* reported that a twenty-year-old student at the University of California had just received a Bachelor of Arts degree in *magic.* Enjoying his brief moment of fame, the magician cum laude explained to the press that his is a valid field of scholarly investigation, since magic is actually quite real, though it does not as yet "fit in with any of the known laws of the universe."

There was a time when magic consisted simply of phenomena "which do not yet fit in with any of the known laws of the universe." Naturally, in such a time, there were practically no "known laws" of anything. In the Stone Age, magicians were simply the local hunters and warriors who seemed to be performing great magic by inexplicably killing god-like beasts with nothing more than sharpened sticks. Such sticks, or spears, became the archetype of the magic wand, and the mysterious red liquid released by the spear signaled the primeval life force whose function seemed thoroughly mysterious and therefore magical. Though the "magic" of the ancient hunters is now realized for what it is, even today, blood and sacrifice remain synonymous with magic ritual.

The hunter did not hold the only claim to magicianship in primitive times. Clever and ambitious individuals, discovering the properties of drugs and hallucinogens or capable of deducing that the gathering clouds would soon bring a storm, became the shamans and rainmakers, the healers or destroyers of ancient society.

The first magicians were masters of another previously unexplained phenomenon: the mystique of sex. Dancing or swaying around the seductive firelight, suddenly, as if by some subtle magic, the unsophisticated male quite naturally gave way to tumescence, and he flaunted an erected phallus that immediately signified, especially to the womenfolk, all the vigorous and magical powers of life. Is it any surprise that the phallic mystique and the mysteries of darkness and the dance have been passed on to the present and incorporated into the practice of magic and sorcery?

Sympathetic Magic

The ancients, lacking known laws of the universe, regarded everything as inexplicable. Rain, fire, flood, war, and love were to them manifestations of mysterious supernatural powers. To cope with the unfathomable, ancient man worked out a primitive but durable methodology. Thus a spear plunged into the one-dimensional belly of a bison painted on the wall of a cave would, by this act of "sympathetic" magic, be endowed with the same accuracy and precision on the actual hunt. The painted animal, thus venerated, was in a sense a god. The act of subduing the god became a form of ritual magic and an archetype of religious god-sacrifice; an archetype eventually consummated in the West by the crucifixion of Jesus Christ. Such a ritual, heavy as it was with homage and awe, was intended to bring about "the answer to one's prayers," and prehistoric man, rather than relying solely upon mechanical hunting skills or sophisticated weaponry, preferred to depend upon the attributes of sympathetic magic. The spear-pocked paintings on the walls of prehistoric caves of Lascaux, Altamira and Les Trois Frères, among others, give ample evidence of the sympathetic ceremony described above. Indeed, modern aborigines are reported to practice similar rituals in Africa and Australia.

Early Magic Cults

Prehistoric man was obliged by ignorance to rely upon magic ritual, but early civilized man used magic as a means of keeping the masses in ignorance. This is one of the reasons that religion, not science, developed so fully in ancient days. The inexplicable was explained by means of the myths and methods first concocted in prehistoric times. Even the animal gods of the Stone Age remained as leading dramatis personae of the ancient pantheons. The Egyptians venerated animal-headed gods; and in more modern times, Christ was worshipped as the *lamb* of God.

The confrontation of man and beast, first enacted on Stone Age hunting grounds, is an essential religious archetype. Modern witches, no less primitive than their Stone Age counterparts, seem to "remember" this age-old trauma as they venerate a horned goat in Central Park or ascribe to common cats and birds the qualities usually reserved for the ancient Egyptian deities. Perhaps a few of these modern mystics actually do respond to what Jung has called "the collective unconscious," passed on from prehistoric man to the modern mind. More likely, most mystics have learned about the ancient rituals from books. It is no wonder that they are therefore ignorant of the essential difference between the early magic cults (called pagan cults) and the nonsense they practice today. That difference is dualism: the belief in an equally matched conflict of good and evil. Until around 600 B.C., man regarded evil as a subordinate force in the presence of good. There were demons and devils and troublemakers of all sorts, but these detractors were minor in comparison to the great, good gods who ruled heaven, earth, and the sea. Unlike the dualistically deluded Captain Ahab in *Moby Dick,* ancient man did not pursue his prey in order to destroy its evil force. The villains, after all, were doomed to defeat because they were, from the outset, inferior to the mighty gods. And so, though inspired by and indeed formulated in terms of magic, ancient religion did not need to draw a distinction between white magic (the good) and black magic (the evil). The activities of demons did not represent a separate sphere of power, since they were an integral part of the divine scheme. Ancient religions, polytheistic as they seemed, were in fact monotheistic, empowering unity to the reigning gods (who were, in a sense, simply various aspects of the same god) and recognizing the singularism—as opposed to dualism—of the universe and its creator. Perhaps this long-abiding monotheistic ideal is best summed up by Isaiah, who, speaking for Jehovah, says: "I form the light and create the darkness. I make peace and create evil." (Isaiah 45:7.)

The teachings of Zoroaster, a semi-legendary Persian divine (c. 600 B.C.), brought dualism into full formation. His concept of Ahriman (the adversary) passed into the Hebrew canon and was translated as "satan." The Hebrews gave no prominence to this adversary; he was only one of the many demigods subordinate to Jehovah (witness his role in the Book of Job). But Christianity, an inherently dualistic faith, enlarged, expanded, and elevated the adversary of Job into Satan, the Prince of Darkness, the evil adversary of God. Thus he remains, and thus he was worshipped and glorified by the Satanists of the Middle Ages, who regarded him simply as the perverse aspect of God, no less glorious or divine. To this dualistic condition, replete with conflict and grandiose schemes of universal mastery, occultists have appended the magical traditions of ancient times. The most influential of these basically nondualistic ideologies are those of Egypt, Mesopotamia, and Greece. Each had its own particular characteristics that remain evident in modern magic in practice and design.

Ancient Egypt

One of the earliest concepts of the afterlife and of resurrection was formalized by the Egyptians at the time of the pharaohs and emphatically set forth in the legend of Isis and Osiris, who were husband and wife, the chief Egyptian gods of fertility and industry. Isis was a supreme magician. The villain of the tale was the desert god Set, brother of Osiris. Numerous times Set tried to destroy his fertile antagonist, finally succeeding in dissecting Osiris into fourteen pieces, which he then threw into the Nile. Beside herself with grief, Isis gathered up the dismembered parts—although she was unable to find the phallus, which rumor says was eaten by a crab—and by means of magic and incantation, she reunited the parts of her husband's body and brought him back to life. She fashioned a wooden phallus to replace the missing member, thereby injecting the phallic mystique even in the otherwise ascetic Osirian cult. The resurrected Osiris, who had turned green in the process, no longer wished to be part of the living world, so he took to the nether regions, where he became lord and judge.

The precise magic and the actual incantation that Isis employed to perform her great miracle have been lost in time (although many a modern charlatan will tell you he knows the formula). Nevertheless, the impact of this stupendous achievement remains, and the belief that magic can indeed restore life to a corpse—even to a dissected one—is one of Egypt's most resounding contributions to the sorcerer's cant.

The efficacy of magical spells and incantation, an efficacy apparently proven by Isis, is another aspect of Egyptian religion that never lost its influence. When Louise Huebner, the self-proclaimed official witch of Los Angeles County, chants her love spells for the television cameras, she is in essence taking her cue from Isis, the original spellbinder. And when Miss

Huebner writes her incantation on a piece of parchment, later to burn it in the fire of a red candle, she is likewise aping the magic of Egypt. For centuries, Egyptian formulas were carefully penned on parchment by priests and scribes to serve as amulets for the living and protection for the dead.

Here are two such formulas reputedly found in papyrus scrolls known as *The Book of the Dead.* To be protected from noxious animals one invoked this incantation:

> Help me, Lord of the Gods,
> drive away from me the lions
> who come from the earth,
> the crocodiles issuing from the river;
> stop the mouths of all biting reptiles
> who come from their holes.
> Stop the crocodile called Mako, son of Set.
> Make him not wave his tail,
> make his arms powerless,
> do not open his mouth . . .

Since the soul could not live if the body deteriorated, the Egyptian mummy had to be preserved perfectly. It was therefore advisable to have the following formula close at hand in the grave as protection from the ravaging beetle known as Aphsait:

> Depart from me, oh thou
> with the lips that gnaw.
> I am Khnemu, Lord of Peshennu.
> I come armed with the words of the gods
> and I bring a message to Ra . . .

Like their prehistoric counterparts, the Egyptian sorcerers practiced sympathetic magic, resorting to the painted image and the effigy. Here is the method by which Egyptian priests might overpower the monstrous crocodile Apep, who lurked on the underside of the world ready to devour everything from a man to a god to the sun itself. The following, adapted from *The Overpowering of Apep,* is the precursor of many similar medieval and modern voodoo ritual incantations:

If you wish to destroy Apep,
read the incantation over an image of
Apep which has been drawn in green ink
on a new sheet of papyrus.
Read it also over a wax figure of Apep
on which his name has been incised with green pigment.
Then lay them [papyrus and image] on the
fire which will consume
the enemy of Ra [the sun] . . .

Mesopotamia

The Mesopotamians, a generic term that encompasses the people of Assyria, Babylon, Sumer, and Akkad, infused their magic rituals with worship of celestial bodies, thus paralleling modern astrologers. From the heights of their terraced ziggurats, or temples, they assiduously studied the movements of planets and the formation of constellations so that they might be able to answer the riddles of the universe and to discover what destiny planned for them. As mentioned earlier, modern astrology owes its basic conceptualization to the Mesopotamian system of celestial scanning.

Their studies, grave as they were, did not imbue the early Mesopotamians with even a semblance of scientific rationalization. Unable to explain such obvious phenomena as the eclipse of the sun or moon, they followed the prehistoric pattern of attributing nature's basic manifestations to mythology and extending these manifestations into the realm of magic and incantation. The following excerpt is reported to be a Babylonian invocation conceived to forestall the adversities of a lunar eclipse:

I, son of [name], whose god is [name],
whose goddess is [name], in the evil
of an eclipse of the moon,
which in [name of the month] and on
[date of the year] has taken place;
in the evil of the powers,

of the portents, evil and not good,
which are in my palace and my land;
have turned toward thee [the god]
. . . listen to the incantation . . .
intercede for me!

The evils spoken of in this appeal were represented in Mesopotamian cosmology by the maskim, a collection of seven demons. Among other things they abetted the giant dragon who —it was assumed—devoured sun and moon on the periodic occasions of the eclipse. Magic, in the form of exorcism, was invoked to keep such creatures at bay. Here are two such incantations, the first from Chaldea (later Babylon), the second from Akkad (the northern part of Sumer); both deal with the maskim:

1. They are seven! They are seven . . .
   They are not male, they are not female.
   They dry up the moistness of the waves.
   They do not love women,
   They have not begotten offspring.
   They scorn kindness and justice;
   Spirit of the sky . . . spirit of the earth, remember them!
   Conjure them!

2. They are seven! They are seven!
   In the depths of the ocean,
   they are seven!
   In the brilliancy of the heavens,
   they are seven!
   . . . they are strangers to benevolence . . .
   . . . Spirit of the heavens,
   may they be conjured . . .

Mesopotamian magic was not restricted only to the formal rituals of incantation, which in a sense foreshadowed modern prayer; specific magical methods were also employed for even such mundane problems as headaches. From Babylon comes a forerunner of the cold compress for a headache; the method advises the sufferer to take a cloth, knot it in various ways, "divide it twice in seven little bands, gird the head of the invalid with it . . . seat him on his bed: pour on him enchanted waters."

Somewhat less tangible means were offered for ulcers; in such cases only the gods could help. "Poignant ulcers, enlarged ulcers, excoriated ulcers," begins this prayer from Akkad, "ulcers which spread, malignant ulcers, Spirit of the heavens, conjure it!"

Note that the verb conjure in these incantations stresses the magical aspect of the prayer; ancient man deemed himself incompetent as a conjurer, since magic was the province of the gods. Western man, however, assumed the prerogatives of conjuring and thus the powers of divinity.

Greece and Rome

The Greeks and, later, the Romans developed a more dualistic approach to magic and magic ritual. In their philosophy, probably influenced by Zoroastrianism, evil and good became distinctly separate, and, as a result, the blacker aspects of divination began to invade religious life. In Greek ritual the demons as well as the gods were invoked to favor the sorcerer and his clientele. A scroll of the fifth century B.C. calls upon "the holy ones . . . mighty arch demons: dwellers in Chaos, Erebus, and the unfathomable abyss . . . perform my commands." The commands implied empowered the sorcerer so that he or his client might gain sudden riches, love, health or even the power to manipulate the curse of death itself. Socrates was cognizant of these powers. "There are certain incantations," he is quoted as saying in the *Memorabilia,* "which those who know them chant to whomsoever they please, and thus make them their friend . . . there are also love potions which those who know them minister to whomsoever they will; and are in consequence loved by them."

Aeschylus reminds us that righteous vengeance pursued

Orestes in the form of evil demons known as the Eumenides. Theocritus (c. 310 B.C.) in his *Idyls* causes the maiden Simaetha to invoke the archwitch Hecate of Hell to restore the love of Delphis. Under Greek influence the invocation of devils and the free use of malicious curses and spells apparently flourished in Rome to the extent that Pliny the Elder lamented the course of events: "We are all afraid," he wrote, "of being nailed by spells and dire curses!" Such spells could have a variety of consequences: they could ultimately prove fatal to the individual or could merely ruin his crops. Regardless, Roman law proscribed arcane practices, as Apuleius reports in his *Apologia,* because "magic is secretive and foul and horrible . . ." Of course the magic referred to is of the blackest variety, the magic practiced by the vengeful Medea, who inspired the Roman poet Ovid in his *Metamorphoses.* Again Hecate and the demons of night are invoked as Medea seeks to rejuvenate her father-in-law (only to kill him thereafter). "Oh night," she cries, "most propitious for mysteries . . . and you, triple Hecate . . . and all you gods of the night, be my aid."

Piercing someone's name with a nail, sticking pins in wax images, curses of death, and demon worship continued to be prevalent in Rome well after the first century A.D., and these traditions passed almost unaltered into Christian society. The demons invoked by Medea and catalogued by Greek philosophers before Christ were recognized by St. Augustine in the fifth century, as being "like the gods . . . corporeal, immortal, with passions like any man." St. Jerome, a contemporary of Augustine, was no less cognizant of the dualistic forces besetting the world. "Some arouse wrath and madness," he wrote in *Commentaries of Ephesus,* "others rule over and provoke hatred among men." Yet although these creatures were malignant, dualist tradition insisted that they were nonetheless equal to the beneficent forces of God; every man or woman who sought power and mastery by magic was obliged to depend on them. Significantly, as Origen wrote in the first century A.D., "no good spirit obeys a magician." The alternative is self-evident.

The Early Christian Period

The dualist philosophy underlies all Christian concepts of magic and sorcery. To these concepts, modern man added the rituals and mysteries of pagan cults. But paganism as practiced in Europe before and after Christ was basically a singularistic ideology, unrelated to the parallel conflict of good and evil forces. The Celts, Druids, Odin worshippers, and such, like their Egyptian and Mesopotamian counterparts, eschewed the Satan concept passed down from Zoroaster through Greece and Rome to the Christian faith. Nowhere in the old ideas was there a figure like Satan, who quite literally stood face to face with God (or Christ), battling for the souls of men and dominance of the universe. Christian dogma, of course, accepted—and in the orthodox view still accepts—this creed. Like Zoroaster, the early church fathers never doubted the ultimate triumph of God. The terrestrial victory of Satan as described by St. John the Divine in Revelation is only shortlived, for Satan shall ultimately be "cast into the lake of fire and brimstone . . . and shall be tormented day and night for ever and ever." (Rev. 20:10.)

But suppose this prophecy was false; could it be that no one knew for sure whether God or the devil would triumph in the end? This was the question posed in the third century A.D. by the Persian monk Mani, who had decided that in the struggle between good and evil, the outcome was forever in doubt; only the strictest ascetic could be assured of salvation after death. Though Christianity fought and successfully debilitated Manicheanism, the insidious logic of Mani's premise could not be squelched. The Gnostics, dissident Christians, eventually inculcated the Manichean heresy, the dualistic dilemma, and many of the blacker aspects of Greek and Roman underground philosophy. To them the sure path to salvation was not so sure as Christianity advised. Right and wrong, good and evil, wisdom and doubt were churned up and spinning about in the baffling universe. It thus became their prerogative to unmix the puzzle and chart a new course, not necessarily as Christ described it, but in a fresh way, a quasi-existential, magical fashion that placed man and his cunning high above natural phenomena. To know and thus to master became the Gnostic creed.

The climate was ripe for the next step in the dualistic delusion. Zoroaster had avowed that the universe was simply a battleground on which both God and Satan vied with equal strength. Orthodox tradition fully accepted the basic formula but asserted the triumph of God as a foregone conclusion. At the end of time ". . . there shall be no more curse (evil); but the throne of God and of the Lamb (Christ) shall be in the river of life . . ." (Rev. 22:3). Unfortunately for the Church, dissident tradition (Manicheanism) proclaimed that the dualist battle would forever be in doubt, not only in sheer force of arms but in destiny. As a result of such doubts, a new rebellion arose, not (like Gnosticism) from *within* the established Church, but rather from beyond, from among the oppressed, miserable, and disillusioned minions of the early Middle Ages. The new philosophy admitted that good and evil were at odds but that the outcome was quite evident: "Look around you: Satan, not God, will triumph at the end of time. The curse (Christ) will be abolished so that the true Heaven, which the Church calls Hell, may be established throughout the universe." Thus the angel Lucifer (who, according to legend, fell from celestial grace but nonetheless crept into respectable Christian theology through the dualist trail), this fallen demigod and enemy of Christ, becomes the *theos* of his own religion: Satanism. He is the author of his own codes, laws, ethics, and principles, all of which, upon examination, are revealed to be mere inversions of the Christian creed. There is no original sin, say the Satanists, for man was always evil; that is his nature. Christ is therefore a fraud, for if he atoned for a sin that did not exist, he atoned and died in vain. Knowing this, Satanism shall free Europe from the grim, gray burden of Christ and bring to every Satanist pleasure, power, triumph, and joy. Satanists thought that magic and sorcery would, in fact, convey these glories to the world. What if the Church abhors magic and the invocation of demons? This is proof enough of their value and usefulness, for, according to the Satanic philosophy, the Church has always perverted the truth. If by reciting certain formulas, by drawing circles and signs, and using drugs, herbs, or powders, a mortal can rise to godhood and glory, and if by doing so he infuriates the Church, then let him. The triumph of Satan will only be accomplished when the dualist dilemma is obviated and when one single force, Satan, rules supreme. When all the Satanists of the world are magically empowered, surely the day of Satan's victory will arise. This vision and ambition eventually became the fundamental Satanic influence in medieval Europe and laid the ground for the full-fledged Satanic religion known as Witchcraft. While sorcerers practiced their arts in secluded places and without benefit of organization, the Church pursued them only passingly. When they organized as witches, the problem could not be so casually contained. (The story of witches will be told in the following chapter.)

Magic remains, by and large, a means of personal aggrandizement. In this function it produced the whole complicated panoply of medieval sorcery and divination; a panoply of "evil," for it was not the magic of Isis or the Mesopotamian astrologer that was invoked by the Christian or ex-Christian sorcerer. He was related far more closely to Medea, who worshipped Hecate just as *he* worshipped and catered to Satan and his demonic horde.

A Primer of Medieval Sorcery

"A sound magician is a mighty god," announces Dr. Faustus in Marlowe's play. Mastery of the sorcerer's art was indeed the surest way in medieval times to master the universe and challenge God. Anyone with sufficient fortitude and zeal could play.

"Oh men! Weak mortals!" proclaims the *Great Grimoire,* a medieval handbook of sorcery, "transport your spirit beyond your sphere, and learn from me that before any undertaking you must be firm and steadfast and attentive in observing scrupulously all disadvantage, confusion and total loss . . . If you observe scrupulously what I say, you will come forth from your lowliness and poverty, completely successful in all your enterprises . . ."

To the countless thousands of downtrodden young people of the eleventh, twelfth, and thirteenth centuries this appeal was extremely seductive. Applying themselves to the lessons of the grimoires or apprenticing themselves to established sorcerers, they were soon exposed to the secret methods and philosophies of the forbidden art. From the grimoire known as the *Lemegeton,* for instance, they could discover the names of more than sixty demons, some of whom, when summoned and harnessed, could torture hapless victims by inflicting them with festering sores or wounds; pander for the magician and bring beautiful ladies to his bed; call up visions to please or to terrorize; or maliciously change wine into rainwater. The novice needs only to learn the proper method of conjuring these powers, harnessing them to do his will, and finally releasing them so that they will not turn their malice back on him. The overall procedure is as follows:

1.   The Pact. A pact is made with Satan and his horde. This pact may be oral or written in ink or blood. To begin, one invokes the archdemons by name: Lucifer, the king; Rofocale, the chief minister; Prince Beelzebub; the Earl of Astorath, and so forth down the line. Next, one appeals to their favors and begs them to appear and honor the agreement; finally, one swears his absolute fidelity, adding as a token of faith the pledge of a certain sum of money (a form of commission) or in extreme cases the promise of one's immortal soul. A plethora of arcane names and words is appended to the pact. Some of these are biblical: Elohim, Emanuel, Adonai; some come from the realms

of Eastern and Christian mythology: Lucifer, Astorath, Ariel; others are anagrams, like the Hebrew AGLA (*aieth godol leolum Adonai*), meaning "Great forever is the Lord"; some are simply gibberish, for example this excerpt from a pact recommended in the *Key of Solomon:*

> So come forth instanter! Or I shall torture
> you endlessly by the force of these powerful
> names of the Key: Aglon, Tetragram, Vaycheon,
> Stimulamation, Ezphares, Retragrammation,
> Olyaram, Irion, Esytion, Existion, Eryona, Onera,
> Orasym, Mozm, Messias, Soter, Emanuel Saboot . . .

In the pact allegedly signed between the priest Urbain Grandier of Loudun and the devilish horde led by Satan, Beelzebub, Lucifer, and a few others, sexual gratification was the chief element promised by the demons in return for Urbain's fidelity, to wit: "And we promise him the love of women, the flower of virgins, the chastity of nuns . . . he will fornicate every three days . . . and in return will offer to us once a year a tribute marked with his blood: he will trample underfoot the sacraments of the Church and he will say his prayers to us." It should be noted that this exuberant contract, which is displayed in the Bibliothèque Nationale, Paris, was notarized by a certain Baalberith, listed as "recorder," and duly sealed.

After the pact has been concluded, the sorcerer is ready to consecrate himself for his central task, the summoning of the Satanic force. First a series of elaborate preparations are undertaken.

2. The Preparations. Before he is ready for his religious rituals, the sorcerer, like any priest, must consecrate his body and soul, thereby setting himself apart from the mundane. There is reason to believe that medieval sorcerers purified their bodies in a mixture of water and blood and spent at least one day prior to their incantations in fasting, meditation, and sexual abstinence. During these consecratory preparations, the sorcerer is advised to burn camphor, thus purifying the very air

around him, just as a Catholic priest purifies the air during the Mass. In all, the aspirant is enjoined to heighten his sensitivities for the enormous task before him and, when possible, to do so in seclusion, surrounded by a desolate ruin, a graveyard, or a gloomy forest. Above all, to protect himself from the very forces he seeks to conjure, the sorcerer is instructed to concentrate on God and Christ, who as enemies of Satan would hold Satan at bay.

As he also prepares his body and his soul, the sorcerer must lay out before him the numerous accessories that will be required in his conjurations. All should be new and freshly wrought, so that they contain the unspent powers of newness and virginity. His knife or sword is a brand new weapon, never dulled by use; his wand, a hazel branch, varying in length but always freshly cut, preferably at sunrise so that it may capture the added vigors of the reborn sun. Both the knife and the wand may be sprinkled with fresh blood for further invigoration.

Ready with dagger and wand, the magician is now required to dress himself as befits a mighty priest. Like Aaron in the Bible, the medieval sorcerer is advised to don only the purest white linen, and an ornate girdle upon which holy names are embroidered, preferably in gold. Like any bishop—whose vestments also originate with Aaron—the sorcerer will wear on his head a miter inscribed with acronymic names of God, YHVH (Jehovah) or El (Lord), on front and back. Whereas the accessories just described should be new and fresh, it is advisable, if not mandatory, for the sorcerer to secure the robes of some former divine, especially if he was a successful conjurer. The powers and talents of the former priest somehow cling to the robes and will pass into the newcomer in some inexplicable, and therefore valid, process of osmosis. Details of costuming in the grimoires include descriptions of the type of shoes, gloves, and undergarments the sorcerer should secure.

Once he is satisfactorily adorned, his equipment collected, his body and soul properly purified and sensitized, the surroundings permeated with energy, only then should the sorcerer begin the actual rituals of divination. Before all else, he is required to draw upon the ground a huge circle so that, standing within its unbreachable bounds, he will be amply protected from the blind, vengeful powers he seeks to call. The drawing of the magic circle is one of the more spectacular thaumaturgic preparations, rich in allegory and enigma.

3. The Circle. According to most authorities, the circle should be nine feet in diameter (nine is the last digit), drawn on the earth with the point of the new knife or rod, or upon flooring with chalk. A second circle, eight feet in diameter, is drawn inside the first. Neither circle is drawn closed, for the time being, so that the sorcerer can move in and out of the protective confines as necessity demands. The sorcerer places certain benign objects and signs around the outer circle, and, for utmost protection, the names and anagrams of beneficent gods should be placed around the edges of the inner circle, thus forming a protective border.

Objects useful beyond the outer rim may include rosaries, crucifixes, and bowls of holy water—in short, any Christian item despised by the fiends that will therefore keep them, in their blind fury, from moving in on the sorcerer himself.

The nineteenth-century sorcerer Eliphas Levi, who supposedly returned to the twentieth century as Aleister Crowley, favored another sort of protection. Because he reasoned that fiendishness is its own greatest deterrent, he reportedly decorated his outer circle with the head of a black cat that had fed on human flesh; a bat drowned in blood; the horns of a goat that had copulated with a girl; and the skull of a parricide. So horrible are the vibrations sent out by these objects that not even Lucifer will venture too close.

Useful names to scrawl in the protective border include those of Christ, God, the Virgin Mary, and various sacred anagrams, acronyms, mottos, and codes; *Dominus Adjutor meus* (God protect me) is the most dependable.

Circles were not the only protective forms the medieval sorcerer might draw. Triangles were effective as protection, and a circle inside a triangle—the Triad of Solomon—was a double force for good. Pentagrams (figures of five points) and hexagrams (of six) were appropriate since the five-pointed star symbolized the five wounds of Christ (whom the demons despise), while the six-pointed star combines the all-powerful symbols of fire Δ and water ∇ and represents the Star, or Shield, of David.

According to the grimoires, the mightiest geometric pattern that the sorcerer can employ is the Double Seal of Solomon, which combines the signs already discussed; it is a hexagram (two triangles) inside a circle. The acronym AGLA is arranged letter by letter around the outside of the star, and a tau is placed at the center, where the sorcerer stands. The tau is a form of cross related to St. Anthony, who successfully defended himself against a frightful horde of demons.

Before the sorcerer steps into the center of his magic design, closing the opened arc behind him, he should light an incense burner or a series of huge black incense candles. These will provide him primarily with odors considered nauseous to demons and secondly with billowy clouds of smoke with which the demons may form semblances of themselves. Another possibility exists concerning the burning of incense at this point. Since henbane, opium, and hellebore were among the herbs most commonly suggested for burning, it may be assumed that a certain amount of intoxication was required by the sorcerer in order to conjure *not* the devils he sought, but rather the hallucinations that would make him think he had succeeded in his conjurations.

Drugs in the forms of incense, ointments, potions, and such play a major part in the history of witchcraft, magic, and sorcery. The use of drugs explains, to a great degree, why there is such a consistency in the fantasies of occult practitioners. The combination of ritualistic procedure, replete with arcane and quasi-religious mystery, and the inhalation of potent drugs quite possibly caused the sorcerer to conjure up more lifelike "devils" than did any incantation.

4. The Magician Enters the Circle. Now the summoning begins. The sorcerer is advised to take with him into the circle a small young animal for sacrifice. The blow of death involved in sacrifice and its age-old magical reminiscences are intended to affect the morbid demons one seeks, because sudden death, according to sorcery, emits a shock wave of enormous energy and attraction. Most often a hen or a young goat is used for this phase of the ritual, but the imaginative Aleister Crowley sometimes preferred a little boy "of perfect innocence and high intelligence," who provoked—in Crowley at least—an orgasm at the moment of sacrifice.

The latest purveyor of evil for evil's sake is the San Francisco Satanist Anton Szandor La Vey, who forbids not only human but also any animal sacrifice. Any magician worthy of his name, says La Vey, "will be uninhibited enough to release the necessary force from his own body instead of from an unwilling and undeserving victim." The body force referred to is orgasm, so it follows that masturbation should be substituted for sacrifice, at least in La Vey's grimoire.

With the bloody business done and the shock waves permeating the atmosphere, the sorcerer may begin at last the actual invocation of the deadly but all-powerful subterranean forces. Over and over again, in rising intensity, he repeats the incantations until the desired effect is achieved and the demon arrives like a genie roused from primordial sleep.

There are many incantations to choose from, of course, but all are designed to cause the demon to come forth peaceably, visibly, and without delay.

It should come as no surprise that very often the demons fail to appear, even after repeated summoning. In such cases, the sorcerer threatens to curse the recalcitrant creature and render it impotent. The grimoires offer various threats that are anathema to Satan's hordes. "O wicked and disobedient spirit,"

says one of them, "because thou hast not obeyed my commands
. . . I curse thee into the depths of the Bottomless Pit, there to
remain . . . until the Day of Wrath." Saying this, the sorcerer
writes the demon's name on a scrap of paper, seals it in a box
tied four times with wire, and throws both the name and the
box into a sulfuric fire. According to the old concept of sympathetic magic, imprisoning and burning the name is literally the
same thing as imprisoning and burning the demon himself.

Such threats usually force the miscreant to appear submis-
sively. The sorcerer, safe in his circle, then begins the major part
of his work, the actual ordering of the spirit. All this ritual, the
fasting, bloodshed, and incense burning would be of little purpose if it weren't for that moment, for this is the point at which
man becomes God, wreaking vengeance upon hated enemies,
securing power, wealth, and love, or unlocking the very secrets
of the universe. Naturally the grimoires do not have much to
report on this phase of the ritual. Each sorcerer must handle his
demon as he sees fit. However, according to the occult view of
history, all the great and awesome events of former times were
the work of successful sorcerers whose demons have done their
bidding. Victories, defeats, discoveries, and failures were attributed to the magician's skill and the demon's prowess. According to de Givry, author of *The Anthology of Occultism,* it
was sorcery that built the old bridge at St. Cloud near Paris and
several bridges in Germany. And the intricate ironwork that
covered the left and right portal doors at the entrance of Notre
Dame de Paris before the nineteenth century reconstruction,
according to the followers of sorcery, was clearly the work of
a demon sculptor named Biscornet, who was harnessed by the
Church to perform as no mortal could.

5.   The Dismissal.   Once the demon has been harnessed and
commanded and his task has been completed, the sorcerer is
obliged to dismiss the Satanic forces he has called into prominence. It would be a fatal error, the grimoires warn, for a
magician to consider himself master of the situation simply

because he has dominated the devil for an hour or two. Such an over-confident sorcerer, stepping from the safe confines of his circle, is sure to be struck dumb—or worse—by the infernal force. The grimoires have provided a formal dismissal to be uttered by the sorcerer as he completes his work. "I am pleased and contented with thee, Prince Lucifer," begins one such farewell from *The True Grimoire,* ". . . leave thou in peace now and go in quiet and without trouble . . . and may our pact be upheld. Go now but return when called by me . . . or I shall blast thee with my wand."

With these words, or words similar to these, the demon departs. Only then may the sorcerer step from his guarded confines and gather his paraphernalia. It is prudent and advisable to utter the dismissal incantation even if one thinks no demon has appeared. Some evil spirit may be lurking in the atmosphere ready to destroy the unwary sorcerer as soon as he steps out of his protective barrier.

The ritual having been completed, the successful sorcerer sets about to build his reputation and to reap the rewards of his power. The unsuccessful sorcerer merely goes back to the magic circle for another try.

How did the practitioners of these improbable feats regard their enterprise? Were they self-deceiving fools, liars, victims of hallucinogens, or a combination of them all? In most cases, self deception played the largest role in the mentality of "professional" sorcerers. Simple hallucination was no doubt a prominent part of the delusion as well. In addition to these basic explanations, there is the complicated factor of human psychology to consider. Such fanatical devotion, such belief and ambition that was apparently possessed by sorcerers throughout all time, doubtlessly drove the individual into a state of heightened suggestibility. This condition is evident today, for example, in the delusions of megalomaniacs, political demagogues, or self-styled Satanists and witches. The very consorting with evil and with forbidden rituals seems to have a power of its own. As Crowley wrote, "If a man summons the devil, the devil comes . . . ," whereupon the suppressed fascination of the self-perpetuating Satanic force washes over the individual in spite of himself. The surrender to illicit or heretical practices in this way becomes a form of possession. Thus, the act of submission, not the practice itself, is in the end the only demonic aspect of any consequence.

Varieties of Magic

Aside from mingling with demons and wreaking untold powers over friends and foes, the traditional sorcerer was capable also, by means of the Cabala, of ascending through infinite emanations of the universe back to a supernatural unity with God Himself. The truly accomplished cabalist could achieve this divinity without the usual necessity of dying. Cabalism, a complicated blend of Jewish terminology, Christian dualism, and Buddhistic discipline, promised such unusual cosmic mastery that death itself was obviated in the splendid sphere above and beyond all mortal description. The modern definition of the cabalist as an involuted mystic given to complicated and secretive arcana connotes an accurate picture of this creed.

Not quite so lofty as the "I am God" cabalist was the "lead into gold" alchemist, another stepchild of sorcery. Through tedious magic and a primitive form of chemistry, the alchemist attempted to concoct the Philosopher's Stone, a lump of mysticism that was simultaneously fire, air, earth, and water. When properly compounded, the Philosopher's Stone transformed all it touched—including lead—into the purest gold. Carl Jung envisioned the alchemist as a lofty divine attempting to purify himself as well as the base metal. However, most medieval alchemists also expected to make a profit by turning base metal into gold, and they often hired themselves out to impoverished aristocrats or greedy kings. When the process worked—as it rarely did—nature's own gold had certainly been liberally mixed into the sorcerer's brew, presumably on the theory (still believed) that gold begets gold.

Cabalism and alchemy are rarely pursued as such in modern times; but the popular search for magical elixirs of life, health, love, and youth—part and parcel of the sorcerer's equipage— still continues today. The elixirs are as phony now as they were when peddled to the gullible peasants of the Renaissance. In most cases the old sorcerer's elixir consisted of heady wine mixed with potent herbs or hallucinogens. The Irish had one such brew that actually is nothing more or less than good old-fashioned Irish Whiskey.

It is part of man's tenacity to grasp at any fanciful panacea, whether it is the thirteenth-century prescription of Albert the Great—who recommended as an aphrodisiac periwinkle "eaten powdered with earthworms in meat"— or the copper bracelets and anklets currently on the market.

W. S. Gilbert, the librettist, doubtlessly had the last word on the subject in the operetta appropriately entitled *The Sorcerer* (an early collaboration of Gilbert and Sullivan). John Welling-ton Wells, Gilbert's man of all magical trades, is no less a faker than his medieval or twentieth century counterparts, and, like them, he promises a plethora of magic wonders "already in stacks," white magic as well as black magic, including "love philtres, hosts of ghosts, creepy things with wings, crowds of shrouds"—all available at discounts for quantity, plus ten per-cent deducted for payment in cash. The chicanery of Mr. J. W. Wells is, however, perfectly excusable in the ethics of sorcery. Anton La Vey heartily recommends that the shrewd sorcerer utilize trick wires, mirrors, and other stage effects so that he can "save his force for self-aggrandizement." Why not be a fraud, asks La Vey, since you'll be accused of trickery in any case?

The Sorcerer's Mass

Although sorcery is primarily a Satanic device, relying as it does on demonic forces, it remained fairly independent of Sa-tanic religion—witchcraft—until the early Renaissance. The major jump occurred when sorcery stepped out of the circle of Solomon and into the Black Mass of Satanism, the apogee of which did not occur during the witchcraft centuries (thirteenth to sixteenth) but, rather, afterward in pre-revolutionary France and in nearly every Western culture since 1800.

The old cult witches of earlier times regarded the Mass as simply one phase of their religious experience. In contrast, as the sorcerer's mise-en-scene, the seventeenth and eighteenth century Masses became complete religions unto themselves, enhanced with huge doses of sex, drugs (hashish and opium as opposed to mere incense), and hate for hate's sake. What emerged was the apotheosis of magic as an evil force, which, though convened to glorify Satan, functioned above all as a perverted form of group therapy and mutual masturbation.

Rossell Hope Robbins, in his *Encyclopedia of Witchcraft and Demonology,* insists that the "Black Mass, as something that historically occurred, is one of the biggest intellectual frauds ever imposed on the lay public." As Robbins sees it, the Inquisition concocted the whole obscene ritual and forced, by torture, persons accused of witchcraft to confess all the sordid details as definite proof of the ritual's reality. It will be shown in Chapter 4 that such a Mass actually did take place in the context of witchcraft and that Robbins goes too far in his well-advertised purpose of assessing the entire witchcraft phenomenon as a fraud perpetrated by Church and civil authorities. The Black Mass, as an element of the witch cult ritual and as an independent function of Satanism and sorcery, still exists, and the fact that most of these diabolic exercises—especially modern ones—are convened more for perverse pleasure than for religion does not diminish or nullify their reality. The sorcerer's Mass—as opposed to the cult Mass—was obviously embellished from year to year with all the eccentric fantasies that evil can provoke. No doubt even some of the enormities dreamed up by the Church (for they did fictionalize at least *some* of the evidence) found their way into the esoteric rituals of eighteenth, nineteenth and twentieth century Satanists: the drinking of urine instead of consecrated wine is one such grotesque practice which, though concocted by some sick imagination, nevertheless eventually became an actual practice in at least a few selected coteries.

One of the most vivid descriptions of the Satanic Mass is offered by the Marquis de Sade in his *Justine* (1791). Robbins dismisses this and other similar accounts as merely "a literary creation." But nearly one hundred years before *Justine,* the Chambre Ardente Affair in France revealed atrocities that were quite obviously much more than literary creations. Even Robbins admits that the lecherous Abbé Guiborg and the infamous La Voisin, the two protagonists of this scandal, did at least conduct what he calls a "simple and guileless amatory Mass." The so-called amatory Mass, in which a virgin's naked body was used as the altar, also included—according to eye-witness testimony at the trial of La Voisin—the kissing of the altar by the priest, the inserting of part of the Host into the altar's vagina, and—for utmost communion—an act of copulation between altar and priest. If Robbins accepts the verisimilitude of these amatory practices, why does he insist that embellishments on the basic scene are either "intellectual frauds" or "literary creations?" Surely anyone who can imagine a young woman used as a sacred altar can quite easily go the next step and insert the Host into the altar. This is precisely what happens in *Justine.*

> The monks made (the) virgin strip and lie down flat on her belly on a big table. They lit the holy candles and placed a statue of our Lord between her legs, and had the audacity to celebrate the most holy of our sacraments on the buttocks of this young girl . . . (One monk) seized the host, that sacred symbol of our venerable religion, and pushed it in the obscene entrance he used for his perverted pleasures, abusively pressing it in; then he ignominiously crushed it under the repeated lunges of his monstrous tool and, shouting blasphemies, emitted the foul surges of the torrent of his lubricity over the very body of his Saviour!

De Sade's description, except perhaps for the belly-down

position of the altar, parallels a 1694 account given at a witch trial in Aquitaine and is strongly reminiscent of the excesses reported among nuns and priests in Loudun (1634) and Louviers (1647). It also follows the same course as described by the eye-witness at the trial of La Voisin (who was, by the way, the accused woman's daughter). The Marquis de Sade did not concoct his Mass purely from his infamous imagination. (Knowing the Marquis's biography, we can safely say that he was not content merely with imaginary fantasies.) The high priest of modern decadent literature, Joris-Karl Huysmans, based his famous Black Mass description in *Là-Bas* on the actual proceedings recounted to him by the Abbé Boullan, a nineteenth-century Parisian Satanist.

In modern times, the San Francisco Satanist La Vey was, like Boullan, also a "technical consultant" on the subject of devilry, in this case for the filming of *Rosemary's Baby.* La Vey brought to his work a fair amount of expertise, having himself conducted Black Masses in the style of de Sade in which, according to an article in *McCall's* magazine, "a red-haired girl lies nude and artfully exposed on a fur rug . . ."

The excesses described by de Sade and various witch trial witnesses, or as hinted at by the cautious La Vey (in his *Satanic Bible*) are hardly beyond the realm of human possibility, despite Robbins' insistence on fraud and literary fantasy. The generation of people that grew up with the terrors of World War II and with the details of murder, rape, and assassination common in the daily press does not have to be convinced of the reality of a Satanic Mass. Such proceedings—some surpassing de Sade—are regularly held in Europe *today.*

Take the eerie case of the Sorcerer of Marsal, Maurice Gerard, reported in *Newsweek*, January 5, 1970. Gerard's temple of sorcery was in Paris, where he conducted Black Masses in the company of his wife and a large following who came to receive the benefits of his healing powers and other benefits the Black Mass usually affords. According to *Newsweek:* "A year

ago, two of Gerard's four children disappeared without a trace
. . . One was deaf and the other had a bone disease . . . Investigators have been probing the walls of Gerard's temple for traces
of the children, hinting they were sacrificed during a Black
Mass . . ." Is this too, we wonder, merely a "literary creation"?

The Real Meaning

In the introduction to La Vey's *Satanic Bible,* we are told
that "many people . . . would like to know how to start Satanic
cults and ritualize black magic. This book," the introduction
continues, "shows them how to go about it and fills that need."

What is really being said—and this applies as much to the
past as it does to the present—is that many people would like
to indulge in sexual experiments, try their luck with drugs, and
generally submit themselves to anti-social activities—and "this
book shows them how." But like all grimoires and bibles of
sorcery, the *Satanic Bible* falsifies basic human desires by cloaking them in the vestments of religious cults and magic mumbo
jumbo. It is similarly a method of elevating basic lust into the
most arrogant "holier than thou" affectation. The medieval
sorcerer lusting after power and gold was no better than the
common medieval warlord and highwayman with the same
ambitions. Similarly, the Black Mass priest—and his "altar"—
who consider their rituals to be highly elevated and meaningful
evocations are, in fact, on a par with participants of the everyday orgies that take place in brothels, frat house basements, and
suburban living rooms. Except for their trappings, the Satanists and satyrs are brothers under the skin.

4

"Once There Was a Wicked Witch . . ."

Two definitions of "witch" are in popular usage: the wicca, or white variety, and the Satanist, or black witch. Both types purport to be great wizards and magicians; therein lies their fallacy.

Wicca is an old English word once commonly used to describe a type of medieval folk doctor, or medicine man, who lived apart from the general Christian community. He worshipped minor pagan deities, brewed potions and salves, and, in the case of wicca women, functioned as midwives for the poor. Though these loners attempted to practice a certain degree of magic in their endeavors, they could hardly be termed sorcerers, for the incantations they mumbled over a bubbling mixture of fennel, henbane, and snake tongue were more the result of ageless superstition than deference to any rigid thaumaturgic creed. From generation to generation these eccentrics passed on their knowledge of medicine and their tales of spirits, fairies, horned gods, and the like to offspring and neighbors. They knew no formal organization or cult, and in most cases they stayed far from the clutches of the law. They usually did nothing more anti-social than digging up a few old skeletons and grinding the bones for some potion or poultice of their fancy.

True, some wiccas boasted of powers beyond the ordinary imagination; transvection, or magical flight, was one of their more frequent claims. In this way they identified, willingly or unwillingly, with eleventh and twelfth century nightriders and moon worshippers, who were non-Christian practitioners of vestigial pagan ideologies. Unfortunately the business of flying on broomsticks brought the usually harmless wiccas into public attention at the beginning of the twelfth century. Such fantastic claims, plus the usual aloofness and cragginess of the typical wicca, rankled many pious individuals; eventually, wiccas fell victim to Church censure under counteractive canons issued against the "delusions of abandoned women" and others who thought they could fly. In comparison with the furious attacks on witches that followed in the fifteenth and sixteenth centuries, these canons were relatively mild and surprisingly tolerant. However, with their enactment, the basically innocuous wicca became, in the thirteenth century, a social pariah and a potential scapegoat for hypocritical reaction. Indeed, when the witchhunts began in earnest, those who resembled wiccas—old, aloof, peculiar in habit and appearance—were the first to be rounded up, and countless thousands were executed.

In the modern metamorphoses, the wicca retains his or her pagan inclinations, worshipping archaic, often apocryphal gods, burning colored candles, and mixing herbic brews. One modern advocate, who holds forth on 14th Street in New York City, musters over 150 varieties of herbs for concoctions, including something called Devil's Dung. Despite this nominal deference to Satan, past and present wiccas consider themselves forces for good. They could be wild and wicked if they chose, but evil is not their style. Wiccas prefer to protect children, to stimulate fertility, and to bring love to the loveless rather than to perform the usual Satanic deeds.

Not quite so harmless is the admitted Satanist witch, or warlock. In the strictest sense this variety was and is as religious, as devout as any medieval Catholic, but his religion is the specific worship of Satan as god; consequently, he worships evil as a force for good.

In the past, the Satanist witch (or black witch) attended sacred services, masses, and baptisms. Like any religionist he followed a liturgy, celebrated holidays and—more than most—suffered continuous religious persecution as a heretic and anti-Christ because he attempted to practice magic and sorcery, which is usually outside the boundaries of traditional religion. This witch was often driven to acts of immorality, upon which his reputation in history rests.

Though both pretend to be magicians or sorcerers, the white witch insists that she (or he) derives her power from the beneficent forces of nature, while the black practitioner allies herself or himself with the devil and the fiendish forces of hell.

The question, of course, is whether magic—black or white—exists as an actuality in either case. Without the efficacy of magic, all witchcraft is merely a form of clannishness or bizarre group therapy. One need not include it as such in a discussion of the occult. But since witches of all varieties assert their magical powers (this indeed is their definition), they must then be investigated and debunked.

Historically, witchcraft is Satanic, and the "white witch" is a misnomer. In the previous chapter, the Christian sage Origen was quoted as saying that "no good spirit obeys a magician"; conversely, all magic springs from the devil. It does not seem to matter greatly, therefore, whether a white witch tries to turn a toad into a man—presumably a beneficent act—or whether a black witch maliciously attempts to transform a man into a toad. Both resort to the fallacy of magic; both employ unorthodox means of harnessing their alleged powers, as the sorcerer does, and both base their philosophies of life on supernatural delusions. In short, a large amount of Satanic fascination and dependence are indispensable in the witches' schema, along with a huge amount of fraud, no matter what the alleged color.

The non-Satanic witches, rather than being called "white," or benign, would probably be best defined as the library book variety, those who pick and choose among the many books concerning occult subjects in order to create for themselves a respectable yet secretive, beneficent yet potent form of self-centered religion. Unfortunately, this creation usually turns out to be a confusing hybrid of paganism, sorcery, wicca herbology, Zen Buddhism, and drug cultism, replete with the messages of love, faith, and back-to-nature simplicity. The obvious question concerning white witches of today is: why, when they could find love, peace, and strength in any of the established religions and even in those of a more unorthodox variety, have they chosen the ancient cult of witchcraft?

The answer concerns Satanic fascination: the blandishments of evil that lurk beneath *all* magic ritual and thus fulfill certain basic needs. Among them are:

1. The need for power, the hope that one may harness unearthly forces to produce wealth and to dominate man and the universe. This was the sorcerer's primary motivation.
2. The need to act out an anti-establishment fantasy; the chance to cut loose sexually, morally, and otherwise, while excusing one's anti-social behavior by saying that it's all part of the sacred ritual.
3. The desire to thumb one's nose at science and reason by steeping one's "faith" in astrology, sorcery, and the prattlings of cultism.
4. The craving for danger, for psychedelic experience.
5. The need to belong, even to an outcast but nonetheless disciplinary clan.

These and other considerations are the fundamental attractions of witchcraft, past and present, white and black.

Even the avowed Satanist of today is seduced largely by the deceptive and neurotic propensities mentioned above. The fact that he may admit to the more lurid and diabolical inspirations of his faith—and thereby pay the devil his due—does not disguise the taint of fraud. Like most white witches, most black ones have learned their practices from the yellowing pages of volumes found in the basements of old bookstores and junkshops.

In short, the modern witch (white and black) may be one of two varieties. The first is the "mixed-up kid," to whom the anti-social aspects of Satanism offer a background for minor experiments in drugs, crime, perverse sex, and violence. When least harmful, such an individual becomes a member of a local coven, or cult, and once a month he prances about nude with his fellow witches, smokes a joint or two of marijuana, enjoys a little down-to-earth group sex, and satisfies the animal instinct which occasionally surfaces in everyone. At worst, however, such a "kid" becomes Charles D. Watson, who returned from the Sharon Tate holocaust and, according to his testimony in court, announced to his master, Charles D. Manson: "I am the Devil, doing the Devil's work."

The second type of modern witch may simply be a charming fraud who gets himself—or usually herself—on television talk-shows and the like by peddling an apparently innocuous grab-bag of love potions, clairvoyance and dynamic "vibrations." In passing, this type usually prattles about family tradition ("Grandma was also a witch"), beautiful people, and wondrous happenings. Always implied is the ever-ready ability to work lawful magic (white magic that is), which brings about health, happiness, love, and all the reputed glories of the Age of Aquarius.

Are There Witches?

In view of the above definitions, how does a serious person answer the question so often heard nowadays: are there such things as witches? What is actually implied by those who ask is whether or not the witches in question can fly on brooms, cast spells, conjure the devil, and, in short, perform a myriad of wonders and magical acts. To this it is safe to answer: no, there are no such persons, and there never were, even in the Middle Ages. Like so many aspects of the occult, witchcraft is riddled with fraud and wishful thinking. The existence of the magician or the witch does not automatically prove the existence of magic (black *or* white). Too often, because some eccentric or neurotic person claims to be a witch, a wizard, or a wonder worker, the mere audacity of his pronouncement creates in many minds the illusion of his prowess. For years Aleister Crowley captivated the popular press and a large part of the public with his opinions of evil, sorcery, and phenomenal events, until his private delusions seem to have become public fact. The battle between Crowley and another eccentric named Samuel Mathers for control of a mystic (Satanic) cult called the Order of the Golden Dawn was one of the best publicized and longest running pieces of news in the early 1900s. The public hung on every detail: how Mathers sent a bloodsucking vampire to destroy Crowley, how Crowley demolished "her" (the vampire) with her own force of evil; how Crowley invoked the demon Beelzebub to revenge himself on Mathers. In 1918, when Mathers died, a great many believers were convinced that black magic, in the hands of the "Great Beast," Aleister Crowley, had finally destroyed the Master of the Golden Dawn. By the time Crowley died in 1947, his reputation as an evil doer and social monster (even Mussolini expelled him from Italy in 1923) had grown to staggering proportions. Even today, he is venerated by those who worship the occult. The popular television witch Sybil Leek was dazzled by Crowley and, as a "curious" girl, she attended his Black Masses in Paris. Though a purported white witch herself, Mrs. Leek nevertheless considered the Black Master Crowley something of a mentor, since he once predicted to her grandmother that Sybil would be the one to take up where he left off. Whether this has happened or not is hard to say; certainly Mrs. Leek is extremely popular with the media and in this respect, at least, she has indeed taken up the master's wand.

It is patently clear, after some three thousand years of civilization, that witches cannot turn men into toads or fly on brooms. They don't conjure spirits or produce effective love potions unless assisted by narcotics and hallucinogens (which they often use). When they want to kill or destroy, they do so not by sticking pins in wax figures but by willful homicide. The Manson cult of California obviously had no use for such parlor games but like Satanic witches throughout history, they took up their weapons and proudly, under the banner of evil for evil's sake, broke into a private home and murdered. This was and is the true essence of witchcraft—not its supernatural powers but its rigid philosophy of evil, its auto-intoxication, its uncanny dualist belief that Satan is God and that negative deeds produce a beneficent result.

Because this Satanic fascination is so essential to all varieties of the witchcraft delusion, it requires a brief survey and demonstration before we proceed to the antics of the cult.

The Satanic Fascination

In the early days of the Church it was essential to convince believers that the devil himself had set snares for them at every turn, relentless snares that lured the innocent victim with the bait of sin. Only if Satan was the progenitor of evil, the purveyor of Original Sin in Eden, could Christ eventually triumph at the end of time. Without a foe, where was the fight?

In drumming the cadence of Satan into the superstitious brains of its adherents, the medieval Church succeeded in its purpose more than it had dared to dream. Not only did the average man live in fear and loathing of Satan and his horde, but he also began to personify the devil, to identify him, and to build up a panoply of names, faces, events, and fantasies in which the Prince of Darkness (or Lucifer, Beelzebub, or

Mephistopheles) was at the nucleus "in shape and gesture proudly eminent . . . ," as Milton writes.

With such emphatic fantasies entrenched and delineated in myths and liturgy it was inevitable that the resulting fear and loathing of some should be manifested as attraction and admiration in others. Thus the fallen angel of Christian faith became, over the centuries, the god of a new and closely organized religion: the anti-Christian but nonetheless dualistic religion of Satanism.

Some deny entirely that such an actual force ever existed; these people call it a "fantastic mythology," as does Hugh Trevor-Roper. In his view, the myriad details surrounding the witch cult and witch behavior can be attributed to the cynical imagination and deception of the Church. In order to crush dissident enemies, goes his argument, the Church needed a "scapegoat for social frustration" and therefore concocted a monstrous red herring: the scourge of witchcraft. Under the banner of salvation from this scourge, the Church piously burned and otherwise slaughtered every shred of opposition and discontent. There were no witches, no Satan cult, no Black Masses, orgies, sabbats, and so forth. There was indeed nothing but the warped delusions of Church fathers, Church jurists, and Church historians.

This approach—shared by Rossell Robbins—is an offense to logic. The Nazi horror, within the memory span of most adults, reveals how Satanic the human soul can become. In addition to the contemporary atrocity of Hitlerism, there is ample evidence of Satanic activities discernible in almost every culture.

All this is not to imply that the Church was either justified in its reaction or totally innocent of deception and fraud. In the context of history, however, Church "violence" simply matched the violent threat of witchcraft, at least as viewed by the Church. Why do the excesses of the Catholic and Protestant inquisitors and the civil courts (which also participated in the witchhunts) by some inversion of logic prove that witchcraft did not exist as an organized cult? The modern witchhunter Senator Joseph McCarthy attacked and prosecuted many persons who were not Communists and certainly not Communist spies. But the malicious incompetence of McCarthy does not automatically indicate that actual Communist spies and agents were not at work in the United States during the McCarthy era.

To deny the reality of the medieval cult is to insist that for three hundred years or more certain devious churchmen and jurists perpetrated a monstrous deception without being detected; this idea seems to belittle historic possibility. To scoff at the stories of sabbats, Masses, evil brews, and other Satanic manifestations is to ignore the inherent perversions of human nature. To ignore the reality of witchcraft as an influential social phenomenon is likewise to ignore its revival—in one form or another—and thus to be inured to any new witchhunt that may ensue. And so it is proper while debunking the magic, the power, and the fascination of witchcraft to set the record straight about its reality, its true place in history, and its very real specifications. The exposure of one depends integrally on the proving of the other.

Isobel Gowdie's Confession

In 1662, a Scottish woman named Isobel Gowdie voluntarily confessed to a series of witchcraft charges. Her evidence was preposterous in the extreme—or was it?

First, Isobel revealed how the devil, in the shape of a small, black, hairy man, forced her to renounce her baptism and how she subsequently pledged her body to him. Then the devil— with cloven hoofs—baptized the novice in his name and put a special mark on her shoulder. Under his aegis, Isobel committed a variety of atrocious deeds, including the murder of more than a dozen adults and children. She and other members of her cult tore up the fields of a local farmer while the devil led the way on a plow fitted with a wheel of spikes.

All was not work. Isobel and her sister witches enjoyed the

favors of the devil, whose genitalia were "exceeding great and long." Unfortunately, in intercourse he was as heavy as a sack of malt, and his huge member was as "cold as ice." The fluid he ejaculated was as cold as spring water. Consequently, some of the witches complained of pain during sexual relations with the devil, but others, the young and pretty members of the group, had no complaints.

When the witches assembled for the sabbat, Isobel revealed, they would put a broom or a three-legged stool in bed with their husbands so that they wouldn't be missed. Then they flew out the window or up the chimney. Each of them could raise the wind, cause storms and tempests, and each could transform herself into a cat, a crow, or a jackdaw. The devil could likewise take on the appearance of a deer, a roe, or some other horned animal. Isobel's sister witch Janet Breadheid confirmed Isobel's testimony and added that in order to kill, they first fashioned images of clay that they roasted until the desired effect was achieved.

Rossell Robbins regards Isobel as "clearly demented," but Professor Margaret Murray, the foremost modern scholar of witchcraft, deals directly with her testimony and much similar testimony, and from it she developed the thesis that Isobel Gowdie, although possibly demented, was in fact a witch, and that Isobel revealed exactly what she believed to be the truth. Preposterous as it may seem, the details described above in the testimony can be related to specific and very real aspects of the witchcraft religion. Even the devil was real; his member was often as huge as Isobel stated; murder and destruction were his stock-in-trade. His witches assembled to pay him homage, flying and assuming the appearance of animals and other creatures, even as he assumed the horns and skins of a forest animal.

Who the Devil Was

The devil was a man, specifically, a priest, the parochial leader of the cult. Nowhere is it assumed that this devil was, in fact, Lucifer or Satan. Like any Christian priest, he represented his Lord, but in doing so, he achieved great rank and authority, much like a bishop. Although a man, he was no ordinary man. He did not appear in public like some common laborer; rather, he dressed his clerical part. It is clear that the medieval cult leader favored dark clothing and cloven-shaped boots, a formerly outrageous style that eventually became quite fashionable among the elite in the sixteenth century. Testimony also revealed that the devil was often a strikingly handsome man of imposing presence. He was reputed to speak with a mysterious voice. An English witch named Joan Wallis, testifying in 1646, referred to her devil as "a large man in blackish clothing, but with cloven feet." The story was the same abroad: in France Jeanne Hervillier (1578) confessed that her leader was a "huge man dressed in black and booted." The Salem witches of Massachusetts (1692) also venerated "a black [garbed] man in a high crowned hat."

The hat, or hood, was in medieval times a distinctive mark of rank. Horns attached to such headgear gave the wearer even greater prominence. Murray believes that the devil wore such horns in deference to the pre-Christian pagan worship of goats, elks, and horned deities, but horns are symbols also of the dualist dilemma and as such may have fulfilled a Jungian need in the Satanic veneration. Pennethorne Hughes, a disciple of Murray, adds that often the devil wore masks and body coverings made from animal skulls and skin; it was natural to retain the horns in such regalia. The mask idea gives a basis in fact to the persistent references among witches to the devil's hollow, husky voice. A German witch in 1589 described "eine gemachte falsche Stimme . . ." (a falsely made, or hollow-sounding, voice). A Suffolk witch named Thomazine Ratcliffe confessed that the devil "spoke with a hollow, shrill voice."

If the devil wore a full body costume of leather, papier mâché, or metal, this would explain the frequent references to his coldness (meaning lifelessness). Not only Isobel Gowdie but also numerous confessants quoted by Murray refer to the cold hardness and hairiness of the devil's body. The Belgian witch

Digna Robert (1565) said that the devil "était froid dans tous ses membres" (was cold in all his parts). This may indicate that Goya's painting *The Sabbath* (Prado Museum), which shows a bevy of women reverently seated around a huge horned goat, is more realism than surrealism. In his artificial animal costume and headdress, the cult leader probably resembled Goya's figure in every detail.

Being a priest, the devil administered religious sacraments, however perverse. As Isobel revealed, he baptized his initiates after they had renounced the Christian faith and, in some cases, to emphasize their renunciation, he made them trample on the crucifix. After the pledging and avowing were complete, the devil stamped his followers with a recognizable mark—the devil's, or witch's, mark. Such an insignia helped to identify bona fide witches lest any interlopers attempt to invade the sabbat. The devil bound his adherents to the faith by the blackmail of such a stigma, for if any tried to rebel or escape, they could be referred to the Inquisition, for whom the witch's mark (whether authentic or coincidental) was undeniable proof of guilt.

Evidence indicates that the devil's mark was tattooed on the shoulders or sometimes on the thighs. In design it varied from country to country. An English confessant in 1618 spoke of a broad "spott"; other evidence likens the design to the foot of a hare or a rat or to the teeth marks of the devil himself. A French account refers to a mark with "several filaments in a circle," or one that resembled a "little black dog." Crab-like is still another description from the Basses-Pyrenees (1609). It should be pointed out that when the Church and civil authorities found out about the "devil's mark," they quite naturally found an abundance of such evidence wherever they looked, whether it was an authentic mark (made by the cult) or simply a natural development of the skin. Papillomas, hemangiomas, blemishes, warts, welts, and common moles were seized upon as authentic witch's marks, and these marks invariably determined the destiny of the suspect.

After the devil had initiated, baptized, and marked his followers, he introduced them to the mysteries of the witch cult faith, an elaborate half-Christian, half-pagan ritual that encompassed the activities revealed by Isobel Gowdie and her associates: the flights, the sabbats, the evil deeds, and the orgiastic bacchanals.

Perhaps the best way to explore the complicated ritual of witchcraft and, at the same time, to assert its basis in reality, is first to present the traditional outline of the procedure and then to elaborate on it with what we may infer from the actual witch trial testimonies preserved since the Middle Ages. As a result, the Satanic basis of witchcraft will become apparent, and the current myth of beneficent, or "white," witches will be exposed.

The Witch's Sabbat

The witches assembled on given dates, in specific places, in order to celebrate their congregations, or sabbats (sometimes sabbaths), a word that may have come from the French *s'ébattre* (to leap or frolic) or that may be derived from the Judeo-Christian "day of rest." According to their strict beliefs, the witches flew to these convocations on broomsticks or other substitutes. Significantly, before their flights, the convocants massaged their bodies with greasy flying ointments given to them by the devil or by other members of the cult.

After they had arrived at the sabbat site, the Satanists assembled to pay homage to their leader, usually by kissing his feet, or by bowing backward to him, thus reversing the usual forward bow of genuflecting Christians. New members were initiated at this point, and Satanic baptisms were administered. Very often, the devil would take the occasion of homage to assign specific deeds to his followers; these were malicious acts because evil equals good in the perverse world of devil worship. Confessions were often taken in conjunction with these assignments, and woe to the witch who was unable to answer properly the question "what harm hast thou done to date?"

Assignments, confessions, and the enactment of evil deeds were also the function of the less formal esbats (business meetings of the cult), which were held independently of the sabbat and were comparatively less crowded. Sticking pins in figurines, brewing potions and poisons, and concocting pranks such as plowing up a farmer's field with spikes were the typical items on the agenda of esbats. Much of the black magic of witchcraft, renowned throughout history, actually took place at the esbats, not at the sabbats. The witch leader probably thought it wiser to restrict his magic wonderments to a few trusted cohorts, lest he expose his inevitable incompetence (since magic is impossible). Professor Murray relates the following incident: at Forfar, Scotland, in 1661, it was rumored that the devil and his horde had caused the bridge of Cortaquhie to collapse as the result of a malicious spell dreamed up at an esbat. Unfortunately for the reputation of magical Satanism, a certain Helen Guthrie later confessed that she and the devil, along with a few of his most trusted followers, crept up to the bridge when no one was around and by thrusting their shoulders against it, eventually brought down the bridge. More muscle than magic in Forfar.

After the business had been completed, some form of religious activity followed at the sabbats. In most cases this was the Mass, not quite the lurid Black Mass of the eighteenth and nineteenth centuries but more of a rustic parody of Christian sacraments, replete with mocking representations of the holy water (goat's urine), the communion wafer (a black-stained piece of turnip), and the Roman Catholic liturgy ("Our Father who wert in Heaven . . ."). In conjunction with the parody were the more serious aspects of devil worship, which, like the worship of any god, is a somber affair. The vestigial ceremonies of paganism persistently remembered by country folk were also conducted.

Most sabbats provided a feast and a dance following the religious part of the assembly. Food was brought in baskets or stolen from farms (in fulfillment of the evil vow), and it was usually eaten al fresco. Only bread and salt, symbols of purity and preservation, were scorned, but often sweet wine, red meat, fruit, and pastries made up a typical sabbat meal. Of course the Church belittled this aspect of the rival religion. The food, they said, turned to ashes once tasted, and meat was nothing less than human flesh carved from helpless infant victims of sacrificial rites.

Sated with wine and rich food, the congregants began to kick up their heels as the cult orchestra of fife, fiddles, and flutes struck up a round dance. The unconventional witches joined this frolic with gusto and exuberance. Drunk, "stoned," and generally debauched, many flung off their garments and pranced about in their "sky clothes" beneath the venerable moon. Quite naturally, couples paired off for sexual activity. Licentious behavior was heartily condoned by those merry and irreverent souls. Perhaps an orgy ensued, something resembling a frat house "ball" early on Sunday morning after a warm night of necking and drinking.

The sex rites associated with the cult and specified over and over again in testimony were sometimes a part of the general bacchanal, but more usually they composed a separate event, cloaked in quasi-religious ideology and performed with reverence and suspense. The women of the cult, who by all accounts outnumbered the men, earnestly sought intercourse with their leader, since sexual congress was, in their view, a form of communion.

Besides, many of the humble women desired the glory of becoming the mother of an authentic devil child. One might view this as a perfectly natural, albeit Satanic, Madonna complex. In addition to the reverent and mystic aura surrounding the fertility scene, pure and simple libidinous drive cannot be overlooked. The women of the cult were frustrated creatures, shackled to the soil, to the drudgery of kitchen labor, and to loveless childbearing. Any chance that came their way to enjoy unashamedly the vigorous pleasures of sex could not and would not be scorned, especially when it was an integral part of a vital religion. And so, it appears, sometimes thirty or forty women eagerly lined up to copulate with the devil as he stood tumescent in his awesome mask and robes high on the rock altar that was his throne, "abler for them sexually than any man could be," said Isobel Gowdie.

When cult members had exhausted themselves in revelries, reverence, and irreverence and the sun appeared in the east, the sabbat came to a close. The giddy, sleepy congregants stumbled home, with only one hope to keep them going through the dreary days and nights to come: the next sabbat.

One need only employ simple logic and modern parallels to flesh out the descriptions offered above, for no matter how improbable the medieval practice of witchcraft may seem to certain timid souls, there exist in recent history too many similar rituals—also of a Satanic nature—to deny the perennial human inclination to such activities.

Flying

But accepting the sabbat as such—and who can deny the instinct of coreligionists to congregate—how do we then explain the persistent notion that witches flew to the sabbats on broomsticks or other objects? The explanation is probably a medical one. According to chemists, some of the recipes for flying ointments preserved from medieval times strongly point to the possibility of psychedelic stimulation, especially where hemlock, belladonna, henbane, and aconite were utilized. In the 1930s, Prof. A. J. Clark of London University reconstructed one of the traditional witch ointments, which contained hemlock and aconite, and he reported that "mental confusion, impaired movement, irregular action of the heart, dizziness, and shortness of breath" were common reactions—especially when the ointment was massaged into the vaginal membrane. In short, the flying ointment was, for the witches, a delusionary narcotic, producing the effects of what is currently known as a "trip." Most likely, only a selected few of the witch group were allowed to use the precious ointment. Having rubbed the mixture between her thighs and having soon after become numb or faint, the "flying" witch was carried bodily by her friends or transported in a cart to the sabbat site. There, the drugged individual was eventually roused, her head swimming with dazzled notions of flying through the air. There are reports, by the way, of medieval judges watching a suspect who had been rubbed with the ointment as she tossed in delirium on the floor. Questioned later, the victim insisted that she had "flown" to her sabbat and returned, although she had in fact never left the room.

The effect of drugs on past and present witches has manifold ramifications. Wild visions, unworldly sensations, and lingering fantasies imbued the congregants with a sense of possession by supernatural forces and a feeling of unreality that transformed the dreary world into a wonderland. Above all, the drugs strengthened the witches' faith in witchcraft as a unique and fulfilling way of life.

On the other hand, the influence of drugs produced in the ancient worshippers the same addicting dependence and susceptibility that the Manson "witch girls" experienced. Henbane and hemlock, two of the plants most frequently used in witchcraft ointments and brews, are powerful hallucinogens and narcotics. The botanist Norman Taylor in *Narcotics—Nature's Dangerous Gifts* reports that henbane was used for centuries "in all-but-unprintable rites, ages before (its) legitimate use in medicine." Jimsonweed, a related plant, has been known, Taylor informs us, "to break down the will of girls attempting to resist prostitution." The pale purple flowers of hemlock can be seen in almost all the areas of Europe in which witchcraft flourished. According to the analysis of Professor Clark, "the action of hemlock usually is to produce a gradual motor paralysis . . . [and sometimes] delirium and excitement."

Ergot, the principal source of lysergic acid diethylamide

(LSD), was commonly employed in medieval times by midwives as a muscle relaxant administered to women in childbirth. It is a blackish substance that grows chiefly on rye. Proper proportions of ergot have been occasionally used in combating migraine; in some cases corollary changes in the brain and nervous system were produced as well as symptoms of drowsiness and confusion. With LSD the results are not narcotic but psychedelic (producing hallucinations). In 1943, one of the developers of the acid, Dr. Albert Hoffman, described losing all control of time and space when he experimented with a moderate dose of the new "mind changer." He wrote that the effects of the extract made him feel as though he were "outside his own body"—almost as though he had died. Considering the prevalence of ergot in ancient times, we may assume that some devil cults actually mastered its hallucinatory properties and used them to produce fantasies and space-time deliriums on those witches who desperately craved unearthly and "magical" experiences.

Current newspapers frequently report cases of LSD users "flying" or "walking" out of high windows. Even alcohol can produce a sense of levitation. When an individual believes, or wants to believe, in magical transvection, a chemical stimulus is more than adequate to produce the desired effect.

The drug-induced illusion of flying and, indeed, drug-oriented hallucinations of many forms relate not only to the past but also to current history. In the early 1950s the French town of Pont-Saint Esprit was visited by a horror that seemed, to some, a particularly cruel example of the devil's malice. Indeed, the whole population of Pont-Saint Esprit seemed bewitched by illusions of flight, demonic creatures, flaming flowers, and assorted apparitions of a decidedly medieval description. The cause of the disorder was a huge dose of ergot that had accidentally been mixed into the local bread.

The full story of Pont-Saint Esprit is told in great detail by John G. Fuller in *The Day of St. Anthony's Fire.*

Assignments

The assigning of evil deeds to bind the witches closer to the cult is a peculiarity that requires little imagination to justify in modern times. The devil figure Charles Manson apparently instructed his worshippers to commit murder and carnage in fulfillment of what was called "doing the devil's work." The Manson cult evidently conducted esbat sessions at their California hideaway in order to plot murder and upheaval in exactly the same way as did the Forfar witches and Isobel Gowdie.

Baptism and Other Rituals

The specifics of baptism, the Mass, communion, and the liturgy enacted by the medieval cult are not unique even to non-Christian faiths. Baptism, after all, originated as an esoteric Hebrew practice several years in advance of Christianity; the Mass is as old as Noah's sacrifice after the flood; communion between men and their gods, using bread and wine, is also a natural manifestation of the religious experience. Hebrews have the blessed matzo (the Bread of Affliction) and sacramental wine at Passover. Modern communes and cults glorify bread; they often consume wine in veneration of communion (sexual as well as spiritual). The fact that Satanists pursue such activities further verifies the religious basis of their creed.

Feasts and Dancing

There is hardly any need to explain the feasting and dancing of the sabbat ritual; few large groups congregating for celebrational purposes can avoid the joys of eating together and enjoying the communal experience. The question of the Satanists' eating human flesh, preferably a baby's, does not pose any problem in a logical analysis. One or two cults probably did experiment with the perversion of cannibalism as a result of some sudden barbarous impulse. Even modern men, when hungry enough, have been known to dine upon each other, and anthropophagy for its own sake is recorded by modern psychiatry as a rare but not unheard of manifestation of insanity. To cite the atrocities of baby sacrifice and cannibalism as proof that witchcraft never existed (since such perversions are also apocryphal) is naive. By such a rationale, future historians could dismiss the entire scourge of Nazism as a hoax invented by the Nuremburg court, simply because the practice of making lampshades out of human skin is considered utterly unrealistic as a human endeavor.

The Orgy

Isobel Gowdie's observations about the huge genitalia of her devil, his ice-cold body, and his frigid semen and her description of the pain she and her sisters experienced during ritual coitus may at first seem less explicable in logical terms than are the preceding elements of the cult. Indeed, many who deny the historical reality of witchcraft point to these "exaggerations" concerning sex and the orgy as proof of their contentions, since such happenings, they assert, have been perpetrated through the centuries by raving lunatics, lascivious priests, and irresponsible scandalmongers.

Because of the research of Professor Murray and others in the last three decades, we can verify logically even Isobel Gowdie's testimony and the numerous similar references to sexual oddities that appeared in the confessions of European witches.

A fertility ritual, culminating in coitus, was obviously part of the sabbat program—probably its finale. The women of the cult lined up before their master, the youngest and most beautiful at the head of the line, and prepared to give themselves to him. Taking the young women to a secluded spot, the devil copulated with them in the usual manner. Significantly, the young ladies serviced in this way never complained about their liaison with the devil; as Isobel reports, they "had great pleasure" with him. Indeed there was the young French witch in the fifteenth century who freely confessed, as she was led to the stake, that she would not have had it otherwise; "I find too much content in my condition," she announced, "I am always caressed." The women who suffered pain and shock and who seem to cast an air of incredibility over the entire sexual side of the sabbat were apparently the riper, older women of the cult. Even the best of devils could not—or would not—accommodate them in the usual way, especially after having satisfied four or five of the more desirable novitiates. Exhausted yet still responsible for servicing many older women, the leader fitted himself with a large false phallus or had an effigy similarly geared. The older women, who were probably drugged, were roughly impaled upon the phony metal or leather penis and told that the devil had penetrated them. In many cases they even experienced "his" ejaculation, a trick simulated by substituting cold water for semen. Naturally the witches found the false appendage crude and uncomfortable, as so many testified. They could not overlook the coldness and grossness of the artificial penis, since such coldness meant not only physical frigidity but, moreover, the absence of life and, therefore, of normal pleasure.

The artificial penis theory is the most logical explanation of the pain experienced in Satanic sex. Of course, the use of dildos is not unknown in either ancient or modern times. The Bible speaks of them (Ezek. XVI: 17). In Greece and later in Rome, centuries before the medieval witches, there were cults of Priapus. These too employed a huge false phallus upon which virgins were impaled in order to surrender their innocence and to pay homage to the gods.

Even Montague Summers, the orthodox exponent of true magic and mysticism, seems ready to accept, at least in part, the dildo theory: "The coldness of the Devil and the repeated assertion at the trials that his semen was nipping and gelid," he writes, "would seem to point to the use upon occasion of an artificial penis."

In any case, the point here is to establish that even the sexual excesses of the cult were not necessarily fantasies or delusions but very real and viable practices.

Modern Varieties

The witch cult was real; Satanism was and is a reality. Modern witchcraft without cultism and Satanism is not witchcraft at all; it is merely a gratuitous form of paganism. Even modern witchcraft, when it is cult-directed and devoted to evil, is calculated and artificial. The medieval tradition is dead. Its revival is an academic exercise of which the essential functions are titillation or the seeking of profit-making publicity. Neither white nor black witches today, as in the past, are capable of performing magic or sorcery. Their spells and incantations are patent frauds; their rituals, perverted parlor games. Only a very few of those who call themselves witches have anything to contribute to the development of culture and thought. In spite of his sham, Doctor Gerald Gardner, the founder of the Gardnerian (white witch) craze, at least established a useful witchcraft museum and library on the Isle of Man (England). Gardner's philosophy, however, sounds more like an alibi for an orgy than the basis of a flourishing faith, especially when he states that the ultimate source of power, or magic, is built up through the sexual glands, which should therefore remain uncovered (and tumescent) during coven rites.

The American Scene

American witchcraft today flourishes in over four hundred functioning covens located mostly in Boston, Detroit, Los Angeles, and New York. A recent report gives some intimate details of one such coven that regularly meets in Chicago, under the aegis of a high-priestess named Carol. She, like her colleagues, works naked; perhaps for this reason, Carol insists that outsiders watch the proceedings in reverse through a mirror, although she says it's really because otherwise they might inhibit the psychic powers of witchcraft by their possibly negative reactions. Carol preaches from the *Book of Shadows*, a grimoire allegedly passed down from ancient times. After she recites the liturgy, she reaches for her whip, and she performs what was described by one mirror-gazing observer as a "token whipping" of her male and female followers. This bit of erotica, according to Carol, symbolizes purification and "serves to tone up the body and increase its psychic voltage." The flagellation is usually followed by a series of enchantments, one of which recently attempted to abort magically the pregnancy of a young woman accidentally fertilized by one of the coven members.

Less lurid aspects of the craze are touted by many Establishment types. To the *Wall Street Journal,* for instance, "Witchcraft (that is *modern* witchcraft) is casting its spell on thousands," even on the stock market itself. According to one broker, witches are now applying for positions as stock market advisors; they enter armed with amulets, astrology charts, and other occultic paraphernalia. This should not be too surprising; the material values of the world have long been sought by those engaged in sorcery and the "true" religion.

Money, thrills, old-time religion: in modern witchcraft there is something for everyone. The popular Long Island cult of Raymond Buckland and his wife (Gardnerians from England) offers what is described as "an attractive religion" to its followers, far more attractive, say the Bucklands, than Christianity and certainly more ennobling, especially in the purity of sky-clad (nude) communion. For Sybil Leek, witchcraft is more or less a one-woman affair, more inclined these days to the writing of popular books and appearances on television. For a growing number, sexual kicks and bizarre practices are the sine qua non of the new "old" religion. For a smaller group, the whole delusion is merely business. This is true of a storekeeper in Manhattan who, though skeptical of witch magic, nevertheless stocks a huge supply of monkey skulls, black candles, Dragon's Breath Powder (a chemical that makes fire blaze up with an eerie green light), ointments, oils, charms, and *fith faths* (ritual dolls) with accompanying pins.

In a few cases, serious adults approach the subject for the purpose of academic investigation. Such interested individuals can study *Witchcraft, Magic, and Astrology* at New York University, the University of South Carolina, the University of

Alabama, and several other educational institutions. Such classes are usually filled to capacity, mostly with the curious but occasionally with a few actual practitioners, who soon tire of the academic viewpoint, preferring, it seems, the dark secret confines of the coven to the glaring light of critical study. Indeed, few old-fashioned Fundamentalists are as dogmatic, fanatical, or closed-minded in their thinking as are modern "witches."

Though adults usually make up the membership of the most current cults, young people are naturally attracted to the anti-establishment attitudes, to the indulgence in drugs and sex, and above all to the unexpected novelties of the craft. Daniel St. Albin Greene, in the *National Observer,* wrote that "Messing with the unknown is plainly the grooviest thing about witchery." Accordingly, high school students have begun to form covens in otherwise sleepy suburban towns all over the country. Regarding themselves as free spirits, these youngsters don't mind dabbling in black as well as white magic. As Greene reports: "In the privacy of bedrooms and basements, they are whipping up love potions and jabbing pins into wax images of rivals, antagonists, and teachers." Their real aim, however, is to "improve the world and to help people, whether they [the people] know it or not." These are not the wild-eyed Manson followers speaking: they are generally clean-cut kids bored with tradition and fascinated by the continuous publicity given to occult phenomena.

Above all, the ancient lore of gaining power through magic draws the uninformed to the alleged achievements of witchcraft. How many uninspiring souls there must be who become excited to think that by sticking pins in a *fith fath* they may bring disease or death to an enemy. Young and old, they thrill to the idea that mystic vibrations pulsate all around them, waiting to be harnessed for good or evil. To peer into the future, to pray to forbidden gods, to know the ecstasies of the sabbat and the ultimate secrets of all time are only a few of the promises offered by the modern witch cult. Added to these fairly harmless propositions are the continuous use of drugs in the cult tradition, the necessary disdain for morality, and the exaltation of evil as the true definition of good. Frequent orgiastic sex is also not exactly a deterrent for the thrill-seeking novice.

The last word about the modern witchcraft revival has not been written or said. New cults, new excesses, and new atrocities will appear cloaked in the old medieval jargon. Every halloween brings a plethora of newspaper articles and countless radio and television interviews on the subject, most of which focus on purported witches and their achievements. In short, the modern craze will not subside until our popular culture shakes off its basically anti-scientific propensities. It will persist in the dualist atmosphere that sees God as dead and the devil reigning supreme.

Is a witchhunt the answer? No. Witchhunting is as much a recourse to delusion as is witchcraft itself. A little logic would help. White or black, frivolous or serious, witchcraft remains a complicated delusion, a deception that attempts to answer life's inconsistencies in terms of the greater inconsistencies of a medieval concept of the universe. Followers of this concept, in their disaffection for and alienation from the Christian God, turn for salvation to the Christian devil. At best this is a "cop out," at worst a menacing perversion.

5

Above and Beyond: Spiritualism, Precognition, and ESP

THE preceding aspects of the occult, astrology, numerology, witchcraft, and sorcery, fall into the general province of popular delusions and allegedly harmless fads. To be sure, there are quasi-scientific astrologers and numerologists who can outdo Einstein with mathematical theorem. In addition, as was mentioned in the previous chapter, a Satanic witch cult of several thousand members is actually thriving in the United States and seems, at least for the time being, to have assumed more than faddish proportions. In contrast, however, and for full-blown scientific investigation, the general area known as parapsychology, or psychic research, cannot be matched for gravity and awesomeness. Three subdivisions form the basis of the occult delusion of parapsychology: spiritualism, precognition, and ESP.

Spiritualism is the doctrine that involves the practice of communicating with spirits, usually dead, who manifest themselves through mediums, or sensitives "gifted" with the ability to reach beyond the mortal sphere. The basic fallacy of spiritualism is that it claims knowledge or proof of precisely what happens to man after death. Spiritualists accept the notion of an afterlife very much like the present life—with the same joys and sorrows—and by extension, they naturally accept the existence of ghosts, ectoplasmic phenomena, and similar paranormal and superstitious canards.

Precognition, or prevision, is the ability to read the future by means of intuitive flashes, voices, and images. To accept this premise one must believe that the future coexists in some material form with the present and that it simply requires the right exposure to be seen and evaluated. Precogs, as people possessing this ability are called, perform this wonderful feat, not by gypsy-like methods of reading omens in cards or tea leaves or by examining the entrails of a bull, but rather by sober, often eloquent prophecy. Practitioners of this sort often manage to capture the attention of presidents, kings, and the television audience of America and have made themselves the "superstars" of the occult conceit.

ESP—extrasensory perception—has, in recent years, been magnified out of all proportion to its actual significance. In its most modest application, ESP concerns the reported ability of certain sensitive people to describe images on cards that are sealed in envelopes or otherwise hidden from view. At its most phenomenal limit, ESP purports to enable a gifted person to move large objects across the floor merely by the will of his mind (psychokinesis, or PK). In some cases the large object may be a human being who is levitated several feet off the floor without apparent trickery but only by mind power or by some similar extranormal, but nonetheless veridical means. (See Levitation in Chapter 6.)

As will soon be seen, the most modest and not the more phenomenal claims of ESP, are those that form the basis of this subject.

The Parapsychologist

There are many sincere and cultivated researchers in the area of parapsychology, including educators who have developed functioning departments of psychic research in various universities. Predictably, most of the psychic superstars rarely allow themselves to be tested by scientists; they prefer the stage of television talk shows to the testing lab. The one or two who have volunteered to become psychic guinea pigs are the ones who themselves maintain a degree of skepticism about their propensities. The late Eileen J. Garrett, founder and president of the Parapsychology Foundation and a subject of testing at the once flourishing Parapsychology Laboratory at Duke University, although a professed medium and psychic, candidly admitted: "If the whole, strange, mystifying psychic gift could be snatched out of the darkness of seance rooms and put into the capable, probing hands of science, everybody would feel much better about the subject and the world of science and philosophy would be enriched."

Dr. Joseph B. Rhine, who directed the Parapsychology Laboratory at Duke University and whose research will be touched on in this chapter, is not himself a psychic, but he quite positively asserts man's mysterious capabilities and the unlimited reaches of the human mind. Most critics do not find fault with Rhine or with his successor at Duke, Dr. J. G. Pratt.

But when one regards the inconclusive evidence that scientists such as Rhine have accumulated over the last few decades and hears the logical arguments that can be made against parapsychiatrics, one wonders how or why investigators began their efforts in such earnest and with such high hopes. Not only have they unwittingly given over their arenas, in many cases, to quacks and liars, but they have also helped to perpetuate and dignify two of the most cruel delusions of modern times: the notion that the future is ineluctable and therefore can be read by mentally superior seers and precogs; and the belief that loved ones who have died and "gone over" are somehow capable of communicating with those they left behind. Imagine the false hopes and sorrows these two delusions inflict on the gullible and grieving individual. Envision also the power and profit that befall the perpetrators and practitioners. "When I consider life," said Dryden, " 'tis all a cheat; yet fooled with hope, men favor the deceit."

The First Deceit—Spiritualism

Some say that the whole delusion of spiritualism began not in a mysterious Transylvanian castle or graveyard, but in a simple two-story cottage in Hydesville, New York, in 1848. In this farmhouse, two sisters, Kate and Margaret Fox, supposedly established a rudimentary method of communication with a murdered peddler named Charles B. Rosma, whose spirit apparently could not rest.

It was twelve-year-old Kate who hit upon the method after many nights of being plagued, she said, by inexplicable knocking and rapping. "Do as I do, Mr. Splitfoot," she called out to the unseen force, presuming it to be the devil. She then clicked her fingers several times and discovered that "Mr. Splitfoot" did likewise. A code was established between girl and "ghost," and by an elaborate formula of letters and numbers, Kate— with Margaret by her side—eventually worked out the peddler's name and learned that he had been robbed and murdered by a former occupant of the house.

News of the contact spread rapidly throughout the area. Before long, queues of curious and hopeful visitors had formed at the Fox cottage. Fame and notoriety settled on the entire family, and they began a tour of the country. For over thirty years the Fox sisters and their associates presented living proof of the spiritualist phenomenon in all the centers of American and European civilization.

The wonders of spiritualism proliferated in the 1860s, when thousands of grieving parents flocked to the Fox seances with the hope of hearing a word, or even a click, from their soldier sons who had died in the Civil War. The humble and the great made pilgrimages to witness the miracle. Sir Arthur Conan Doyle, creator of detective Sherlock Holmes and a psychic researcher of renown, regarded the Fox phenomenon as "one of the great points of psychic evolution," absolute proof of the supernatural world that he so avidly sought toward the end of his career. When we recall that imitation is the highest form of flattery, we can appreciate how highly praised were Kate and Margaret Fox. Seances, mediums, and other spiritualist phenomena appeared all over America and Europe during the second half of the nineteenth century. Of course not all the spirits rapped or clicked, as the Fox ghost did; most spirits preferred to establish their own personalized system of communication. Some, for example, caused tables to rise and float in space; others could blow trumpets or shake tambourines; "ghost writing" appeared on walls and blackboards; and in some cases the ghosts themselves materialized out of ectoplasm —an imaginary cellular emanation produced by spirits.

If March, 1848, was the birth date of spiritualism, October, 1888, should have been the date of its demise, for in that year a much harried and apparently repentant Margaret Fox confessed all to the *New York World.* The whole thing, she reported, had been a galloping hoax. The young sisters had, in 1848, been trying to concoct an April Fool's prank to play on their parents when they hit upon the rapping idea. But how were the mysterious noises made? It was simple, Margaret revealed, ". . . the result of a perfect control of the muscle of (my) legs below the knee, which govern the tendons of the foot and allow actions of the toe and ankle bones that are not commonly known." She continued: "The toes may be brought down to the floor without any movement that is perceptible to the eyes. The whole foot, in fact, can be made to give rappings by use only of muscles below the knees."

Margaret demonstrated her trick toes to a committee of physicians who fully concurred with her "perfect control" analysis. But Margaret would not stick by her confession, and in 1889 she repudiated all she had said. She had probably been coerced by the spiritualist cult, which, by then, had developed into quite an industry. Retraction or no, Margaret's demonstration before the physicians stands. Unfortunately, despite this evidence and subsequent exposure of mediums by scientists, police authorities, and magicians themselves, the spiritualist fraud continues to grow. In March, 1970, the *New York Times* reported an estimated 24,000 spiritualists working in the United States, most of them capitalizing on the poor and gullible.

According to recent figures put out by the National Council of Churches, over 400 spiritualist churches now exist, with a membership of at least 150,000 practicing congregants. Descendants of the eccentric nineteenth century Theosophy cult and of Rosicrucian mysticism, these updated spiritualists eschew the Fox sisters' rapping technique as well as similar theatrics. For them the disembodied spirit, or "discarnate," remains just that, disembodied and invisible. No longer are tambourines heard or ectoplasmic masses seen floating in limbo. Only by the agonized expression on the medium's face, or by the twisting and contorting of her body, do the congregants know that contact with the spirit has been made. In the second half of the twentieth century, the spiritualist delusion has assumed the proportions of a religious movement, in which faith, not proof, is the sine qua non.

To add to its religious flavor, modern spiritualism boasts the participation of several ostensibly orthodox clerics, or former clerics, including the late ex-bishop of the Episcopal church, James A. Pike, and the late Reverend Arthur Ford, described by one admirer as "the world's most famous medium." It was Ford who allegedly contacted Pike's dead son Jimmy during a taped television seance in Canada. The audience saw Ford relay disjointed messages from "the other side" to the eager ex-bishop. In the modern fashion, the spirits themselves remained invisible.

Tricks of the Trade

Motivated by self-preservation, modern mediums have abandoned the old tricks and maneuvers since the antics of the past were, at best, simply feats of prestidigitation and, at worst, were easily exposed even by the medium's own credulous clientele. During the 1920s, when seances were almost a national hobby in the United States, some of the following ruses were employed both by well-known and insignificant mediums.

In a darkened room, the medium touches the smallest finger of each hand to the thumbs of her clients to her right and left. While they are all thus connected, mysterious rappings are heard, shrill trumpets blow, and the table rises from the floor. How is it done?

Slowly, the medium withdraws her right hand from its contact, while simultaneously she extends the other so that the thumb of her left hand eventually takes the place of the pinkie of her right hand. The clients do not notice the movement and therefore continue to feel contact with what they believe to be her pinkies while, in fact, she has one hand free to play music, move tables, and rap on wood.

In most practices of spiritualism, accomplices are used. This explains the far-away voices and floating faces once employed in almost every seance. Accomplices also take care of ectoplasmic appearances by slowly removing from a black silk bag a piece of gauze cloth soaked in phosphorescent paint. They then dangle the cloth in a beam of ultraviolet light where it is blown about by a hidden electric fan.

Sometimes unwitting clients create the ghostly mood themselves. Overcome by fear or autosuggestion (or both), the nervous participants suddenly "feel something" or "see something" in the darkened chamber. Every medium is ready to include any such gratuitous assistance into the act.

Houdini's Exposé

The greatest exposer of spiritualists and occultists was the remarkable performer Harry Houdini, who made it a regular part of his career to debunk the fakes that had given the art of legerdemain an unsavory reputation. An inimitable master of tricks and illusions, Houdini never presumed to possess psychic or mystic powers of his own, even when Sir Arthur Conan Doyle insisted that Houdini, the exposer of mediums, was indeed the greatest medium of all. Perhaps he came to this conclusion because of Houdini's attempts to communicate with his beloved deceased mother. Such attempts were invariably failures, as in the following case.

Lady Doyle, Sir Arthur's wife, practiced automatic writing, in which spirits allegedly write their messages through the medium's pen. She once prevailed upon Houdini to attend a seance where, she said, his mother had appeared. The event took place in a dimly lit hotel room, with Houdini carefully watching as Lady Doyle shakily wrote his mother's "message." Unfortunately, Houdini pointed out to the medium, his mother had never communicated to him in English, as Lady Doyle had done, but rather in their native German. Of course, Lady Doyle had the typical answer of occultists caught in the act. Neither language barriers nor any other earthly barriers, she insisted, applied to the spirit world.

In the early 1920s, in order to give strength to his debunking, Houdini joined the Committee for Psychical Investigation, organized by the prestigious *Scientific American* magazine. The committee was prepared to pay $2500 to any occult practitioner who could not be proved a fraud. The prize was never paid, mainly because Houdini was so thorough and so knowledgeable of the charlatan's repertoire. Levitation he exposed by revealing the use of trick ropes and knots or long curved loops that allowed one to pass his hand under and over the levitated body without jolting the invisible suspension. A medium who tied himself with sixty feet of rope and then, in the dark, performed magical feats was completely helpless when tied by Houdini.

One of the master's most sensational exposés concerned the prominent seance mistress of the 1920s, Mina Crandon, better known as Margery. To her many followers and clients, Margery appeared to be the epitome of probity and respectability. Because of her basic lack of sophistication, her "gifts" were said to be clearly extranormal in origin. During her dark-room seances, somber bells would ring, rappings would sound in the darkness, the table would levitate, and the voice of Walter, Margery's dead brother, would boom through space. At all times Margery's hands were firmly clasped by her clients. If any trickery occurred at all, which was dubious, it was leg work, not hand work that Margery employed. To all who observed her, or sat by her side, there appeared to be no motion whatsoever of either her legs or feet. Many on *Scientific American*'s committee felt that the $2500 prize was at last in jeopardy.

Houdini rushed to the challenge and later wrote up his precise examination in great detail (italics are his):

> Anticipating the sort of work I would have to do in detecting the movements of her foot, I had rolled my right trouser leg up above my knee. All that day I had worn a silk rubber bandage around that leg just below the knee. By night the part of the leg below the bandage had become swollen and painfully tender, thus giving me a much keener sense of feeling and making it easier to notice the slightest sliding of Mrs. Crandon's ankle or flexing of her muscles ... As the seance progressed I could distinctly feel her ankle slowly and spasmodically sliding as it pressed against mine while she gained space to raise her foot off the floor and touch the top of the box [on which Margery sat] ... When she had finally maneuvered her foot around to a point where she could get at the top of the box, the bell ringing began and *I positively felt* the tendons of her leg flex and tighten as she repeatedly touched the ringing apparatus. There is no question in my mind about it. *She did this.* Then, when the ringing was over, I plainly *felt her leg slide back* into its original position with her foot on the floor beside mine. . . .

Though exposed and denied her prize, Margery insisted that Houdini had proved nothing, and that his further assertion that Walter's booming voice was simply her own in a male falsetto was not proof, she said, but conjecture. Predictably, Margery continued her practice with almost as many followers as before. Houdini and most other sensible observers were convinced of her chicanery, especially when her famous ectoplasmic manifestations were exposed by two Harvard professors as consisting of specially treated lung tissue apparently obtained by her accomplice-husband, a surgeon. Another famous medium of the period, exposed in much the same way, was Eusapia Palladino, from Naples, who died in 1918. At a seance held under the collective eye of a group of academicians from Columbia University in New York, it was discovered that Eusapia had adroitly used her foot to produce the knockings and kinetics ascribed to spirits from the other world. When that exposé and others were reported in the press, Eusapia's followers parried by insisting that the great woman had reluctantly resorted to patent trickery in order to maintain her popularity. She was, they averred, nonetheless a psychic phenomenon.

A word should be said here about Houdini's own alleged reappearance to his wife after his death; the story is dubious at best. Before his death of peritonitis in 1926, Houdini stated that he would try to transmit a secret message to his wife from the afterlife, if indeed the afterlife existed.

It was Arthur Ford who convinced Mrs. Houdini that her husband's spirit had indeed performed this wondrous feat by contacting Ford in 1928. So convinced was she that in 1929, Beatrice Houdini swore out an affidavit confirming that Ford had conveyed the secret "in the agreed sequence . . . prearranged between Mr. Houdini and myself."

The message was really a word code employed by the Houdinis in a fake mind-reading act they had performed years before on the stage. It went: "Rosabelle (Mrs. Houdini) Answer. Tell. Pray. Answer. Look. Tell. Answer. Answer. Tell." This, verbatim, was the message that Arthur Ford allegedly presented while in a trance in front of a group of witnesses. It is significant that Mrs. Houdini was not present at this first seance because of illness. The alleged spirit message was conveyed to her afterward by associates of Ford. When she acknowledged its veracity, a second seance was arranged in her home. Here, Houdini, by way of Fletcher, Ford's control spirit, reportedly thanked Beatrice for her compliance and then asked her to reveal the single word which the ten code words equated. That word: *believe.*

There are various explanations of this apparent reappearance of the great Houdini. The magician Milbourne Christopher in *Houdini: The Untold Story* suggests collusion between Ford and Mrs. Houdini. This Mrs. Houdini vehemently denied, but, according to Christopher, she also later denied the entire revelation *and* her affidavit. Whatever the case, supernatural factors certainly do not seem to have been involved. For one thing, Mrs. Houdini admitted that the "secret" code she and her husband used in their act was, in fact, published and known to several people, including various backstage personnel. It was a typical mind reader's device. The word "pray" meant A; "answer," B; "say," D, and so forth. Knowing the basic code, someone could easily figure out the conformations of the message word "believe," *if* he knew that *believe* was the word.

If only Beatrice and Harry Houdini knew that word, is it possible that Mrs. Houdini unwittingly projected it at the time she first received the message? It is important to note that prior to her affidavit she seemed to have questioned the accurate transmission of the message. Being ill and at one point delirious, she could have accepted as true a code that was only partially accurate. Did she then unwittingly rearrange it to form the word "believe," thereby automatically revealing the secret? Might a shrewd guess on someone's part have figured out that *believe* might be the likely word transmitted from a "spirit" to the doubting world? The possibilities of normal explanation are numerous, especially in face of Mrs. Houdini's admission that the code itself was known to several individuals.

However, Ford's control, Fletcher, seems to have cast the greatest doubt on the whole affair. Caught up in an apparent exuberance of triumph, he supposedly exhorted Mrs. Houdini to "tell the whole world that Harry Houdini still lives and will prove it a thousand times and more . . ." Unfortunately for Mrs. Houdini, the thousand and more proofs were not forthcoming. From 1929 until 1943, when she died, Bess Houdini never again heard from her famous husband—nor was Arthur Ford so favored.

Continuing Delusions

So many spiritualists have been exposed as frauds that persistence in this profession—even among updated spiritualists—seems to be an act of sheer defiance. The idea that modern psychics, or mediums, still receive spirit voices and messages indicates that belief in ghosts and ectoplasm prevails today, in the space age. Of course there is no scientific documentation to support the archaic notion that the dead float about the earth in some tangible and perceptible form. This is said despite alleged ghost photos that have been produced by ghost chasers and exorcists. Nine times out of ten such phenomena are hallucinations or illusions produced by slide projectors, mirrors, light blurs, lasers, radio beams, powder blasts, treated gauze, and so forth. The tenth case, it should be hastily added, could be exposed just as easily, but it falls into the category that scientists term "pending explanation." (See Chapter 6, Apparitions.)

Although there are no such things as ghosts, spiritualists continue to bilk and delude the innocent (and some sophisticated people as well) on the basis of valid ghostly or spirit appearances. Eileen J. Garrett tells of a particularly cruel, indeed criminal, fraud perpetrated on a mother whose son had been killed in World War II. Through the agency of a spirit, the medium to whom this mother went "discovered" that the boy was not dead at all but alive in a Japanese prison camp (five years after the end of the war). The grieving mother was told to bring $100 a month to the medium, who would then "apport" (or magically transmit) food and clothing to the prisoner. The mother scraped together the requisite sum, and she entrusted it and her faith to the medium's prowess and ghostly authority. "When I see miserable, ignorant people so brutally victimized," Mrs. Garrett wrote, "I am moved to tears of rage."

But tears of rage and psychic research are not enough. What is needed is more of Houdini's technique. Under such scrutiny, all occult delusion will fall away like the black bag that hides the ectoplasmic gauze. Stage trickery, not psychic power, is the basis of the spiritualist deceit. Houdini the magician said it: "Many things that seem wonderful to most men are the everyday commonplaces of my business."

The Second Deceit—Precognition

The assassination of President John F. Kennedy had ramifications that went beyond the apparent political and social considerations. Indeed, the awful events of November 22, 1963, became a sort of benchmark for practitioners of precognition, who appeared on television or in print blatantly announcing and documenting the fact that they had predicted the tragedy —often in great detail.

The subsequent assassinations of Martin Luther King and Senator Robert F. Kennedy similarly became precognitive landmarks in the popular mind. Indeed any seer who had predicted one, two, or all three of the tragedies had certainly earned his psychic reputation.

Prophet Jeanne Gardner even went so far as to confront President Kennedy in the White House in early November, 1963. According to her autobiography, she was eating a chicken dinner with Mr. Kennedy when suddenly she saw the events of Dallas looming up in a precognitive flash before her eyes. "A part of me wanted to warn him," she wrote, "but an even stronger part of me refused to speak." The stronger part naturally prevailed, and two weeks later John F. Kennedy was murdered.

It boggles the mind to conceive of a situation in which a seer has the attention of a president and yet neglects to warn him of what certainly would be of the gravest significance to him and to the nation. But the evasiveness of this incident is endemic, if not essential, to the phony profession of precognition, which manages to impress millions (and to rake in millions as well) by a series of clever and subtle rationalizations, evasions, and double entendres.

Ancient Precedents

Precogs attempt to bolster their reputations by reminding us that predicting the future is as old as the Bible and has been venerated in every age with almost religious ferocity. The prophets of the Bible, especially Ezekiel and Jeremiah, they contend, were precogs whose clairsentient messages came directly from God, in much the same way that Jeanne Gardner and Jeane Dixon receive their divine pronouncements. Of course neither Ezekiel, Jeremiah, Isaiah, or the others were prophets —that is, future casters—in the popular sense. Jeremiah, for one, was a religionist whose prophesies about the fall of Jerusalem were no more extrasensory than someone today predicting the onset of a third world war. Ezekiel was a preacher who couched his message in elaborate poetic imagery, which his followers could interpret as they chose. Ezekiel preached the themes of redemption and revival; his was a realistic message of patent probability, not a prophecy as such. The great Hebrew prophets never claimed clairsentient or clairvoyant powers of a supernatural nature; their purpose after all was not future-casting but religious instruction. Though they reportedly experienced visions and flashes of insight, we must remember that their fallacies and wrong guesses were not recorded by their followers who, like many biographers, may have glamorized their subjects so as to make them appear infallible. Besides, many of Ezekiel's visions, like those of St. John the Divine, are submerged in obscurity and as yet remain ostensibly "unfulfilled."

The Delphic Oracle

The Delphic Oracle of ancient Greece, another noteworthy predecessor of modern precogs, was simply a priestess of Apollo, not alleged to possess any inherent powers of her own. Seated over the so-called "navel of the world," the Holy of Holies in the temple at Delphi, the Oracle would inhale the fumes and drink the waters from the bubbling Spring of Massotis that ran directly beneath the "navel." Having done so, she would eventually fall into a mantic ecstasy, mumbling and shouting largely incoherent words and phrases, which the Delphic priests seized upon as divine and infallible decree.

It is quite obvious that the Oracle was simply intoxicated by some form of narcotic that had been naturally or artificially dissolved in the waters of the spring. The pertinent factor, however, especially as it concerns modern precognition, is the subsequent interpretation given her ravings by the Delphic priests. Most often these interpretations were offerings of good advice on matters of war, marriage, finance, and the like. But when the priests were asked for specific predictions—the bane of all seers—they cloaked their reports in clever ambiguities that, coupled with the ambiguous condition of human life, served as an effective ploy. Thus the name of a king or prince babbled by the Oracle might mean prosperity or calamity for the kingdom or personal harm (or fortune) for the king. If the king was later involved in a crisis, either good or bad—as kings or rulers are wont to be—the priests could take credit for a significant prophecy; something, they would say, was in the air concerning their king.

So it continues today. The precog speaks of a black cloud descending on the White House. Time passes; the president is assassinated; the prophet and his followers rush to the television studios to remind the public that their predicted cloud was in fact the specific act of regicide. And the gullible public believes.

Nostradamus

The most famous precog was probably Michel de Nostre-Dame, better known as Nostradamus, born in France in 1503. There is no doubt that Nostradamus was a remarkable scholar and physician. Unfortunately for his modern following, however, he was also something of a fraud. His highly vaunted prophecies, which appear in the poetic tome *Centuries* (1555), are again exquisite examples of ambiguity, aided by a keen sense of history. The fact that Nostradamus foresaw the phenomenon of modern aircraft dropping bombs on civilian populations, for example, is no more than a crafty deduction based not on supernatural insight, but on the work of Nostradamus' great contemporary Leonardo da Vinci. A decade before Nostradamus was born, Leonardo had designed numerous flying machines and bomb-like weapons, which were never used but were nonetheless recorded on elaborate blueprints by the master. Assuredly, the clever Nostradamus knew of these inventions and merely applied them to his hunches concerning future historical development. In the same vein, anyone today can safely "prophesy" great moon cities in which former earthlings will live in perennially sunlit, air-cooled crystal cocoons and will move about on conveyor belts or by means of jet-propelled footwear (all of these "prophecies" have been previewed by modern technology).

His cleverness notwithstanding, Nostradamus occasionally stooped to the practice of outright deceit in his prophecies, as in the case of his recorded revelation to Catherine de Medici of France. Inviting the superstitious woman to his canopied chamber, Nostradamus is reported to have shown her several significant visions that seemed to float in space. These Catherine believed to be prophecies concerning the future of the Medici throne. About 100 years ago, a French optics expert, sifting the details of the famous prophecy, proferred a probable earthbound explanation. The industrious Nostradamus had simply used mirrors, arranged periscope fashion, to reveal his "visions" to the queen. One mirror, into which Catherine was told to gaze, reflected the image of another mirror hidden beneath the ceiling canopy. This second mirror, in turn, picked up the images of several accomplices in another room, who portrayed the details of what Nostradamus wished the queen to believe. Whether the prophecies came true is highly debatable, but Nostradamus was no fool, and his precognitions, like those of many of his modern counterparts, were always tinged with realistic possibility. Steeped in a supernatural, emotion-charged aura, such prophecies penetrate the susceptible mind in such a way that, later, they quite convincingly seem to come true. The real events and the earlier prophecies may have very little, if anything, in common, but the credulous client has blocked out the mundane details and the discrepancies, and he remembers only the magical ambience of the original prediction.

Does It Work Today?

One might think that the best way to debunk alleged precognitive abilities is simply to analyze the predictions made by precogs and to show how rarely they actually come to pass. This is not as easy as it may seem, since, as noted, visionaries purposely cloak their prophecies in evasive phrases or make such obvious and patent observations as to defy contradiction. In many cases, in fact, clever precogs do not even bother to prophesy at all, but merely utter what is nothing more than a logical eventuality. Jeane Dixon's continuous talk about the threat of Red China and the subsequent military alliance of the United States and the Soviet Union is regarded by some as prophecy, but it is in fact political conjecture similar to that which frequently appears in the writings of news analysts or historians.

Just as it is difficult to pin down the precog and force him to prophesy chapter and verse in specific details, it is impractical to trust the records and reports these precogs have made in their notebooks or spoken to friends to verify their claims.

Although we will analyze and explode some of the latest prophecies of famous seers, for now the best procedure in debunking them is not to show how false their conclusions are, but rather how fraudulent and transparent are their methods.

By and large, popular precogs utilize any or all of the following procedures in concocting their claims:

1. They depend on prior information that is a result of research or information given them by accomplices, either intentionally or unintentionally. In most cases this is information as yet unknown to the public and the press.

2. They prophesy in glowing generalities about the most obvious observations, carefully couching what they say in an armful of ifs, ors, and similarly self-protective phraseology.

3. They cleverly utilize the suggestibility quotient of their clientele or resort to outright tricks (mirrors, cameras, tape recorders, accomplices, etc.) to learn what they need to know. In some cases they may even employ the potent techniques of hypnosis.

4. They depend on inherent instincts and shrewd perceptiveness in guessing personality types, probable needs, and problems. They are, in this maneuver, no more omniscient or prescient than the palmist who tells a nailbiter, for example, that he suffers from nervousness.

5. They finesse their gifts and capabilities, denying any personal power, by putting the blame or glory entirely on God (or the devil). The reference to God may also serve to remove them from the taint of fraud that they would otherwise exude in profusion.

Examples: The Use of Prior Information

Nostradamus' apparent reliance on Leonardo's private blueprints for his predictions of wartime flying machines is a good example of this maneuver. Similarly, a popular modern seer who is the perennial guest of Washington, D.C., cocktail parties is privy to numerous items and rumors that quite often turn into "news," such as the marriage plans of a presidential widow. The friendship between Evangeline Adams and J. P. Morgan, noted earlier, probably afforded Miss Adams a good deal of stock market "clairvoyance" that less well-connected prophets never displayed.

Accomplices are often indispensable to the prior information technique. When they are invited to appear on television talk shows or to attend private parties, for instance, many precogs or their accomplices scout around for days in advance, finding out who is likely to attend the party or to appear on the show. They then dig up details about the people that "only the subject and his family would know."

In one such case an individual known as a "warlock, precog, and seer" learned that Mr. M.—a well known celebrity—would be at the party to which the seer had been invited. A friend, an attendant at a nearby hospital with access to its files, informed the warlock that Mr. M. had, about three years ago, rather surreptitiously entered the hospital to combat an illness. The friend informed the precog further that the symptoms of the illness consisted of large red blotches on the face and torso. The cause of the ailment was excessive drinking, a fact that the prestigious Mr. M. preferred to hide from public view. The warlock added this piece of information to the news that Mr. M. was once again hitting the bottle quite publicly, and thus he went well-armed to the party. There he simply confronted his subject with the following discreetly worded prophecy: "I see red blotches, like splashes of paint, appearing all over your face and torso. I cannot tell what they are or where they come from. All I know is that they will soon appear." Mr. M. at once put down his highball, dumbfounded with amazement. Only later did he deduce the real "inside" nature of the prophecy; by then the warlock had gone on to other conquests, fairly confident that Mr. M. would never spill the beans (at least in public).

Medical prophecies are a popular item in the precog bag of

tricks and can be usually explained by the prior information device. Cures for disease and advanced surgical techniques are, of course, frequently written about in the popular press, but only *after* the fact, when the cure or technique has been approved by the medical profession. However, doctors are continually experimenting and speculating on medical developments as part of their overall research. Sometimes their speculations are published in professional journals or delivered as papers at medical conferences. The precog who specializes in the "I-see-a-cure . . ." school garners these speculations in the same way the aforementioned party going seer maneuvers in her Washington circles. Epidemics are frequently predicted as a result of this "precognition" technique.

The prophet Criswell, who, in preparation for Doomsday 1999, sleeps in a coffin, predicted for 1970 "a ringworm epidemic . . . sweeping the nation from Mexico and the South." His calculations, which proved faulty as far as medical knowledge is concerned, may have been based on his reading of esoteric medical journals or—more likely—on his discussions with doctors and researchers, some of whom may have spoken of increased incidence of ringworm in Mexico or in the southern United States.

Obvious Observations

Maurice Woodruff, a popular astrologer and precog, thinks he can dazzle a great many followers with his blatant "prophecies" about the miniskirt and the maxiskirt. Neither will be popular to the exclusion of the other, he asserted in the spring of 1970. Rather, some kind of compromise will be agreed upon in which "skirts will be just below the knee." In addition, he stated, "they will be flared and quite full." There is hardly need to explore the glaring generality and simplemindedness of this prophecy. It was similarly foreseen by fashion designers from the very first. However, Woodruff doesn't always deal in generalities but sometimes sticks his neck out quite a way. He predicted in March 1970 that Governor Ronald Reagan of California would lose California in the 1970 election. (Reagan's winning plurality was in excess of half a million votes.)

Perhaps one of the most noteworthy examples of obvious generality was offered by Jeane Dixon on a television talk show in the summer of 1970. When eagerly asked by her host what her overall prognosis for the immediate future was, she stated quite unashamedly that "in some ways the world will get worse; in some ways, better . . ." Drug use, campus riots, race conflicts, and such will continue, she said. But there is also hope: various diseases will be cured (which ones she did not specify); living conditions for some will improve; and we may infer, I assume, that babies will be born, and elderly folks will die in their sleep.

Because she is so popular, Mrs. Dixon has to endure a good deal of public debunking. Her publicized Kennedy predictions, including the election victories, the assassinations, and future episodes in the lives of the former Jacqueline Kennedy and Senator Edward Kennedy, fall into the category of evasive guessing and generality. This applies even to her specific prediction made in 1967 concerning the assassination of Robert Kennedy. Reportedly she told a Washington friend that "something terrible is going to happen to Senator Robert Kennedy . . . [specifically] he is going to be shot." At the same time there were many ungifted persons who feared for the life of the New York senator. In the spring of 1968, for instance, an equally famous lady also told a friend that she couldn't be very happy about Robert Kennedy's intention to run for President; "I know he's going to be shot," she said, ". . . they're going to shoot him." The prophet in this case was Jacqueline Kennedy, the senator's sister-in-law, who, out of personal experience and sorrow, well knew the hazards of political life.

The writer Gordon Prentice, who conveyed the above information in *The Psychic Reader,* has several similarly cogent things to say about the vague and sermonizing elements that make up most of Jeane Dixon's prophecies. The fact that Robert Kennedy became a presidential candidate just prior to his death, Prentice reminds us, went completely unmentioned by the famous seer despite her specific predictions of his impending assassination. Nor was Lyndon Johnson's decision not to run for office part of her "election day special." Not that Mrs. Dixon ignored LBJ. Here are her evasive observations about him given in the spring of 1968: "I feel President Johnson is seeking, for the first time since he entered the White House, divine guidance rather than depending altogether on his circle of advisors . . ."

As Prentice puts it, "the reader must decide for himself just where the prophetic aspects of this sermonette may be found." Regarding another president, Mrs. Dixon was similarly bland and evasive as she observed that Richard Nixon, in the 1968 election, would face "powerful forces, both foreign and domestic, hard at work to bring about his defeat." The shallowness and gratuity of this prophecy are self-evident. As Prentice concludes, referring again to Mrs. Dixon, "If you make a sufficiently large number of prognoses, and if they are worded vaguely enough, several of them will come true—particularly if, in retrospect, you fit specific events into a general prediction." His words apply not only to Mrs. Dixon but to all practitioners of the precog delusion.

One of these was the celebrated seer and prophet Edgar Cayce, sometimes called the "sleeping prophet" because he allegedly uttered his many predictions while in a somnolent state resembling sleep. Although Cayce dabbled in outright precognitive forecasts, such as foretelling the destruction of New York, Los Angeles, and San Francisco and the subsequent reappearance of the legendary continent Atlantis, he also baffled and amazed many by his more credible medical evaluations and his formidable remedies.

It should be pointed out that a great deal of what Cayce prescribed in his role as a psychic physician is merely folk medicine, more amazing for his naivete than for its supernatural force. The persistent use of castor oil, which he authorizes for warts and blemishes, and his remedies for baldness, which include rubbing the scalp with crude oil and "Listerine twice a week" are hardly supernatural. Notions about adding more seafood, carrots, onions, and garlic to the diet to grow hair or to improve eyesight can be found in any farmer's almanac or handbook on folk medicine. What made Cayce seem so marvelous was his apparent ability to spot an illness or diagnose a disease by merely gazing at the subject before him. But even this was the product of the well-developed perception that Cayce no doubt possessed. Old country doctors, long schooled in practical medicine, are often just as competent in assessing that a yellowish complexion indicates a diseased gall bladder, or that yellowing sclera shows the likelihood of a malfunctioning liver.

The fact that many untutored persons can sit down at a piano and play a melody that they've only just heard or that some preschool children can quickly add up the most complicated column of figures is rationally regarded by psychologists as nothing more than a highly developed, albeit unlearned, intuition, probably hereditary and not supernatural. Cayce's prodigious success with medical diagnosis and other forms of personality analysis has many of the earmarks of this same untutored intuition.

According to his obituary in 1945, Cayce suffered from doubts as to the source of his prophetic visions. Was it from God, he wondered, or did it originate with a less desirable force? Cayce's quandary points up the sincere confusion of many psychics and other occult practitioners. Not all of them, after all, are outright frauds as are the dime-a-dozen readers and advisors, the fly-by-night seance swindlers, and the phony faith healers and medicine men. Nor are all of them of the more subtle variety, who carefully cover their tracks and stay within the law by ambiguous and relatively innocuous prophecies, readings, and assorted visions of a grandiose but legal formulation. This last type never advertises any more than he delivers, thus protecting himself frcm the accusation of criminal fraud. The fraudulent aspect of this subtle deceiver, however, is the fact that he *knowingly* employs outlandish and discredited systems of "magic," under the guise of viable truths.

There is a third category of practitioners, composed of the sincere, if confused, individuals who truly and deeply believe in their alleged gifts and powers to the extent of almost total self-delusion. Often this type develops a form of Messianic inspiration quite early in childhood. Lucky guesses and intuition are thereafter regarded as supernatural guidance; unusual powers of perceptivity or deduction are viewed as second sight; and sheer neurotic exuberance becomes an aspect of the Divine.

Once embarked on their mystic careers, a few of this ilk probably realize the fragile ground upon which they are walking. It is then a question of personal integrity whether they remain or withdraw. If they remain, they are eventually obliged to transform themselves into caricatures of their original purpose or into schizoids wavering between Messianic inspiration and the realization of sham. The medium in the film *Seance on a Wet Afternoon* was one such pitiful character. She insisted that she formerly possessed great psychic gifts that unfortunately waned. As a result, she was gradually reduced to criminal fraud and near murder by dint of her frustration and greed.

Tricks of the Trade

Kreskin the mentalist is candid about the showmanship aspect of mind reading and future casting, which, as he publicly reports, have nothing at all to do with the occult. He, like all clever mentalists, picks up clues and cues from his subjects and subliminally introduces into their own mentality ideas and episodes that he will later "read" or prophesy to the amazement of all. Undoubtedly, the suggestibility of most subjects and followers of the occult plays directly into the showman's hands. A hypothetical example illustrates this point. We are at a public mind-reading precog demonstration. A heavy-set, attractively dressed young woman steps up to the stage for a psychic reading. She is probably unmarried—no wedding ring; her weight problem bespeaks some emotional difficulty, perhaps romantic. The quality of her clothes indicates a good income or perhaps a spendthrift nature if her income is low. Around her neck is a fine old watch on a gold chain, and the cover of the watch is engraved with initials. Obviously it is a man's watch, an antique, given to her probably by her father (the last initial is the same as her last initial). She often toys with the watch reverently and affectionately. Was she unconsciously in love with her father?

The trained psychic has almost at once culled a mass of useful information with which to begin his reading. On top of everything else, he sees in his subject's eager eyes a willing spirit, susceptible to his ploys and no doubt imbued with reverence and dependence on astrology, numerology, the Tarots, and other aspects of the occult.

"You are troubled" (and overweight), he begins. "Life today is not what you want it to be (that's why you eat so much), and you are usually lonely (why else would you come alone to a show like this?). There was, once, a dominant man in your life not too long ago (her father, presumably dead, or else he would still possess the watch). But now he's gone (I know all this from the slight nod of your head and the sigh that escaped your lips when I mentioned the dominant man). But soon a tall, dark stranger will appear in your life—perhaps he already has (that is why you are taking such care with your clothes). There is bound to be a change in your affairs (there usually is with everyone). Don't give up even though you are often tempted to do so (as most people are). And, above all, do return for a further reading when more will be revealed by the psychic force."

The woman would be sure to return, despite the vagueness and limpness of the prophecy just described. For even if he lacks accuracy and precision, the precog is, after all, a man of great appeal, and for the first time in a long time someone has shown an interest, someone seems to care.

The shrewdness and seductiveness of a successful psychic were interestingly portrayed in a 1950 film called *Whirlpool,* in which José Ferrer played the part of Caldwell, smooth and sinister, famous as an astrologer and psychic of all persuasions. At a chic cocktail party, Caldwell astonished everyone by accurately "reading" the character of a pompous Italian count who had only recently—and secretly—tried to commit suicide. Vain even to the point of his own exposure, Caldwell glibly explained his techniques to the assembled guests. The morose, tense, and excitable features of the Count's personality were evident to the trained eye, he told them; one need but study the subject's high-pitched voice, bulging eyes, and flushed appearance. As to the suicide attempt, anyone who looked closely could spot the freshly healed scars across the subject's wrists. "You are also a Sagittarian," Caldwell added as a footnote to the astonished Count, "born in late November." This piece of clairvoyance, we later learn, was plied from the Count's little girlfriend, who also happened to be a protegée of Caldwell. Not knowing this, the gullible Italian at once becomes a convert to Caldwell's blandishments. Yet, still amazed by his powers, he asks: "All this you learn from the stars?" "Not the stars," Caldwell candidly admits, "from my eyes!"

Caldwell's stock-in-trade, however, is not merely astrology, mentalism, or clairvoyance. Above all he is an expert hypnotist, as are many of his counterparts. Often the psychic's expert use of hypnosis has engineered what later will seem to be a marvelous demonstration of mind reading and precognition. In such cases a variety of hypnotic techniques is used. Susceptible subjects may quickly and privately be brought under hypnotic influence by the expert even as he interviews them before the "reading." While in their trance, they are asked to reveal numerous details of their personal life and fantasies. The hypnotist then dismisses all memory of his strategem from the subject's mind and proceeds—usually in public—to rattle off the numerous details that "only the subject could have known." In another version of this ploy, a post-hypnotic state of heightened susceptibility is created, in which the credulous subject involuntarily confesses to the veracity of the psychic's enumerations even when they are false. This is comparable to the common compulsion to say no when one means yes or to the common tendency to acquiesce to a strong and dominant personality despite the shallowness or foolishness of his behavior.

The tendency toward self-deception and self-hypnosis in otherwise sophisticated persons is related to the strains of modern life. Indeed, there are numerous cases in the annals of psychiatry in which seemingly external problems are shown to be entirely self-produced by the apparently innocent subject, who appears quite incapable of deceiving either himself or anyone else. Freud discusses the self-hypnotic tendency in his analysis of prophetic dreams. In one case an intelligent and truth-loving woman came to him distressed and amazed by an ostensibly supernatural incident. Freud described the visit:

> She related that she once dreamed that she had met a former friend and family physician in front of a certain store in a certain street, and next morning when she went downtown, she actually met him at the place named in the dream . . . Careful examination definitely established the fact that there was no proof that the women recalled the dream in the morning following the night of the dream—before the walk and before the meeting. She could offer no objection when this state of affairs was presented in a manner that robbed this episode of everything miraculous, leaving only an interesting psychologic problem.

In other words, the patient had convinced herself retrospectively that she had dreamed of this rendezvous, but in fact she had dreamed no such thing. Freud discovered why this particular meeting had caused his patient a kind of *déjà vu.* The family physician, she admitted, had awakened memories of a lover, who was also a friend of the doctor. Because she had long ago invested her clandestine affair with mystery, the patient tended now to associate all persons who had known her lover with similar dreamlike qualities and mystery.

Freud's report is an example of how the mind can play little tricks on the susceptible subject. Imagine the tricks that are played when the subject is manipulated or instigated subliminally by the clever and deceptive psychic.

Failing to master the subtleties of psychology and hypnosis and lacking well-developed perceptivity, most precogs, mentalists, and others who profess clairvoyance or clairsentience, resort to the old-fashioned tricks of the trade that Houdini enjoyed exposing so much.

When the psychic act is done in a theater or a public place, accomplices mingle with the audience in advance of the show to catch any uncommon names and pertinent details that may be useful in the act. A mother calls out to her daughter in the lobby: "Iphigenia, come over here or you will get lost!" Later during the show the seer covers his eyes and in a mysterious voice exclaims: "There is someone in the audience whose name begins with I—I—f—no Iph—Iphigenia!"

Electronic devices function as silent accomplices in the auditorium and in other areas of the theater. Hidden television cameras in the ceiling scan such things as the contents of a lady's purse when she opens it to take out a handkerchief; supersensitive listening devices hidden in many of the chairs pick up everything from names, addresses, and social security numbers to the date of Aunt Millie's latest attack of lumbago.

Backstage, the mentalist assembles this information for the type of "telepathy" demonstration usually associated with carnivals and nightclub routines. Precogs evaluate similar information in a more deductive, long-range manner. A casual remark about possibly moving to California or contemplating the purchase of a new station wagon is perfect grist for the precog's phony mill.

The Gift from God

Jess Stearn, a popular writer about psychic and many other subjects, waxes poetic in his *Adventures into the Psychic* concerning "God's power" and what he calls the "psychic milieu" that has recently been developing to "help man resolve the problems (that) the intellect has failed at." Given the anti-scientific and anti-intellectual propensities of our time, we should not be surprised to find followers of the occult groping after medieval notions of God and the Divine as they seek to fill the void that a lack of courage and logic has created. Afraid of death, which according to Stearn "is lurking as never before" in the form of man's "technical know-how" (for example, the nuclear bomb) and ill at ease with rational philosophy, many moderns have outdone even old-time religion by investing their faith in the clairvoyant and supernatural powers of people who are regarded as God-chosen vehicles of divine guidance. To challenge the veracity or validity of these seers is to challenge God; to follow and believe their dictates is to do no less than the ancients did in following Elijah, Jeremiah, Isaiah, and Christ.

What is evidently overlooked by these devotees is the fact that claims of divine inspiration in terms of prophetic gifts are likely to be cynical deceptions that attempt to preclude contradiction by their claim of sanctity. How many times we have heard the pious disclaimer uttered by cornered psychics and seers that "what I do is a gift from God" or "it's not I who make these prophecies; it's some higher force."

A typical version of the "God-chosen" finesse is the one in which a prophet claims two kinds of inspiration: direct (from God) and indirect. The direct, God-given prophecies are unalterable; the indirect ones, clouded up as they may be by the prophet's own human fallibility, can be altered and changed by man's "free will." How do we know which predictions are divinely ordained and which may be mere human assumptions?

Simple—the ones that come true belong to God, while the ones that fail are attributed to human error. Such convenient strategy saves many a prophetic face. Similarly, the complexity or peculiarity of many predictions can be attributed not to the derangements of personal psychology, but to God's own "wondrous ways," for His omnipotence is never questioned by the devoted precog on earth. Jeanne Gardner, the West Virginia prophet, puts it this way: "You must understand that I believe only what I am told by the Voice (God). I have no desire to seek outside verification, because I trust in the Voice." Her trust is so very great that it enables Mrs. Gardner to overcome any confusion that may logically arise whenever she asks herself why God should have chosen her to be His holy instrument on earth. "Maybe it is because I am a simple being," she says, "one who would listen, that I was chosen for this work."

Jeanne Gardner is just one of many seers who not only were ordained by God Himself but also quite literally were visited by Him and shown the entire formulation of His divinity and universal scheme. Such seers are usually linked closely to the Christian faith. Jeane Dixon—who usually receives her precognitions while at morning Mass—predicts that the state of Israel will one day, in gratitude to God (and apparently in penitence for its long religious ignorance) convert to the Christian faith. Mrs. Gardner is no less emphatic in her indisputable Christian view of God, Christ, and the afterlife. The Voice itself has told her of these mysteries in terms reminiscent of the *Apocalypse.* "I am the Alpha and Omega, the beginning and the end," the Voice has announced. Heaven is the place where everything is glorious, where there is "No sickness. No pain. No sorrow. No tears. Only many glad tomorrows." In such a paradise, the faithful Jeanne will receive, in due time, her great rewards at the hands of God Almighty Himself. "Ye have worked hard, Jeanne," says the Voice, "and ye will win." Later—dropping the formal "ye"—he states: "I will be with you. I will let you know dates; I will let you know times [of future events]. I will keep you and those who help you safe."

In another message the Voice gives us absolute proof that the legend of Adam and Eve was no legend at all, but fact, exactly as the preacher preached it. Speaking in verse that resembles the doggerel found on greeting cards, God tells Mrs. Gardner that Eve did in fact eat of the forbidden apple and thereby brought to the world "the wages of sin." Furthermore:

> By tempting her with the apple,
> Old Lucifer the Devil,
> Brought upon the earth
> Corruption and upheaval.
> . . . I then had to thrust
> These two from my Garden fair.
> And they had to find themselves
> An unannointed lair.

This Fundamentalist theology sounds odd and contradictory in the company of precognition, which, under the synonym of "soothsaying," or divining, is most stringently and explicitly forbidden in the Bible, to wit: Lev.20:27 states, "Also a man or woman that divineth by a ghost or a familiar spirit or that is a wizard shall truly be put to death; they shall stone them with stones . . ." Also in the Bible: "There shall not be found among you anyone that . . . useth divination, a soothsayer, or an enchanter or a sorcerer or a charmer. For all that do these things are an abomination unto the Lord . . ." (Deut.18:9). Does Mrs. Gardner's Voice remember these holy prohibitions as he exhorts her to:

> Tell all about Me,
> The things I conceive;
> Tell all the story, so they will believe . . .
> Just do as I ask, leave the doubters to Me,
> Then someday they'll know
> That God has spoken Truth through thee.

ESP

The deceit of ESP is not so much in its validity or lack of validity as in the vaunted paranormal or supernatural status it has recently achieved at the hands of well-meaning scientists and less inspired psychics. Arthur Clarke, the author of *2001: Space Odyssey,* puts the situation in the clearest light. There is nothing really extrasensory about extrasensory perception, he says; it is "just that our senses reach farther than we may have imagined." Freud was inclined to view the phenomena of ESP and telepathy as possibly aspects of an archaic but natural method of communication employed by primitives to convey basic ideas and emotions—in much the same way animals transmit alarm signals to their mates and offspring by odors and sounds that humans cannot understand. ESP tests given to aborigines of Australia seem to support the notion that primitive peoples—and children—have a more developed extrasensory perceptivity than do more sophisticated individuals.

Dr. J. B. Rhine, the patron saint of psychic investigation and the developer of many ESP tests, has said that heightened perception may have served as a form of communication predating the usage "not merely of language and of reason, but even of the sensory functions themselves." As speech and functional motility developed among civilized men, according to Rhine's view, the ESP factor fell into disuse, becoming vestigial in most but remaining dormant in others. These "others" are the percipients today about whom such a great fuss is made when evidence of ESP is cited and around whom a kind of ESP cult is developing.

Unfortunately, defining the subject of ESP is not easy. Dr. J. Gaither Pratt, currently the head of Duke University's Division of Parapsychology, combines telepathy, clairvoyance, and precognition into the general category of ESP. He appends psychokinesis (mentally stimulated movement) as an afterthought. Out of a possible 100 percent, he rates the valid existence of these phenomena as follows: telepathy and clairvoyance—80 percent; precognition—55 percent; ESP, as a combination of telepathy and clairvoyance—100 percent. "I'm 100 percent satisfied," he says, "that it (ESP) has been proven to exist." Psychokinesis (PK) he puts at 75 percent. Pratt does not mean to imply that the evidence he regards so highly is always reliable. Certainly it is not enough to overcome the resistance of skeptics and materialistic scientists; this, says Pratt, is the problem of parapsychology: "our failure to produce evidence that can be repeated reliably . . . The notion of repeatable experiments comes from the physical sciences. The life sciences," he says, "use statistics, which are statements of probability." Pratt then adds, as a lament, "It may be that parapsychological phenomena will not ever lend themselves to specific predictions of specific results . . ."

If Pratt is right about these "specific predictions," we must then conclude that the problem of verifying the ESP phenomenon as a supernatural or even as a natural force will never be fully resolved, particularly when we consider that many psychologists allow up to a 20 percent probability for coincidence or blind luck in ESP tests.

Accepting Pratt's figures—which may or may not include the 20 percent differential—can we always accept the tests upon which they were based? The Zener Card Test, used by Rhine for quantitative experiments in ESP, consisted of five sets of five cards each. Each card was printed with a different geometric symbol (square, circle, cross, five-pointed star, and three wavy parallel lines). The individual being tested for ESP would be asked to read or guess the symbol unseen by him and carefully controlled by the tester, who was often in another room or building. In all his many years of experiments with these cards —a period of roughly thirty years—Rhine discovered only two subjects who consistently called all twenty-five correctly. Hardly a stampede.

Even in those cases where the card tests ran above the predictable 20 percent and where, as a demonstration of basic clairvoyance, the tests ran to 80 percent (according to Dr. Pratt's evaluation), some suspicion must be voiced about the overall validity of the testing procedure. No doubt the integrity of Drs. Rhine and Pratt cannot be faulted; therefore, fraud may be dismissed as a factor. Even so, one may ask how valid is a test in which the five symbols to be perceived have been well-publicized in advance of the test. Apparently the Zener Cards were in the public domain throughout the years they served as the basis of ESP testing. If one knows that he is expected to perceive either a square, a circle, a cross, a star, or a series of wavy lines in any particular sequence, one can simply calculate the possibilities in order to achieve an above average score. The subconscious computer-like procedure in such a case is remarkable, to be sure, but hardly supernatural. Even if the specific symbols were not known and the subject merely advised that assorted geometric shapes or forms would be used, he could probably guess that circles, squares, crosses, stars, lines, or dots would probably be included in such random formations.

J. Fraser Nicol and his wife Betty, writing about the card tests for the Parapsychology Foundation of New York, dismiss the Zener method as a "sheer waste of time" in proving the validity of the ESP factor along supernormal lines. "The level of success," they state "in literally millions of experimental card tests is either nonexistent or so low as to bear little affinity with those psi (psychic) manifestations of mediumship and spontaneous cases upon which this field [of parapsychology] was founded. Even with the *best* of experimental subjects, well over 90 percent of the trials are a sheer waste of time."

But in all fairness to the subject of ESP, we should consider the following. Suppose the object of the extrasensory perception was honestly and completely open ended; in other words, not specifically a symbol or an object or an idea, but any one of these or all three together. If the target of the ESP test was totally unpredictable and fully random and if the results were nonetheless significant, would this not mean that clairvoyance and/or telepathy were in evidence and that ESP is indeed a qualitative, if not a quantitative, truth?

To assess this supposition, one must first examine the significance of such supposedly random tests. Among those under scientific control, there have been some evidently remarkable results. In the Guthrie Series, the procedure supervised by the physicist Sir Oliver Lodge in 1883, several young women employed by Malcolm Guthrie of Liverpool seemed able to transmit among themselves a series of random images in a perceptibly telepathic way. If the agents, or transmitters, drew the figure of a cat, for instance, the reproducer (in this case a girl named Jane), blindfolded and in another room, soon after drew the face of a cat. The drawing of an inverted pair of scissors by the agents caused Jane similarly to draw an inverted forceps, two canes overcrossing, and something resembling a closed umbrella with a long tip.

In these and similar tests, the idea, not the image itself, was transmitted in a way that indicates telepathy more than clairvoyance. In the 1920s, the American writer Upton Sinclair and his wife May Craig conducted similar tests under controlled procedures and reported fairly good results. A fish hook was drawn by Mr. Sinclair and carefully sealed in an envelope which was then handed over to Mrs. Sinclair. Lying on a couch, she would stare at the opaque envelope and proceed to draw her own impression of what she "saw." In the case of the fishhook test, she drew a curved line with a small flower on the end, undoubtedly resembling a hook. Mrs. Sinclair was apparently picking up the overall ideograph of a hook from her husband, who was seated with her in the room. Telepathy more than clairvoyance again seems to be the operative factor in these cases. To test clairvoyance as a phenomenon separate from telepathy, one would have to identify an object or symbol that was totally unknown to the agent and thus incapable of being transmitted telepathically. For example, a picture book that the subject had never seen and the contents of which are completely unknown would be placed in the percipient's hands. If the test were successful, he would be able to indicate that somewhere in the book there were, for instance, pictures of ladies in hoopskirts, children in rowboats, or automobiles on the highway.

This would be conclusive evidence of clairvoyant tendencies since the pictures would seemingly transmit themselves without the intrusion of the agent's brain waves.

There have been tests conducted in universities that utilize the procedure just described, but even in these, the agent or tester knows beforehand what types of pictures may be "seen." The probability of telepathy rather than clairvoyance is therefore indicated. In fact, all cases of clairvoyance may scientifically be explained as unconsciously transmitted examples of telepathy, which are also unconsciously received.

What About Telepathy?

The foregoing evaluation indicates that certain well-publicized features of ESP may actually exist. But this does not mean that they can be considered supernormal or even more than vaguely remarkable in a psychological way, since the basis of ESP seems to be more a question of inbred telepathy than one of extraordinary clairvoyance. Telepathy as a form of conscious or subconscious communication could very possibly exist as a normal function of the mind, a function that reaches further than we may imagine. This possibility of telepathy will be explored, even though it remains a weak possibility regarded as an improbable factor by most of the psychologists who have been questioned on the subject. It is dealt with here purely as a *natural* possibility, evidently taking the form of an electrical transmission much like the sending of electronic patterns from a television camera to a video tube.

Naturally, students of the occult reject the notion that telepathy is merely a form of physical transmission; as the British writer Douglas Hunt stated: "A physical theory of telepathy will not work . . . any kind of physical transmission would have to involve both a material transmitter and a material receiver, and though it is true that the brain itself does emit very faint electrical waves, they are nothing like strong enough to affect another brain, even if only a few feet away."

The instruments that measure such faint electrical brain waves are material transmitters, indicating that despite Mr. Hunt's denial, a material object is in fact capable of picking up the electric pulses of the brain no matter how faint they are.

Suppose the complex and multi-faceted brain is in itself capable of acting as a "material" transmitter and receiver unlike any mechanical structure invented in a laboratory. If so, two brains could function as a sort of radio apparatus by passing signals, or thoughts, between them, in much the same way that some people pass signals to each other by a simple glance.

Mr. Hunt is at least partially willing to accept this view. He cites the work of G. Tyrrell and W. Carington, British researchers in personality who suggest that telepathy is the result of subliminal or subconscious interreaction of two minds (not brains) that transmit telepathy despite distance, space, or time. Occultists prefer this explanation because it *seems* to deal with some intangible, ergo supernormal, factor—namely, the subconscious. However, after half a century of Freudian psychology, one can hardly regard the subconscious as an intangible or even vaguely occultic element. Indeed, subconscious factors probably play the most significant role of all in the various self-deluding "tricks of the mind" of the occult. Submerging the telepathic process exclusively into the subconscious or saying that the transmitting agent is not a brain but a mind is an attempt to cloak a mundane function in a mysterious or supernatural formulation. The fact is that, try as they may, occultists cannot alter the basic psychological and even physiological aspects of telepathy, just as the functional process of hypnosis cannot and should not be relegated by skeptics to some mysterious corner of subscience simply because it does not utilize mechanical factors such as hypodermic needles or X-ray cameras.

Professor Leonid Vasilyev, the late head of the Department of Physiology at Leningrad University, worked on psychological aspects of telepathy for nearly half a century; he regards the subject as a form of energy "as yet unknown" in an empirical way. The word unknown immediately gladdens the hearts of occultists, since to them it is synonymous with the word occult. Dr. Vasilyev's concept of the unknown, however, was carefully predicated by the words "as yet." In other words, he regarded his analysis as only a step on the road to complete empirical proof. Occultists regard the unknown as a permanent factor, impenetrable by mere mortals; or if penetration does occur, it is accomplished in such a way that it transforms the ordinary man into a god and thereby places him and his discovery further off into the unknown and out of the grips of science.

ESP is one of the areas that occultists believe will never and should never be scientifically explained, lest they lose it as a prerogative. Vasilyev's work, as well as other recent experiments, is viewed as proof of the occult, but in fact it is a form of clinical debunking. Take Vasilyev's experiments with telepathy under hypnosis (1962). Placing a patient in a hypnotic sleep, the Russian transmitted to him a series of commands projected from a numbered list supplied by colleagues. The patient reacted in most instances by obeying the subconsciously received instructions: at one point flailing his arms, at another, folding his hands. Vasilyev had perhaps conditioned the patient under hypnosis to a state of heightened susceptibility, because he could not produce the same good results when the subject was awake. Even so, the demonstration is hardly proof of supernormal manifestations; instead it seems to indicate that the subliminal factors discussed by Tyrrel and Carington—and earlier by Freud—were the logically operative factors.

Explanations

There have been, of course, so many stories about instances of mysterious clairvoyance and inexplicable ESP (and precognition, premonition, apparition, and so forth) that to analyze and debunk them all would take volumes. Even so, the effort would be impracticable since many of these stories are mere hearsay, and much of the "evidence" is faulty. Nevertheless, one might safely conclude that in most of these instances a purely psychological (natural) explanation exists, an explanation that may as yet be unknown but potentially explainable under the proper procedures.

For example, take ESP dreams or flashes, known variously as "crisis" apparitions, premonitions, or telepathy, in which someone perceives danger or death befalling a relative or friend before or at the same moment that the crisis occurs. In these cases the following elements are usually reported. The recipient is either sleeping or thinking of something entirely removed from the crisis situation. Suddenly an image, a voice, or sense of reality concerning the person in trouble manifests itself. The recipient sometimes contacts the opposite party only to discover that he or she has just died or suffered some form of catastrophe. In other cases the recipient forgets or dismisses the impression and later learns that his loved one is dead or injured. Numerous cases of this sort have been recorded and cannot be attributed to fraud or deceit.

What seems to be operating in at least some of these crisis cases is conscious or subconscious telepathy—a phenomenon that may be particularly viable between blood relatives. In other cases, perhaps the majority, the self-deception factor discussed by Freud regarding prophetic dreams is suggested. Persons in this condition may actually convince themselves *after the fact* that they have received some form of mysterious prior communication related to the crisis in their lives. I myself have had such an experience. Seated at a restaurant window one day having a late lunch, I believed I saw my grandmother walking across the street, although she lived many miles away. I said to a lady companion: "I believe that was my grandmother across the street, but what in the world is she doing way up here?"

Several hours later news came of my grandmother's fatal heart attack and, soon after, of her death. The restaurant incident at once came back to mind and was, in those days, regarded as a mysterious form of telepathy or premonition. For weeks the idea persisted that grandmother had somehow communicated her crisis miles across space to me. The occultic aspects of this typical incident evaporated rapidly when I again met my luncheon companion of that strange afternoon and asked: "Do you remember how I believed I saw my grandmother and how I had wondered about her presence in this part of town?"

"No," the woman replied. "You never said anything like that. I would surely have remembered it."

There is no reason to doubt the probity or sobriety of the young woman in question. This case, like so many others, is merely one of post-dated wish fulfillment. After a crisis—usually involving death—the bereaved is understandably burdened with loneliness and remorse and consciously wishes he might once again, even for a brief moment, see or communicate with the deceased. Subconsciously he begins to convince himself that in fact he had seen or spoken to, for one last time, the beloved party in some form of very private and mysterious communication. It is a self-preserving mental trick, a tender delusion like the alleged passing of one's whole life before one's eyes in the act of drowning.

Freud, whose interest in this field was extensive and whose analyses were revealing, speaks of the general subject of supernatural visitations in his essay "The Psychopathology of Everyday Life," in which he includes an important reference to the so-called crisis aspect of ESP.

> I am sorry to confess that I belong to that class of unworthy individuals before whom the spirits cease their activities and the supernatural disappears, so that I have never been in position to experience anything personally that would stimulate belief in the miraculous. Like everybody else, I have had forebodings and experienced misfortunes; but the two evaded each other, so that nothing followed the foreboding, and the misfortune struck me unannounced. When as a young man, I lived alone in a strange city, I frequently heard my name suddenly pronounced by an unmistak-

able, dear voice, and I then made a note of the exact moment of the hallucination in order to inquire carefully of those at home what had occurred at that time. There was nothing to it. On the other hand, I later worked among my patients calmly and without foreboding while my child almost bled to death.

ESP is certainly not all it is reputed to be, but it is also not merely fraud and should not be associated, *in its purely scientific definition,* with the dubious areas of spiritualism, precognition, astrology, witchcraft, and the rest. In fact, ESP (telepathy) is a subject that has suffered from its association with the occult, and, as a result, serious investigation about its normal and functional qualities may have been retarded. This is regrettable. Oddly enough, it has *not* been the scientist but rather the occultist himself who has inhibited the field of ESP. To him the mystery and arcana of a subject are indispensable. When scientific explanation replaces the mystique surrounding ESP, it is the occultist who stands to lose one of the most popular booths in his sideshow of the supernatural.

6

The High Cost of Humbug

W<small>E</small> have discussed the intellectual, emotional and moral aspects of the occult conceit. But there is another tangible part of the problem—the financial one. A few demonstrations from actual experiences may offer some enlightenment in this significant area.

A Visit with Madame Vera

A neon sign announces: Mme. Vera, reader-advisor; answers all your problems: Astrology, palm reading and Tarot cards—two flights up, ring bell on right.

You dress in a nondescript fashion so as not to arouse suspicion, and, pretending to be a typical Saturday night tourist, climb the stairs to the reader's parlor overlooking one of the landmark streets in Greenwich Village, New York.

Mme. Vera greets you at the head of the stairs and ushers you into a large, sparsely furnished apartment. The heavy odor of spicy cooking and the crying of a baby hardly convey the mystic impression you had expected. There are no crystal balls, no

165

zodiac symbols—only a few cheap landscape reproductions on the walls and a plastic Madonna statuette on the sideboard near the baby's playpen.

An old woman appears briefly and quickly disappears with infant and bottle as Mme. Vera leads you into the "consulting" chamber. Doing so, she announces her fees in a very matter of fact tone. For a complete horoscope, $15; palm reading plus perusing facial characteristics, $15; the right palm alone, $10; for Tarot, $15; Tarot plus palm, $25. For you, she'll throw in a bit of astrology for the same flat fee. You protest the cost, so she quickly settles for a complete divination for $20. The focus, however, will be palm reading since Mme. Vera descends from a long line of Romany gypsies, for whom reading the secrets of the palm is second nature.

The Romany gypsy is about twenty-five years old, wide-eyed and olive skinned, with a set expression around her mouth and an impatient venal manner that subsides only when she sees the color of your money. Her accent is hard to determine; it could be Caribbean. On the other hand, the reader-advisor industry is largely a gypsy vocation, so you accept the Romany origins, even though Vera foregoes the usual gypsy costume, wearing only a simple tailored dress and a scarf tied tightly around her head.

She leads you to the couch for the palm reading; takes your right hand in her fingers, glances at it, and announces that you have a long life line and a good soul. Studying your face, she rapidly concludes that you are generous, intelligent, and ambitious, but that you are seeking something that you cannot find.

The reading progresses. "Someone very close to you has gone away," she opines, eagerly searching for a clue to confirm her guess. "Could it be my mother?" you ask downheartedly. "She passed away this December." "But, of course," she immediately replies; "someone in your family has died." You feign amazement at her accuracy; this encourages her to philosophical exhortations about supressing one's grief and the promise that the pain will ease and tomorrow will be better.

Better—but not entirely, she warns. And here's the clincher. Two enemies are plotting against you. They can be seen in your palm seeking your downfall at every turn. They must be thwarted, but how? Mme. Vera makes a logical suggestion. As one in touch with angelic forces, she will, forthwith, light a series of special candles, one each day for ten days. These will protect you from the malignant forces and obstruct their detraction. Such candles will be lighted not in her home but in a Catholic Church, and at one dollar apiece they are a psychic bargain.

You balk at the price, but she insists: "I cannot help you without the candles. Only this will work." You try to change the subject by moving over to the Tarot table, reminding her about the astrologic prophecies she promised you. Reluctantly rising, she asks you for the day and hour of your birth and begins laying out the traditional Tarot cards; first in a cruciform, then five under five, and finally the whole Major Arcana. What she sees, in tandem with your Sun Sign and palm, spell out the same relentless truths: you are good natured, sensitive, and ambitious, but hidden forces lurk throughout your life, ready to undo you. One is a man, and the other is a woman. "Tell the truth," she demands. "You know I am right. Only the candles can help."

You want specifics. After all, anyone can tell you about sensitivity, ambition, and the vicissitudes of daily life. "Will I get the promotion I want?" you ask. "Will I have good health? Should I move from my present apartment?"

Hedging her replies, Mme. Vera cleverly brings in the hidden enemy theme and, consequently, the candles to answer every challenge. Yes, you will get the promotion, your health will thrive, and you will make a beneficial move very soon but only if your enemies permit. "Tell the truth," she repeats. "You know I am right. Let me light the candles; only they can help you."

With matching persistence, you try to pin her down, eager to see how she reacts. Pointing to your mouth, encumbered by an orthodontic brace that you've recently begun wearing to correct a faulty bite, you shamefacedly inquire: "Will I ever be rid of this speech impediment?"

"How long have you had it?" she demands. "Since birth," you lie. "Oh," she announces with profound authority, "you will never be rid of it. But you must overcome such things." The Tarot cards have shown her that you are capable of great inner strength; even your speech impediment need not hinder your ambition. But those ever-lurking enemies . . .

Having once more evaded the question of candles, and having turned over twenty dollars, you turn to leave the chamber of enchantment, as the baby's hungry crying begins anew.

A Visit with the Reverend Mrs. Pratt

Mme. Vera is, of course, only one type of occult practitioner. With a better education, more elaborate paraphernalia, and greater perceptivity, Vera could rise to the heights of the occult profession as did the Reverend Mrs. Edna Pratt (name fictitious), who is also a reader-advisor, astrologist, and Tarot diviner, but who works by appointment only, for a flat fee of $30 for fifty minutes. Among Mrs. Pratt's clientele are steady customers of the finest pedigree. Many of them, she tells you, bear household names.

The first thing you notice about Mrs. Pratt's surroundings is their good taste. Here and there, of course, are hints of the occult, but very decorous ones: a Pisces bas-relief over the door, a photo of Mme. Blavatsky, the Theosophist, and shelves of books dealing with everything from amulets to zombis. Mrs. Pratt herself is a middle-aged dowager dressed in black and wearing a rather striking amber pendant around her neck. She may have been an actress, or at least an aspiring one. Certainly she remains devoted to the notion of putting on a show and winning audience approval. Accordingly, her consulting chamber is a theatrically styled example of the Mauve Decade, with heavy drawn draperies on the window, a weighty glass chandelier descending from an ornate ceiling, and faded carpeting covered with Oriental scatter rugs.

You are seated in a huge black leather chair while she takes her place opposite at a small round table covered with a shawl. There is no crystal ball on this table. For props Mrs. P. lays out only a series of astronomical charts, a few pencils, and a pad of writing paper. The room is dimly lit, but a high-powered lamp is focused on the writing area. When she turns it on, the session begins.

She asks the date and hour of your birth. If the precise hour is unknown, she will rectify it by working backward from the known to the unknown. "What childhood diseases have you had?" she demands; knowing you had measles when you were five and whooping cough when you were eight enables Mrs. Pratt to ascertain that you were born between 7:30 and 7:45 A.M. since, on your particular birth date, the astrological factors at play during this quarter of an hour would cause the types of illnesses that later befell you. (I was actually born around 9:00 A.M.)

"Did you ever have pneumonia?" she inquires. As she proceeds, you have the feeling that she asks more of you than she tells, and in fact what she eventually tells is inferred from what she has asked.

The chart is gradually drawn. While drawing it, the seer informs you that she is carefully attuning herself to your vibrations as she works, for she is clairvoyant and bristles with ESP. "Of what good would I be as an astrologer," she confesses, "if I lacked the essential sensitive antennae? Yes, I could tell you your Sun Sign, your ascendant, your potential characteristics and destiny, but the fourth dimension—the fleshing out—would not be there."

The "fleshing out" she refers to consists of random references to the fact that you are sensitive, moody, inquisitive, and sincere (much the same reading rendered by Mme. Vera). But she sprinkles her analyses with references to Carl Gustav Jung, to the mystic Gurdjieff, to cosmic forces and fields, all of which references elevate the simplest deductions to a truly astral sphere. Mrs. P. frequently asserts the scientific infallibility of her art by reminding you of the "correlation between sunspots and the incidence of influenza on earth."

Vague allusions to ambition, career changes, timidity with employers and yearning for acceptance plus warnings about fevers, falls, and crucial journeys make up the substance of the reading. For added dimension, Mrs. P. draws up what she calls a cosmopsychogram of your life curve, including illnesses and recoveries but judiciously avoiding the moment of death. "We are free beings," she explains. "Astrology shows us the potential of our fate, our powers and weaknesses—nothing is truly fixed, nor are the rules hard and fast. The great serene Buddha," she continues, "and the monstrous Hitler were both of the Sun Sign Taurus; one can see how rich and full the influence of astrology must be."

You ask, "If this reading is to be so vague, if astrology itself is so indefinite and controversial, if so much depends on the antennae of the reader, then why bother with charts, zodiac constellations, planets and so forth? Why not simply take a guess and leave it at that?"

This gives Mrs. Pratt the opening she has been waiting for. Grandly rising from her place, she advises you in no uncertain terms that before you can benefit in any way from her talents and from the undeniable truths of her art, you must overcome such obvious skepticism by engaging upon a course of serious study that she will prescribe. "Are you serious?" she demands. "Very well. First there are certain papers and books you must acquire." She reels off a few choice titles: *The Theory of Celestial Influence, Astrological Key Words, Astrology: How and Why it Works,* and these are just the beginning. She further instructs that you must subscribe to several magazines and monthly newsletters, such as *The Aquarian Agent,* published in the East Village, *In Search,* and her own bimonthly monograph *Sidereal Influx.* All these publications and many more are fortunately available at a discount cost from her own collection, which she keeps on hand for the benefit of her clientele. The cost for this basic library, including subscriptions to monthly and bimonthly periodicals, is a mere $45, slightly four times more than Mme. Vera's candles.

You hedge a bit. What else does she offer besides astrology and how much does it run?

To be sure, Mrs. Pratt practices palmistry, but scientifically you understand, none of this gypsy hokum. For $10 she will take a print of each hand and in two days provide a full, five-page chiromantic analysis. She will also give you a numerological scanning for the same figure. This will include a breakdown of all the number factors in your life and a movable wheel showing the best digits to employ on any given occasion. She does not deal in Tarot (which she seems to deprecate), but as for seances, though not a medium herself, she will recommend a very gifted spiritualist who offers private readings and specializes in contacting long-dead and newly interred close relatives.

You decide to buy only a few of the literary offerings; you'll let her know about the rest. She takes your money and fetches her appointment book to mark you down for your next encounter. No one can learn very much, she warns, from a mere fifty minutes.

You turn to her with a wicked twinkle in your eye. "From what you saw in my horoscope," you ask, "do you think I will return?"

Her answer sums up the whole business. "Even if you do not come back, you will want to come back." She continues: "I believe you will fight it, but when you least expect it, you will suddenly have the urge. The influence of Mercury will decide, not you."

With your question thus unanswered, you leave the astral regions and return to the material world.

A Visit with the Police

Section 165.35 of the New York Penal Law holds criminal anyone who "claims or pretends to tell fortunes, pretends to have occult powers" for purposes of gain or compensation (side show amusements are not included). Despite the sweeping prohibition against everyone who pretends to have occult powers, the supervisor in the Confidence Division of New York's Police Headquarters reports that few cases come to trial, primarily because victims are unwilling to complain. "They need to be fooled too much," the supervisor explained, "on top of which they are often very embarrassed to admit the extent of their gullibility."

Nevertheless, by means of their own diligence and as a result of a few helpful leads, detectives in the Confidence Division have managed to process an annual average of 700 fraud cases. These cases concern what are generically referred to as "gypsies"—fortune tellers, reader-advisors, and astrologers such as Mme. Vera. Unfortunately, the police rarely come up against the likes of the Reverend Mrs. Pratt—imagine a Hollywood star turning in his or her astrologer for pretense of having occult powers. Years of misleading forecasts, vague readings, and the like, coupled with thousands of dollars spent in fees, do not add up to fraud and swindle in the mind of the occultnik. Besides, the high-class practitioner never stoops to the desperate and obvious tactics pursued by the old-fashioned gypsy fortune teller. Indeed some may insist that the two are not even remotely related. Comparing the honest psychics with the obvious charlatans, they say, is similar to equating a neurosurgeon and a snake-oil medicine man.

But gypsies on the lowest rung of the ladder and the highclass seers work to each other's advantage. They are cryptic allies. As one detective put it, the celebrities on television talk shows soften up the public for the swindlers who operate in Harlem, Greenwich Village, and similar haunts. Sated with the alleged powers of the Reverend Mrs. Pratt and her cohorts, the average television watcher may be inclined to ascend the staircase of Mme. Vera's dingy establishment for a $5 quickie into the world of the occult. If he is lucky, he will come away disappointed and about $20 poorer. If he is the victim of *bajour,* the gypsy word for "swindle," he can end up stripped of his life's savings. The Confidence Division reports on its records one swindle by a gypsy fortune teller in the amount of $126,000. The victim was a fairly intelligent but extremely susceptible individual with a long history of occultic fascination. Mrs. F., another classic case on the files, was taken for over $20,000 in a mere three months. This is how it happened:

Reading her favorite occult monthly, Mrs. F. came upon an advertisement that immediately appealed to her occultnik instincts and to her personal needs. Sister Bella, an "Indian" (the connotation of gypsy having become somewhat onerous) would for $5 remove all problems from life, assure tranquillity, and uncover and relate the secrets of the universe.

All her adult life, the stars had pointed the way for Mrs. F. The numbers had revealed undeniable truth; a medium had once helped her contact a dead relative whom she believed she had wronged. Besides, every time she saw Jeane Dixon or Sybil Leek on television, Mrs. F. was confirmed in her belief that the occult was the true path to a meaningful, peaceful life. Surely Sister Bella would help her the way she had saved "over 1000 troubled souls."

With her $5 fee in hand, Mrs. F. approached the tenement where the Sister operated. She paid her fee and was given the first perusal. From what the seer could tell—by clairvoyance— Mrs. F. was suffering from some explicit evil, perhaps a fatal disease. To save herself, she must go home and return in one day, bearing a brand new man's handkerchief and a fresh tomato—standard items of gypsy divination.

At the appropriate time, the client returned with the requisite props. Sister Bella spread the handkerchief on the floor, took the tomato and began passing it up and down Mrs. F.'s body like a geiger counter. Her movements were quick and mysterious, so quick that Mrs. F. did not discern the moment when her own tomato was replaced by another preconditioned for the swindle.

This hoax tomato was then ceremoniously placed in the handkerchief, and Mrs. F. was asked to crush it beneath her foot. Quickly she obeyed. There in the bloody pulp of the tomato, Mrs. F., to her horror, saw an obscene black rubber lizard (it could have also been a tiny skull) staring up at her. It was undoubtedly a sign of the evil predicted by Sister Bella only the day before.

Could it be cancer? Could it be an omen of family disaster? Anything is possible, so Mrs. F. must act at once. All such evil, Sister Bella explained, is the result of tainted money; money in the client's possession that was ill-gained, not necessarily by Mrs. F. herself but by someone else who passed it on to her, along with the lingering curse. "Take all your money except a few hundred dollars out of the bank. This money I will convert from evil to good by special magic venerated for over three thousand years. Listen carefully: the money must be brought in cash in denominations from one to one hundred (in Mrs. F.'s case the total was $22,000). It will then be sewn tightly into a bag and placed in a dark safe deposit box for three months. Untouched by human hands or by the rays of the sun, this rotten cash will gradually lose its evil power, and at the same time, the threat to your life will diminish.

"However," the seer continued, "should someone open the bag before the prescribed duration, then the $22,000 will magically transform into a mere $22 or into 22,000 strips of worthless paper."

Mrs. F. was convinced. She had seen the black lizard in her tomato; and the stars, the cards, and the numbers all collided to spell misfortune unless she acted.

With her husband's compliance, Mrs. F. removed nearly all her personal money from five separate savings accounts. This she took in a large envelope to the gypsy's den. Before her eyes it was sewn up in a pillowcase and handed back to her with a ceremonious flourish. She immediately took the bag to her own safe deposit box, where for three months it would be detoxified by gypsy magic. Throughout the three month period, Mrs. F. continued to visit her seer (each time forking over $20 in fees) and was encouraged by suggestive references to improved signs, new vigor, and radiant vibrations.

One week before the three month expiration, Sister Bella phoned her client at home to inform her that family affairs required the seer to leave New York for about a month. While she was away Mrs. F. was not to touch the mystic bag but instead to depend on the omnipresent powers of the occult. When Bella returned, all would be "as though in Paradise."

At first Mrs. F. accepted the separation. But as the days went by, she became increasingly uneasy and alienated. Without her Indian, life was fraught with anxiety, confusion, and doubt. Two days before the three month deadline, Mrs. F. gingerly opened her safe deposit box, removed the sacred bag and undid the stitching.

Alas! As Sister Bella had warned, evil had triumphed. In place of $22,000 only $22 lay at the bottom of the bag—the fate of a disbelieving soul.

Happily for the law, Mrs. F.'s husband was less willing to accept the ineluctable workings of destiny. Suspecting a switch, he reported the whole weird story to the Confidence Division. There he was informed that his suspicions were clearly justified, for the pattern was a familiar one. The vanished Sister Bella had of course switched bags at the critical moment, exchanging $22,000 for $22 in a flourish of mysticism.

Even now, as she sits in Police Headquarters, Mrs. F. refuses to believe that she has been swindled. In fact, at this moment another $2,000 of her evil money, in another bag in another bank, is being purified by another gypsy, this time under a one-year prohibition.

"Another bag!" cries her husband in agony. A quick trip to the safe deposit vaults reveals another typical bajour. $2,000 turned into a mass of newspaper shreds.

Mrs. F. begins to see the light, but only dimly. Turning to her husband with tears in her eyes, she stammers: "It's the bad influence of Saturn. It has brought me in touch with charlatans who tricked me and kept me from those who could truly help."

Will this sad, desperate woman ever give up the search? Probably not. She will continue to seek her savior among the gypsies and the seers, hoping that she will some day meet the eminent astrologer, precog, or medium whose antics she follows so diligently in the pages of *Occult Review.*

According to the police there are about three thousand advisers operating in the five boroughs of New York. There are probably twice that number in Los Angeles, where susceptibility to the occult seems to be a locational disease. Each of these criminals waits for, prepares for, and dreams of the one big bajour that will ensure a sunny future.

Shrewd, talented, often dangerous, these practitioners rejoice in the occult revival of modern times. For them it is the appropriate setting in which to play out their ancient tricks: squashing tomatoes, sewing evil money into a pillowcase, or lighting holy candles. They are not worried about the crudity of their methods. After all, the squashed tomato is not so far removed from the more sophisticated horoscope, Tarot, or crystal ball maneuvers. All are props in a gigantic and illegal confidence game.

7

A Debunker's Miscellany: From Apparitions to Zombis

INCLUDED here are brief descriptions of some of the more popular subjects of the occult not explored in the previous pages.

Apparitions

Accepting the fact that apparitions, or ghosts, are not the ectoplasmic remains of the dead supernaturally surviving among the living, we are left with three logical explanations as to the real nature of the many spectral visitations, phantoms, spirits, wraiths, and assorted apparitions that have perennially haunted the pages of history and the minds of men.

Apparitions as Outright Fraud

The ectoplasmic manifestations frequently encountered at traditional seances were clearly of the fraudulent variety. As previously explained, treated silk or gauze spotlighted by ultraviolet lights and blown around by electric fans in a darkened room was a standard device used for producing phantoms. Optical instruments were also in use at the seances of the 1920s (and are occasionally used today). A hidden magic lantern was often focused on a cloud of steam that acted as a sort of screen for an intangible floating image that quickly disappeared as the vapor evaporated.

In his autobiography, Benvenuto Cellini, the flamboyant sculptor and goldsmith of Renaissance Italy, describes a phantasmagoria of apparitions and demons that confronted him and his companions one night in the Coliseum of Rome. An experienced necromancer was in charge of the illusion, and, like the medium's modern counterpart, he used the sixteenth century version of a magic lantern to create his ghostly effects. Cellini recalls that the old amphitheater was filled "almost in an instant with demons a hundred times more numerous than at a former conjuration." The sudden appearance of the vision suggests the on-off capacity of the projector. Later, as Cellini and his group crept home along the darkened streets, the same demons who materialized at the Coliseum appeared to be accompanying them "leaping and skipping, sometimes running upon the roofs of the houses and sometimes on the ground." Again the explanation seems to be that a portable slide lantern was in use, projecting a rapid succession of stills that looked as though they were moving up and over the house façades and roofs of the darkened street.

In more recent times, I produced a ghost for the edification of weekend guests at a huge country house in Sussex, England, a perfect spot for a haunting. In this case, odorless blue smoke was forced through a pinched rubber siphon, producing plastic shapes and forms such as those conjured up by blowing smoke rings. The effect, however, in a high, dimly lit room was quite spectral, even alarming.

The universal airy and wispy character of apparitions leads one to accept the use of smoke, vapor, and magic lanterns as the actual origin of many spectral creatures. Bulwer-Lytton

natural

oxicated
page as
jewels,
ppeared
haps the
e the air
produc-
rms and
earthly
them the
ointment.
result of
st memo-
g "trips"
stimulant
ilar mind-
s, it is no
fore men's
genic con-

nvoluntary
ed only by
can often
and others
mistry and
dly anxious
ions of the
he boy into
on, that the
l the flames
ral ana
or

l phantom of his acquaintance as "phos-
ike yet not dead." A "phosphoric" object
phosphorescent paint smeared on animal
sed by the medium Margery at her Boston
ors, and tiny beams of light, some of which
es, have been and are currently employed

the Coliseum story, Benvenuto Cellini
ning of "precious perfumes" that were
hancer in charge to ward off the demon
could have been stimulants that helped,
ure the "several legions of devils" that
. In conjunction with a slide lantern,
probably have produced the desired
and his friends, especially as the
"bade him [a colleague] burn all the
he had."

inatory phantoms, spirits, and general
nd history is widely known: De Quin-
f "an apocalypse of the world within
transformed into music by Berlioz in
e—the story of a narcotic delirium;
luced by the philtre that Faustus
" fantasies triggered by peyotl (or
Central America. These literary ex-
hough drug-produced, seem to some
ural.

by reputable investigators demon-
d physiological basis of even the
Ellis, the eminent English psycholo-
is own reactions to "mescal buttons"
1890s. A reader not knowing that Ellis
d and vision with a powerful drug might

think he was describing the quintessence of supe[r]
phenomena.

In a room illuminated only by a flickering fire, the int[
Ellis at first saw pale violet shadows floating over the[
he attempted to write. Eventually "a vast field of golde[
studded with red and green stones, ever changing" [
before his eyes. "This moment," he wrote, "was per[
most delightful of the experience, for at the same tim[
around me seemed to be flushed with vague perfumes,[
ing with the visions a delicious effect." Unearthly f[
colors followed, and Ellis sensed the "removal fro[m
cares," common to psychedelic experiences—among [
hallucinatory effects produced by the witch's flying [

Ellis' experience with apparitions was, as stated, th[
three mescal buttons prepared so as to produce the m[
rable effect. Others have gone on far more astonishi[
with the merest lick of LSD, the chief hallucinatory [
of modern times. With the vast pharmacopoeia of sim[
bending stimulants available since prehistoric time[
wonder that apparitions have so often occurred be[
eyes after the inhalation or swallowing of hallucino[
coctions.

But hallucinations, which may be likened to an i[
functioning of the sensory system, are not create[
stimulants externally introduced. The mentally il[
conjure effects identical to those envisioned by Ellis[
as a result of an internal breakdown of body che[
metabolism. Freud recounts the case of a boy, morb[
about masturbation, who suffered vivid hallucina[
devil. Day and night the fiend threatened to heave [
the hottest fires of hell. So real was the appariti[
subject could smell the pitch and brimstone and fe[
on his skin. Freud diagnosed this as a case of cereb[
which "produces an alteration of character, dem[
hallucinations, and very violent nocturnal, and [

diurnal, states of anxiety." An incident of hereditary syphilis in this particular case, according to Freud, was a contributory factor to the chemical imbalance concurrent with the cerebral disease.

Most of the thousands, if not millions, of people who are convinced they have seen, heard, or felt ghosts and other phantoms are indeed afflicted with some form of neurosis, psychosis, or some specific functional illness that produces hallucinations as a prominent symptom or side effect. It should be noted that in some cases these disturbed individuals appear entirely healthy and therefore seem credible as witnesses of supernatural phenomena.

Hunger hallucinations, which are the result of privation, not disease, are common among vagrants and victims of famine. These hallucinations result from a chemical imbalance in the blood. Lack of sleep can also cause hideous apparitions such as those that befell disc jockey Peter Tripp, who—as part of an experiment in 1959—went for two hundred hours without sleep. After fifty hours of wakefulness, Tripp discovered "cobwebs" in his shoes, specks on tables that seemed to move, and a rabbit that appeared out of nowhere and as quickly disappeared. After one hundred hours, the disk jockey saw furry worms crawling out of the tweed fibers of a friend's suit and a wall clock that resembled the face of Dracula. A few hours later, flames seemed to be spurting out of a drawer as he tried to open it. Finally fearful that he might be buried alive by ghoulish pursuers, Tripp ran naked from his room in the Hotel Astor down the hall, escaping not from ghouls but from the doctors who were testing his nervous reactions. Side effects of Tripp's grueling experiment lasted for several months. Similarly, anesthesia can produce postoperative hallucinations and delusions. In short, the mind itself, whether stimulated by external agents or by unbalanced body chemistry, has doubtlessly conjured most of the fearful visions and sounds before which men have shuddered for centuries.

Tricks of the Eye, the Ear, and the Mind

Less formidable than outright hallucination and far less perceptible than fraud, are the apparitions caused by optical or auditory illusions, natural phenomena, and the interesting psychological tricks played by the mind, by the eye and by the ear.

Wishful thinking can produce a very real apparition, especially when the subject has been grieving over a recent death or wishes to identify with great figures of the past. The imaginary and compliant playmates of most young children are such wish-fulfillment ghosts, conjured not of ectoplasm and winding sheets but of subconscious needs barely recognized by the subject himself. A colleague of Freud, Dr. Nandor Fodor, relates that he and his wife heard at their bedroom door the nocturnal scratching of a pet dog soon after the creature had been destroyed. Investigation found no dog and no source of the noise, but psychoanalytical procedure may have revealed an acute wish in both Fodor and his wife to see or hear the beloved pet once more. Fodor wrote in *The Haunted Mind:* ". . . the psychoanalytic method of approach promises a greater understanding of psychic manifestations than the exclusive utilization of objective methods of research as used in parapsychology and psychical research."

Nathaniel Hawthorne swore to the reality of an apparition that he saw more than once in his private club in Boston. The "ghost" was that of an old cleric named Dr. Harris, who for years had sat in a certain chair by the fire reading his daily copy of the *Boston Post.* Hawthorne continued to see the old silver-haired gentleman even after being told that Dr. Harris had died. The figure of the old man, a symbol of dignity and tradition, seated respectably and pleasantly by the fire, no doubt afforded Hawthorne a sense of security that he needed and cherished. This association, plus the gloomy bent of the author's mind, created a wish-fulfillment ghost. As Hawthorne wrote, "By some subtle connection, this small, white-haired, infirm yet vivacious figure of an old clergyman became associated with my idea and recollection of the place [the club]."

One might compare Hawthorne's apparition to a form of subtle daydream. Wakeful dreams, or instantaneous dreams, offer another explanation of fleeting but nonetheless vivid apparitions. Mark Twain spoke of a ghost he saw leaning against a fencepost in upstate New York. The writer was walking down the road when the specter suddenly loomed up and then as quickly vanished. Being introspective and practical, Twain took some trouble to analyze the true nature of his ghostly visitor and came to this decision: apparently he had dozed off for a second or two even as he was walking and had dreamed momentarily of the nebulous man. The dream, sandwiched between Mark Twain's waking impressions as he walked, merged with them and became momentarily "real."

Upon fainting many have experienced the sensation of a sudden or flashing dream in which they imagine they are falling or flying. An instant later, they find that they have landed on the ground. This is an instantaneous dream.

Such tricks of the mind can be extended to the eye. In cases where retina detachment is indicated, halos of light are perceived around the edges of vision, often producing what one patient described as "hot phantoms" that seem to blaze up and quickly subside. A plethora of ocular disorders, ranging from myopia to strabismus, have produced apparitions, "spots," and other phenomena no more supernatural than a winter cold.

In this same vein, tricks of perception without the faulty eyesight factor have no doubt played their role in the history of apparitions, especially among the gullible and unsophisticated.

Patches of light, strangely shaped shadows, and images reflected in ponds, on the glimmerings of dew and raindrops, or in heat waves are part of the natural explanation possible in certain cases. One only needs to remember the frequency of mirages on deserts or on heat-baked roads to realize how common such things are, no matter how supernatural they may seem to be.

A sheet of newspaper blown up by a gust of wind in the

proper place and viewed by the proper eye can seem to be the white-shrouded ghost of popular fiction. One such "apparition" is reported by de Maupassant in a remarkable short story. A family keeping watch over the coffin of their recently deceased relative was horrified during the night to see a white specter fly through the darkened room as though emanating from the open coffin. Petrified by fright, no one moved until dawn. Daylight clarified the mystery; what the onlookers had seen flying through the darkness were the corpse's false teeth that had sprung out of his mouth as a result of the muscular changes caused by rigor mortis.

With all the possibilities just described concerning hallucinations or tricks of the senses, it is no wonder that in a Census of Hallucinations conducted by the Society of Psychical Research, London, 1882, a good 10 percent of the 17,000 persons polled indicated that they had, while completely awake, experienced "a vivid impression of seeing or being touched by a living or inanimate object . . . not due to any external cause." Adding the current external causation of drugs, the 10 percent recorded in 1882 would probably double or triple by now. It is no wonder that this world has become more and more a haunted realm replete with "things that go bump in the night."

Astral Projections

In some cases, astral projections are described as glowing emanations emitting from the body of a living person; more often, they are thought to be duplications of the living individual, a psychic twin, or *doppelgänger,* that moves about and functions independently of the host. When you have manifested your own astral projection, according to the occultist, the original part of you, the host, remains behind in a trance or in a state of suspended animation. Dying or critically ill persons are supposed to be able to rise astrally out of themselves and to move about the sick room while doctors try to save or revive their corporeal senses.

Perfectly whole people gifted with the ability to project themselves astrally have been said to visit back and forth with friends over hundreds of miles away while remaining entranced at home. Medium Eileen Garrett was one of the persons supposedly so endowed. She could physically be in New York and yet could visit in an apparently corporeal way with a friend in Newfoundland.

In most cases of the astral delusion, those elements previously analyzed under the classification of apparition conceivably apply: hallucination, self hypnosis, intoxication, or basic tricks of the mind and eye.

In some cases—perhaps in Mrs. Garrett's—a form of real or imagined telepathy may be at play, in which the host receives the thoughts of someone far off and infers that he has been bodily projected into a new locale.

Many of us have sensed the illusion of looking down on ourselves as we drift off to sleep. A slight displacement of depth perception or a somnolent confusion of form and image is usually responsible. The effect is not unlike *déjà vu,* which is explained below.

The conditions produced by LSD, described earlier by Dr. Albert Hoffman as "being outside my body," remind one of astral projection and suggest a drug-induced basis for at least some cases.

The alleged astral auras and vibrations that psychics see emitting from certain people may be due to nothing more than faulty vision. The drug factor would similarly produce such sensations, since mandalas or halos of light often appear, at least to those under psychedelic influence, to be pulsing around static images.

In short, the supernatural connotation of astral projection may be classified with similar aspects of apparition and hallucination. Despite any logical explanation, however, astral bodies, like apparitions, will no doubt remain a favorite delusion of occult philosophy. The idea, after all, is extremely intriguing, especially since it seems to answer the eternal question of what becomes of an individual after death. The modern occultnik feels that when the corporeal man dies, the astral counterpart travels to the next plane of existence, where it is judged "according to the eternal laws of balance." A more mundane view is set forth by the anonymous author of the *Encyclopedia of Occult Sciences:* "The astral body, *which never sleeps,"* he states, "is the servant of our dreams, and enables us sometimes to do things in complete sleep . . . It is neither Intellect nor Conscience but the strange and dumb companion which accompanies us until death."

Déjà Vu

The French expression déjà vu literally means "already seen" and refers to a sense of momentarily experiencing an event that seems to have happened before. Although this is undoubtedly a phenomenon with a physio-psychological basis, occultists invest it with mystery because to them it is tangible proof of a former life or of clairvoyance.

There are two broad explanations for this sensation. In one it can be clearly shown that, owing to stress or fatigue, a displacement in the brain (paramnesia) causes current impressions to blend with memory factors, just as two radio stations overlap when the reception is faulty. In such cases, the memory factors cloak first impressions, whether visual, aural, or both, and create in the mind a distinctive sense of passing through, for the second time, the particular scene or conversation at hand. In most instances the percipient has the parallel sensation, during déjà vu, of knowing that he is experiencing a dislocation of some sort. The effect can be and has been reproduced electronically in the scientist's laboratory: a subject has been asked to study a sign while undergoing an electrical charge in the brain. The sign reads: "You will believe you have read this sign before. It is an example of the déjà vu effect."

A more uncommon extension of the phenomenon occurs

when someone encounters a place or an incident for the first time, yet he believes that he has been there before. Some go so far as to describe details accurately in advance of seeing or hearing about them. To occultists this is evidence of precognition on the one hand and of reincarnation on the other.

When the situation is in any way valid—meaning when it is removed from fraud—it should be obvious that the psychological factors of intuition and/or repression are at play.

Unconscious intuition is strongly indicated in cases in which, for example, someone seems to be able, suddenly, to recognize an unknown house in the country, describing rooms, colors, objects, and so forth. Having seen countless old or allegedly haunted houses in movies and picture books, most of us may be expected to guess correctly certain predictable factors in each and every one; peeling yellowish wallpaper, faded velvet furniture, wine-colored settees, garish bric-a-brac, smoky mirrors, and ornamented brass bedsteads. Where the percipient hits on one or more of these coincidental features, these, not his wrong guesses, are remembered, and the occultic explanation of déjà vu is offered.

Subconscious fantasy repression is probable in other similar cases. The Hungarian psychoanalyst S. Ferenczi explains: ". . . the inexplicable feeling of familiarity can be referred to unconscious fantasies of which we are unconsciously reminded in an actual situation. With one of my patients, the process was apparently different, but in reality it was quite analogous. This feeling returned to him very often, but showed itself regularly as originating in a forgotten (repressed) portion of a dream of the preceding night."

In other words, visual or aural stimuli, such as a room, the sound of a band playing in the park, or even an odor, can provoke a set of emotions so unpleasant or threatening that the individual hurriedly and subconsciously represses them by cloaking his current problems in a sensation of past, and therefore harmless, memory. This psychological maneuver is not unrelated to the physiological effect described at the beginning of this definition. In that instance, stress or fatigue creates the déjà vu, in this present case, repression is the distorting factor.

The Evil Eye

"If looks could kill" is a common expression that is rooted in a universal fear of the magical "evil eye," which reportedly fixes on a soul and proceeds to destroy it. Witchhunters of the Middle Ages described the threat as *fascinatio* or *mal occhio* (bad eye) and sought to stamp it out as a source of enchantment. The handbook of witchhunters, *Malleus Maleficarum* (the Witches' Hammerer) of 1486 refers to individuals who can "bewitch their judges by a mere look or glance from their eyes." But the apprehension goes farther back than 1486. St. Matthew announced a similar, more eloquent, warning in the Gospel: "the light of the body is the eye . . . but if thine eye be evil, thy whole body shall be full of darkness" (6:23). The Biblical view probably derives from an old Hebrew fear of the bad eye *(ayin hara),* which in turn may be an extension of an eye cult that originated in ancient Egypt. There, according to legend, the sun god Ra gave his powerful eye to the goddess Isis, which she later used as a charm to resurrect the dismembered Osiris. Very often the original beneficent aspect in magic evolves into a frightening one, especially when life and death are involved; so it has been with the eye of Ra.

Occultists maintain that a fixed glance has enslaved or killed the unwary and has manifested malignant spells. A variety of charms and antidotes have therefore developed against fascinatio over the ages. These include everything from the wearing of garlic and red pepper around the neck to the simple procedure, most popular in southern Italy, of flashing the index finger and the pinkie (the *cornato*) at the alleged perpetrator. This symbol of the devil's horns (also used to indicate cuckoldry) is used to counteract the diabolic factor by a rudimentary functioning of sympathetic magic.

Where there have been alleged cases of bewitchment by an

evil eye, it is clear that hypnosis or autosuggestion has been at work. The baleful reputation of persons supposedly possessed of the evil eye is also a potent factor in causing the desired effect. A kindly old woman with pleasant blue eyes is unlikely to bring about malicious results with fascinatio, but an ugly hag with beady, sickly eyes is already well on the way to success by virtue of her alarming appearance. One need but recall the unwholesome effect of the old man's eye upon the narrator of Edgar Allan Poe's "Tell-Tale Heart." In this case an apparently innocent individual provoked horror and terror simply because his eye was defective; there was no intended fascination or *mal occhio* in that case.

A fixed stare, especially on a brooding face, can and does create discomfort, especially when it is persistent. The best counteraction in such cases is not the superstitious red pepper or cornato (horns) but simply a fixed stare of your own. Even cats, which often seem to stare maliciously, eventually desist when looked squarely in the eye.

Halloween

There are, even today, many adults who persist in believing that the night of October 31 is a baleful time of flying witches, hobgoblins, and supernatural manifestations. Children, being more realistic, accept the holiday for what it should be—an excuse to dress up in fancy costumes, play pranks, and collect candy. Unfortunately, even children can be corrupted when it comes to halloween, especially if they listen to the radio or watch television, since the air waves on that day are filled with stories of real ghosts, actual hauntings, proven witch magic, and other occultic nonsense. One New York television station, in celebration of a recent halloween, invited a ghost chaser to conduct a five-part series on the validity of phantoms and hauntings, augmented with pictures and dialogue. Appropriately, the nonsense was aired at six in the evening when the kiddies are glued to the set.

Halloween can be, and to many is, a deadly serious affair. It therefore needs to be debunked of its supernatural aura. Some might even say that it should be discarded as a serious holiday or, at least, revised to fulfill its more Christian delineation as the eve of All Saints' Day. Certainly it should not be continuously exploited by the media as a sounding board for all forms of occult nonsense and pagan ritual. For pagan it is, having originated with pre-Christian Druids or Celts in Northern Europe, who marked the year by four seasonal festivals. The autumn feast took place on November 1. Early Christians, desiring a part in the traditional festivities, created All Saints' Day to coincide with the pagan rites (a method they followed to create most of their other holidays). Satanists—acting true to form—reversed the Christian procedure. Because November 1 was All Saints' Day (All Souls' Day, November 2, memorializes the dead), Satanists established October 31 as an "All Demons' Night." As surely as the Christian martyrs and saints dominate their own holiday, so did the demons permeate the preceding evening. All Hallows' Eve predictably became a time of spells, curses, and horrors for those who did not believe, but for Satanists, particularly the witches, it was a joyous festival and a major sabbat. So it remains in a diluted form, ironically celebrated by Christian society far more vigorously than All Saints' Day.

While the source of halloween is pagan, the accessories are distinctly Satanic: the broom-borne witch, a deference to the Satanic celebration (she is flying to the sabbat); the ghosts and ghouls who fill the night, enlivening the Satanic concept of *all* demons' eve; garish costumes to hide one's true identity; the black cat in recognition of the witch's dreaded familiar; and the candlelit pumpkin or skull, a remembrance of Jack O'Lantern, the earth demon whose lantern served as a beacon for the sabbat and as a signal to mark those farms and homes that were sympathetic to the Satanists and thus deserving of mercy when the terror ("trick or treat") of the night began.

Any modern evil or disaster that occurs on halloween, when

not the result of malicious pranks, is likely a problem of suggestibility. Those who fear to venture out on that evening because of some lurking supernatural terror are probably the same susceptible persons who see ghosts in abandoned rooms and persuade themselves to become ill as a result of the evil eye.

In all fairness, one cannot blame the weaker ones for a certain amount of legitimate fear when they learn that in New York City, Chicago, or Los Angeles, even in the 1970s, covens and cults dedicated to Satanism gather to celebrate their sacred festival with all the fervor of Christians on Christmas Eve.

Recognizing the widespread use of drugs and dedication to evil that most of these groups purport, added to the general recklessness of modern life, one may indeed be advised to lock himself in his house during halloween. There he may ponder the irony of the whole affair: a "Christian" holiday, the major aspects of which are founded in Satanism—a modern sabbat in which all the quacks and demons of our day take to the air, via radio and television, to advertise their gibberish.

Levitation

According to occult ideology, both objects and people are capable of levitating or lifting off the floor, and in defiance of mechanics and gravity, they may float, fly, or otherwise transvect themselves by means of supernatural forces.

St. Joseph of Copertino, an Italian monk, achieved a widespread reputation in the seventeenth century with his reported flights over Italy. Several contemporary witnesses, including Pope Urban XIII, attested to the Friar's unearthly levitational powers.

A more recent and better documented case is that of Daniel Dunglas Home (pronounced Hume), called by Eileen Garrett "the greatest physical medium ever known." Judging from his reported powers, one would think that Home should have been one of the wealthiest and most influential men in the world. For a time it seemed as though he was just that, mingling as he did with princes and kings and finding special favor with Empress Eugénie of France. Despite his well-placed connections, however, Home was expelled from Rome as a sorcerer in the early 1860s, and in 1866 he was involved in a lawsuit in which he failed to prove satisfactorily his supernatural power and lost out on a settlement of £ 60,000. He died in 1886, neither powerful nor wealthy despite the authenticity ascribed to his wonders by several leading scientific figures of the day.

Home had his detractors as well. The great poet Robert Browning, with Home in mind, wrote a lengthy dramatic narrative entitled *Mr. Sludge, "The Medium"* (1864), in which the poet expresses contempt for Sludge's fraudulent impostures: ("I cheated when I could," says Sludge, "rapped with my toe joints, set sham hands at work . . .").

To occultists, Home remains something of a demigod; his vaunted reputation rests chiefly upon fantastic feats of levitation that were extensively witnessed and studied in the nineteenth century. Sir William Crookes, the physicist, chemist, and founder, in 1898, of the Society for Psychical Research in London, was one of Home's most ardent champions. Here is his testimony written in the prestigious *Quarterly Journal of Science:*

> On one occasion he [Home] went to a clear part of the room and after standing quietly for a minute, told us he was rising. I saw him slowly rise up . . . and remain about six inches off the ground for several seconds. Then slowly descend . . .

On December 13, 1868, at Number 5 Buckingham Gate, London, Home was reported to have opened a window in one room, apparently floated out of that window and appeared standing outside another window in another room—three stories off the ground! The eyewitness on that occasion reported the event in great detail:

> He [Home] told me to open the window as it was before. I did so and he told me to stand a little distance off. He then went through the open space, head first and quite rapidly. His body was nearly

horizontal and apparently rigid. He came in again, feet foremost, and we returned to the other room.

The eyewitness was Lord Adare, Earl of Dunraven, a respected correspondent for the *Daily Telegraph* and President of the Royal Astronomical Society.

Levitation was apparently not the only fantastic feat Home could perform. On various occasions—all of them witnessed— he put his hands and face into an open flame without any obvious harm. He also caused an accordion to play by itself, or to be played by what Lady Crookes, wife of Sir William, described as a "cloudy appearance which soon seemed to condense into a distinct human form, clothed in a filmy drapery . . . I could see the sitters through [the form]."

How did Home do it?

The levitational performances were managed either by the employment of imperceptible flying mechanisms, such as those exposed by Houdini in the 1920s or, more likely, by the use of mass hypnosis. Even though mesmerism, as it was then called, was considered and denied by Sir William Crookes as an explanation of the Home phenomenon, it does remain the only logical conclusion in the face of the evidence.

Here, by way of amplification, is the description of an hypnotic experiment carried out in 1887 by Dr. Albert von Schrenck-Notzing, who had studied hypnotic theory with Freud at Bernheim's school in France. The subject was Lina, an alleged medium. While she was in an hypnotic trance, Schrenck-Notzing told her that upon awakening she would be completely unable to see a certain Dr. S. who was there in the room. This post-hypnotic suggestion would continue until the word "palm" was spoken.

Lina awoke and immediately asked where Dr. S. had gone. She could not see him, although he repeatedly passed in front of her. At one point S. caused her to touch him, whereupon Lina became alarmed, perceiving what she thought to be a tactile hallucination. Schrenck-Notzing next handed a tea cup to Dr. S., who took it and held it at arm's length. Lina gasped and rushed to catch the "floating" cup, since to her the item appeared to be levitating. Finally, when the code word "palm" was spoken, she again saw the once "invisible" Dr. S.

There is no reason to doubt the validity of this experiment, since it has often been repeated in one form or another. The author himself experienced a similar set of delusions under the controlled post-hypnotic suggestions of a professional, who in this case caused me to believe that a harpsichord had "disappeared" from its usual place in my living room.

The intended implication here is that D. D. Home similarly hypnotized his witnesses in such a quick and facile way that the deception was totally unknown to them. It is significant to note that in the testimony cited above, William Crookes makes a point of stating that Home "told us he was rising" just before he actually began to ascend. Was Home signaling a post-hypnotic illusion with these words? No doubt the clever illusionist had prearranged certain code words or phrases with his observers; when he uttered one, they would see him as he was; when he uttered the other, they would see what he told them to see.

In Adare's account of 1868, it is reported that before Home went into the room from which he allegedly flew out of the window, he ordered his viewers not to be afraid "and on no account leave your places" (Adare, *Experiences in Spiritualism with D. D. Home*). Home was apparently being cautious, for if all the viewers began walking freely around the various rooms, one of them might have inadvertently bumped into the "invisible" Home and perhaps, unlike Lina, who believed she had encountered a hallucination, he would have realized the fraud. It is noteworthy that when Home allowed Adare a personal inspection of the window trick, only he and Home were present in the second room.

Even the accordion could have been made to perform, as it seemed to, by post-hypnotic suggestion, just as Lina's teacup appeared to be floating in midair. Lady Crookes described a "cloudy form" playing the accordion on one occasion. It is possible that she had not been thoroughly hypnotized and saw, at least partially, the figure of Home as he performed his illusion.

The medium's harmless exposure to fire likewise indicates hypnosis, in this instance self-hypnosis. Or again, by means of mass hypnosis, Home could have convinced his dupes that the embers he touched were blazing hot when in fact they were cold. In some cases the witnesses were also asked to handle allegedly burning coals. Home, once again, probably prearranged two code words: when one was spoken, the coals would visually appear to be blazing; when the other was uttered, the sensation would be the natural one of coldness.

Without motion pictures, only one absolute control of Home's performances, or any similar performances, could disprove the hypnosis theory—namely, a stopwatch control. By this means the time lapse between the first employment of hypnosis and the subsequent rousing would be perceptible. For example, if it had been nine P.M. when the experiment began and if every minute could be accounted for, no employment of hypnosis would seem feasible. But if somewhere in the hour or so of the procedure four or five minutes could not be accounted for by the witnesses, this would patently prove to them that they had been duped by hypnosis.

It should be noted here that a person may be hypnotized without his knowledge, consent, or cooperation and that he may even be obliged to perform anti-social, illegal, or immoral acts in such a state or in a post-hypnotic condition. Simeon Edmunds, an expert on the subject, mentions these points in *Hypnosis and the Supernormal* (1961). Numerous demonstrations of mass hypnosis (by the Menninger brothers, for example), odd behavior under hypnosis, post-hypnotic status, and illusion and telepathy by hypnosis have been carried out by scientists over the last three decades. Some of these "shows" have even taken place on television for the supposed amusement of the viewing audience.

After a ten-year study, two researchers at Stanford University recently came up with startling statistics about the "hypnotizability" of the general population. One quarter seems highly susceptible to hypnosis, they report, and only one in ten completely resistant.

If supernatural levitation is truly possible, it would seem a most conclusive means to dispel persistent skeptics by time-controlled public demonstration. A man or woman walking on air without the aid of trick devices or hypnotic suggestion is, after all, visible proof of something occult. The late Edgar Cayce was supposed to be capable of horizontal levitation, along with his other gifts. But modern exponents of the miracle are not forthcoming at this time. The champion is still D. D. Home. The question is champion of what: levitation or chicanery?

Ouija Boards

Considered a game by many, the Ouija Board is nevertheless a traditional object of veneration among occultists. Since the rise of Spiritualism in the nineteenth century, this simplistic method of divination has gone through several cycles of popularity, peaking in the 1920s and now again showing signs of a mass revival.

Most Ouija Boards are made of polished wood or glossy pasteboard upon which the alphabet, the numbers 1 through 9 plus zero, and the words "Yes" and "No" are arranged in various designs. The instrument of supposed magic is not the board, however, but the planchette, a small object usually shaped like a rounded triangle, which was, in the past, made of pumice or balsa wood, but which today is manufactured out of lightweight plastic or glass. The occultist believes that spirits of the dead guide this planchette, or pointer, across the Ouija

Board so that it spells out meaningful messages or answers to questions ranging from "Will I marry soon?" to "Where did Uncle Joe bury his money belt?"

Usually two players are asked to place their four fingers lightly on either side of the flat planchette. Because it stands on three little feet—affixed with felt tips—this featherweight object easily responds to the imperceptible tension in the players' fingers and hand. As a result, the planchette, after a few seconds, usually begins to glide toward a letter or number on the board. Once this happens, one of the players will unconsciously (or consciously) begin to spell out simple words that may or may not answer the questions at hand. If the planchette, responding to nervous tension, should move first toward the letter E and then to A, the player's subconscious may impell him to gravitate the pointer next toward the letter T or R since EAT and EAR are logical words beginning with EA. The question posed may have been, "What will I do on my vacation?" The subsequent answer, EAT, can be regarded by some as a gross but nonetheless plausible response. EAR requires a bit of interpretation, which occultists are always quick to provide. "You will go to several concerts on your vacation," they may opine since EAR in this case is obviously a symbolic indication.

Needless to say, spirits of the dead do not guide the planchette any more than they cause tables to rise at medium seances. Those who believe otherwise should examine the results when next they place their fingers on the planchette, only this time *firmly,* not lightly. The firmer the touch, the less likely the kinetic reaction that is indispensable for the functioning of the Ouija phenomenon. A logical observer will then ask why the spirits cannot move a planchette that is firmly held? Or why they require such a feather-light touch along with felt tips on the planchette legs and, as some manufacturers recommend, a damp surface on the board itself? Obviously, spirit-magic should be potent enough to overcome a little tactile resistance.

The name of this game, by the way, derives from two foreign

words for "Yes": *Oui* (French) and *Ja* (German). Unfortunately, the Ouija Board for many, in terms of its psychic powers and occult value, is more a No-No than a Yes-Yes even in the 1970s.

Poltergeists

A noisy ghost, producing some sort of rambunctious supernatural tumult, is known in German as poltergeist (translated as noise ghost). The term seems to have originated with Martin Luther in the fifteenth century, and the word eventually entered the English language in the nineteenth century to denote the "merry ghost" phenomenon.

According to the credulous, poltergeists are the chief haunters of haunted houses; they are the ones who rattle chains, cause boards to creak, and recklessly toss objects around, anything from a shower of stones such as the one reported in the sixth century B.C. by the Roman historian Livy to a ten-pound portable phonograph, which was ostensibly hurled across the basement room of the James M. Herrmann residence in Long Island, 1958.

Robbins states that the existence of poltergeists is evidenced by the following manifestations:

1. Noise or knockings without apparent natural origin;
2. Uncontrolled movement (telekinesis) of small objects, such as dishes or bric-a-brac;
3. Disappearance of small objects and their subsequent recovery in unexpected places;
4. Occasional major disasters such as arson.

Like many other investigators, Robbins cites the relationships of the poltergeist syndrome to the proximity of children. "Where fraud has been positively proved," he writes, "the agency responsible for what seemed supernatural or extranormal acts, turned out to be either a naughty and cunning child or a mentally sick adult." The association of poltergeists and people has been given another meaning by Dr. Gertrude R.

Schmeidler of City College, New York, who believes the "poltergeist phenomena may be created by a living person's repressed hostilities." Dr. Nandor Fodor defines this repression as the pubescent child's "unresolved tensions of sexual stress," which take the form of kinetic energy and thereby cause the chaotic results usually ascribed to poltergeists. Dr. J. Gaither Pratt of Duke says that he has never seen objects move as a result of mental power, but he nevertheless believes, as does Fodor, that "there is some sort of influence of mind over matter."

All this kinetic energy business brings up the popular occultic notion of psychokinesis, or PK, a subject that is often examined in tandem with ESP. Its advocates believe that PK defines a mental but nonmuscular influence over objects—in short, a mind-over-matter effect (levitation is sometimes the result). In PK tests conducted by Dr. J. B. Rhine, dice were rolled by subjects who in many cases were reported to have psychokinetic powers. The combination number of seven was sought. Two rolls of seven in a run of twelve throws was considered coincidence or chance by the testers; higher scores of seven were supposedly related to the PK power of the subject. Though scores above two out of twelve were occasionally achieved by Rhine, the PK series did not prove significant in the long run; it proved less meaningful, in fact, than did similarly structured telepathy (ESP) scores.

The conscious employment of PK is not accepted seriously even by parapsychologists as an explanation of the poltergeist syndrome. Most seem to favor instead the unconscious teenage repression theory. In the Herrmann case, a young boy and girl were in the house during most of the alleged poltergeist antics that occurred in February and March, 1958. Dr. Pratt, who inspected the scene, focused his investigation on Jimmy Herrmann, the twelve-year-old boy around whom many of the disturbances took shape. One problem hampered his work: the father of the family refused to allow the use of lie detector tests.

As a result, Pratt was unwilling to endorse completely even the poltergeist-cum-repression theory. To many newsmen and others on the scene, however, there was no other explanation.

Sonic booms, effects of radio waves, drafts from the chimney, and similar natural causes were checked and dismissed. And so, when it appeared that the Herrmann poltergeist had done its worst (tossing about small items and causing bottle caps to pop off their bottles), the case gradually faded from the public eye. As far as anyone knows, the Herrmanns have not been bothered again.

What explanation can be offered for this seemingly honest and puzzling manifestation of a poltergeist in Nassau County, Long Island?

The most reasonable analysis concerns a simple sewage pipe. After prolonged study, an expert in the field came up with the following conclusion. Running under the single-story Herrmann house was one of the town's main sewage conduits. During the winter, ice had formed around the exterior surface of the huge pipe. When the weather turned warmer, the ice slowly melted. This kinetic action, combined with the normal vibrations caused by the heavy flow of sewage within the pipe and with sound waves created by jet planes that frequently flew overhead, created, at different moments, a barrier of strong vibrations that permeated the house and caused the seemingly supernatural motility. It is important to note that many of the more startling manifestations in the Herrmann home occurred in the basement room, the room closest to the conduit. Also of significance is the fact that the manifestation desisted after March, when the thaw was complete.

Such an explanation, although involved, may be found at the root of similar cases, such as the wind-draft "poltergeist" that showed up in Revere, Massachusetts, just prior to the Herrmann disturbance. In this case, a chimney cap was enough to "lay the ghost." Mystics scoff at such logical explanations, denying the coincidence factor and the generally improbable nature of these kinds of events. As complicated as the sewage pipe theory may be, it is no more improbable than the existence of a disjointed, invisible spirit—a spirit called from his eternal repose by the unconscious sexual repression of an adolescent.

Premonitions

Probably the most common sort of "psychic" experience involves premonitions, the ability to sense, or "see," approaching disaster or sorrow. Parapsychologists consider this factor a mystic Early Warning System, vestigial in most people but highly developed in others. Premonition differs from precognition by virtue of its spasmodic nature; premonition seems to occur only when needed and usually in conjunction with dire events that are imminent. Such great faith is placed in the authenticity of these supposedly supernatural warnings that both in London and in New York, Premonition Registries have been established by parapsychologists in order to cull experiences of premonition from men and women throughout the world. The purpose of these efforts is to attempt eventually some form of control over disasters. If enough people, for example, should contact the Premonition Registry and report the same uncanny vision of San Francisco sliding into the sea, those in charge might conceivably communicate their findings to the proper authorities who would evacuate the city—even before seismologists are aware of the impending doom.

Dr. Louisa Rhine, wife of J. B. Rhine, is very enthusiastic about such preventive aspects of premonitions. Properly used, she says, they could function to the "untold advantage of mankind."

Unfortunately for mankind, the results so far are academic, not preventive. In 1967, 600 premonitions were received by the registry in London; only about sixty of these fit the stringent definition of premonition established by the researchers themselves:

A. they must be reported by credible witnesses, prior to the event foreseen;

B. they must describe in detail the forthcoming events;

C. they must be literally fulfilled.

Of the sixty "definitive" cases of 1967, most were concerned with private premonitions, such as deaths in their families or illnesses of their close relatives or friends. In the intervening years, more universal cases, pertaining to political assassinations, earthquakes, landslides, and so forth, have been recorded. Accepting the authenticity of these reports, can we assume that the alleged premonitions are in fact a form of supernatural or divine intervention, or is there an earthbound explanation?

There is a story that is told by an old New England country doctor whose own analysis of the event is most significant.

It was two A.M. on a bad snowy night. The doctor had been asleep for several hours when he suddenly sat up in bed with the premonition that Bill, a neighbor, was about to knock on his door pleading for help. It was Bill's wife Emily, the doctor thought, who was in trouble—perhaps dying. The old gentleman was pondering this apparent premonition when suddenly there was a loud knocking on the door. As the doctor had feared, there stood Bill, shaking and panicky; his wife had awakened in horrible pain and was now writhing on the floor. At once, Bill had hitched up his sleigh and had rushed through the snowbound road with hopes that the doctor would be able to help him.

Fortunately, the doctor, having been aroused by his apparent premonition, was ready at once to travel. Upon arriving at Bill's house, he discovered that Emily had suffered an attack of bleeding ulcers, and he rushed her to the hospital where she was saved.

After the crisis, the old doctor started to ponder the uncanny events of that snowy night, trying to find a rational explanation of his obviously accurate premonition. Was it really of a supernatural origin, he wondered? Had Bill's anxiety somehow broadcast itself over many miles, thereby alerting the doctor to his task? And—more important—did the old man possess certain extrasensory faculties that had been dormant until this time?

The answer was simple: yes, sensory faculties were involved, but only the usual ones—in this case, the doctor's sense of hearing. What happened was this: as he lay asleep that night, the doctor unconsciously heard the sleigh bells on Bill's horses as they raced toward his house. Thesé bells, which the old man had heard many times before, had a special timbre and quality that at once connoted the person of *Bill* to the sleeping man. In the next few seconds, after the first sound of the bells, the sleeping doctor assembled in his unconscious mind the following known facts: Bill is hurrying through a snowstorm to my house in the dead of night. It must be an emergency. What sort of emergency? Emily is an ulcer patient; she had an attack of bleeding ulcers about six months ago. Has she had another? I had better get up, get ready, and try to save her life.

The distinctive sleigh bells had signaled a chain of logical conclusions that proved correct. No supernatural factor was in any way involved; it was the masterful computer-like action of the human brain that was responsible for the premonitionary sensation.

In Chapter Five, self-deceiving tricks of the mind and other psychological factors of alleged precognition were discussed in relation to ESP, prophetic dreams, and premonitions. Especially in the case of simple (short-term) premonitions, there is no doubt that a huge amount of subconscious intuition and/or self-deception is at work.

So it was in the case of the old country doctor and probably in all similar premonitionary flashes or dreams.

Reincarnation

No facet of the occult provokes greater expectations and hopes than does the subject of reincarnation, a phenomenon that implies a conquest of death by virtue of the continuous reappearance of the soul in different forms throughout eternity. As a religious tenet or as a purely philosophical notion, reincarnation cannot be disputed. One need not argue with ideas believed on faith. But when living proof of the phenomenon is offered in demonstration of the occult, the proof must be carefully examined to attest to its supernatural status or to expose its natural explanation.

The rebirth of a deceased personality or an "old soul" in the body of a living person supposedly took place in the case of Bridey Murphy, an Irish girl long dead, who manifested her presence through the confessions, under hypnosis, of a modern American woman. Though heralded as proof positive of a supernatural miracle in the form of reincarnation, the Bridey Murphy case strongly suggests the possibility of psychological regression, the type of oddity most obvious in such cases in which individuals believe themselves to be various figures of renown. Under such regression, conscious personality is submerged, and the presumed or known characteristics of the imaginary or dead celebrity are adopted. The motivation of this quirk is usually a desire to escape from present life and its problems or to aggrandize a dreary existence. Eileen Garrett tells of a woman who believed she had been Eve, mother of all humanity, in her former life. If she had been, said Mrs. Garrett, "the madness of our world can be easily explained."

There is a difference in degree, of course, between the eccentric who believes himself to be Napoleon or Eve and the Bridey Murphy type who is able to convey details allegedly unknown and allegedly accurate. The case of the famous Count of St. Germain fits this latter category (as did Bridey Murphy up to a point). St. Germain was most prominent during the days of Louis XV. Even then, he claimed to be two thousand years old. He had managed to be reincarnated (with the aid of a magic elixir) over and over again from the time he attended the wedding at Cana in the company of Jesus Christ until his reported death in 1784 (he didn't really die at all, say the believers, but reappeared in the nineteenth century as Bulwer-Lytton, the mystic novelist). Certainly there was a huge amount of showmanship connected with St. Germain, but records of the eighteenth century verify a prodigious fund of knowledge, especially of languages, that, at the time, seemed proof of a former life. The fallacy here is that checking these details is extremely difficult. How can one verify, for example, St. Germain's eyewitness information about the Queen of Sheba when historians even now cannot prove that she ever lived?

A vivid imagination and an intuition about history and foreign localities very often create an illusion of prior knowledge that is taken by some as proof of a prior life. In most opinions, this explains even Bridey Murphy's evidence.

For their part, reincarnationists prefer to believe that the prior knowledge in such cases was achieved first-hand but forgotten over the intervening decades or centuries until stimulated by a tangible factor, such as a sight, a sound, or an odor, or until revealed through hypnosis or narcosynthesis. There are three types of this tangible form of reincarnation, according to the believers:

1. Parts of the personality or characteristics of a former soul return to permeate a part of a present life. Buddhists compare this to a flame of a lamp that has been made by the flame of another lamp.

2. A former soul unwilling or unable to die (St. Germain, for example) reincarnates itself over and over in different forms but is essentially the same soul. This process depends greatly on the magic of something such as an elixir of life.

3. The soul of a child or young person cut short by death simply reappears as another child. This is the "second chance" aspect.

The late General George Patton, one of the victorious American commanders of World War II, believed he had lived a former life, at least partially, as a soldier in the battle of Carthage. When coming upon the overgrown ancient battlefield in North Africa, he sensed and even smelled the clash of arms, the flow of blood, and the general turmoil of the fight, although his companions saw and smelled nothing but an empty field. Patton's experience suggests to occultists the partial reincarnation of a Carthaginian soldier's soul in the living body of an American general. An avid reader on the subject of warfare and a man dedicated to the righteous force of arms, Patton was bound to have read many details of the major battles connected with Carthaginian history. These details, coupled with his vivid and mystic imagination, created in him a sort of computer tape that needed only the right set of stimuli to evince the reincarnation illusion. These stimuli appeared when Patton, on the eve of a great battle of his own, came upon that deserted African field. Without apparent clues as to the specific location of the battle, he no doubt unconsciously compiled the mental data he had in reserve and deduced the correct details. Certainly he knew he was close to the battleground as soon as he passed the well-known ruins of Carthage on his way to the front; also, his need to justify or glorify his own heroic role in history may have been a strong contributing factor to the "I was here before" feeling. Patton's experience is something like that of a tourist who has read voraciously about Paris, although he has never been there; years later, on his first visit, he comes to a quiet street and seems to sense that just around the corner there will be a Gothic church and a small bistro. A combination of probable coincidence and a large mental reserve of facts and photographs about Paris may give the semblance that the tourist has lived a "former existence" as a Parisian of the nineteenth century, even as Napoleon.

The St. Germain concept of reincarnation, while less respectable among believers, nevertheless makes an occasional appearance even today. Some occultniks believe that Herbert Marcuse, the controversial Marxist philosopher of Southern California, is Friedrich Nietzsche reincarnated. The late singer Mario Lanza reportedly believed he was, either in part or in whole, the reincarnation of the immortal Enrico Caruso, who died the year Lanza was born. Aleister Crowley had the same notion about Eliphas Levi, who, Crowley said, died in 1875, the same year that Crowley was born (although Levi's birthdate is uncertain). In all of these cases, as in Patton's, it can be observed that the careers are the same, the ambitions alike.

Frequently a present soul believes he has lived a similar or identical life in another time for the purpose of reinforcing his present goals or justifying his life style: "It was always thus, and thus it should stay," he may argue subconsciously. A larger group of reincarnates identify with heroes and celebrities of the past only because their own lives seem so dreary and meaningless. The playwright Pirandello writes of a wealthy but bored Italian aristocrat who voraciously devours biographies about the German Emperor Henry IV. One day the Italian suffers a skull fracture and awakens to believe he is Henry. Reincarnation is not the theme of Pirandello's play, but the drama does indicate how deeply cross-identification can go, especially as a result of trauma (such as an injury) or under the uninhibiting effects of hypnosis.

Reincarnation is often a sentimental subject, since it assumes that previously short-lived individuals, especially children, somehow transmigrate time and space, forcing their way by supernatural means into a newly forming fetus. Such would seem the case with Shanti Devi of Delhi, who, since the age of three, kept talking about a husband she once had in the town of Madura, some hundred miles away. As she grew older, Shanti identified more and more with a young Madura housewife named Lugdi, who had married and died soon after the birth of her first child. Had this discontented spirit somehow possessed the womb of Shanti's mother, thereby to be reincarnated so that she could continue her life? A great deal of evidence pointed in this direction. European and American psychiatrists studied Shanti Devi in the early 1960s. One of them, Dr. Ian Stevenson, after exhaustive work, declared that the case of Shanti Devi was indeed an authentic instance of supernatural reincarnation. In all his investigations, Stevenson had encountered only forty or so similar cases out of hundreds he examined.

Without faulting Dr. Stevenson's research or doubting his

unimpeachable sincerity we must remember that India, where Shanti was born, is the place in the world given most to speculation and hallucination concerning endless transmigrations of the soul, set forth in the Hindu-Buddhist tradition. Imagine the emotions aroused in Delhi and in Madura when Shanti's story first became public knowledge. This occurred at a time before the scientific investigators reached the scene. Were the neighbors and relatives that she encountered as both Shanti and Lugdi objectively responsible in declaring that everything she said or seemed to prophesy was true? How can an investigator who arrived on the scene after the initial "proofs" took place be sure that Shanti had indeed picked out the right husband, as she was alleged to have done when she arrived in Madura? And if she had actually done so, was it a proof of reincarnation, or had the man in question, overcome with the significance of the moment, made some gesture to signal his identity?

What was the mental status of the young girl? Was she actually competent to convey the ideas she spoke or was she misunderstood? Were words put into her mouth, or had she somehow been subconsciously primed by someone—perhaps a religious teacher who wished to reinforce the reincarnation philosophy or someone who knew of Lugdi and fed the facts of her life subliminally to the susceptible Shanti over a period of years?

The possibilities of psychological or natural explanation, however improbable, must always be considered against the more improbable phenomenon of reincarnation as a supernatural force.

Dr. Stevenson himself tells of a case that seemed, at first, to be a study in reincarnation à la Bridey Murphy. A young man under hypnosis appeared to have been, "in a former life," a member of the ancient Oscan culture of Italy. How else could one explain his ability to babble the long-dead Oscan language? Dr. Stevenson took a closer look at the case. The subject, it was discovered, remembered dozing off over an open book and allowing his eyes to scan hypnotically the pages before him. He subliminally absorbed the contents in spite of himself and stored them away in his memory bank, in which some psychiatrists believe every incident, every memory, and every thought remains intact. The exact pages were found; they revealed a chart of the Oscan language. Clearly, subconscious intuition had been at work. The subject had lived only once, but his storehouse of memory, unknown to him, reached back hundreds of years.

Superstitions—Occult Variety

There are almost as many superstitions as there are people to conceive them. Most superstitions have a practical purpose and are rooted in long standing empirical conclusions. The rule of not walking under a ladder, for instance, belongs to the area of practical purpose. In many ways it is safer to walk around a ladder than under it, especially if someone is standing on the ladder or using it as a shaky platform for a huge can of paint. To give more power to the practical purpose of this superstition, early churchmen related the notion to worship of the Trinity (the three persons, the Father, the Son, and the Holy Spirit, in one God). A two-legged ladder open on the street formed a triad (a Trinity); to walk between its legs was, in a sense, to rupture the Trinity—a supposedly dangerous or blasphemous act.

Three popular superstitions, which apparently have no real practical value and which are, in fact, rooted in the occult are not breaking mirrors, knocking on wood, and fear of the number thirteen.

The mirror business, of course, may be as much an example of practical philosophy as not walking under the ladder. Broken mirrors are messy and dangerous. But this is true of broken dishes, bottles, and windows; why are mirrors singled out for special attention?

From their earliest use in the Middle Ages, glass or metal

mirrors were deemed to be strange, unholy inventions. They catered to the sin of vanity, and they reversed the true position of things, making left into right and right into left. By extension, pious people presumed that mirrors reversed the usual good and evil standards of dualism. In short, they considered mirrors the devil's toy. Paracelsus, the fifteenth century magician and physician, invented a magic mirror in which he could reportedly foresee the future and conjure up visions of persons as yet unborn—two rather impious practices, according to orthodox religion.

In light of such considerations, one may wonder why mirrors were not universally smashed as Satanic instruments, why instead such a fear of breaking them has developed. The answer lies in the supposed supernatural power of a mirror to capture the soul of those who look into it. If one's soul was somehow drawn into the looking glass, to break that glass was to break the soul. Significantly, those without souls, such as vampires or ghouls, cast no reflections in mirrors. The seven year's bad luck handed down as a sentence for those who break a mirror is an addendum conceived to strengthen the prohibition. After all, if someone loses his soul, seven years is as likely a time as any to suffer for it.

Knocking on wood may be called a deference to pagan gods and demons who reportedly resided in trees during the time of the Druids (first century B.C.) in Europe. Pliny, the Roman collector of curiosities, pegged the Druids as "a whole tribe of diviners and physicians." They considered the oak tree sacred, not in and of itself but as the domicile of mighty forces, such as Taranis, a vengeful Zeus-like god who harnessed lightning and held it in the tree.

Early non-Christians accepted a wide pantheon of nature gods and wood demons. The latter resided in trees, and one may imagine they were a deified form of termite: bothersome, dangerous, and costly, but nonetheless quite powerful. To dispel these creatures, especially when they might be eavesdropping on human dialogue, one merely kicked, hit, or knocked on the tree. Similarly, all wooden objects (doors, beams, tables) became appropriate for the little ritual, since it was believed that merely by cutting down the tree one did not necessarily vanquish its inhabitants.

Today most people knock on wood when they speak well of a situation or pat themselves on the back. The vengeful wood demons are apparently listening and must be thwarted. The early English expressed another technique of propitiation in an old rhyme: "Turn your cloaks, for fairy folkes are in old oakes." Venerable and quaint as it may be, the wood knocking superstition was nevertheless conceived as a deference to the supernatural. We may hope that it won't signal a return to other Druidic rituals, particularly child sacrifice.

Fear of the number thirteen, sometimes referred to as trisadixaphobia, has no discernible function. Yet even today, many office buildings and apartment houses eliminate the thirteenth floor, several airlines do not schedule a flight thirteen, and one shopkeeper in Greenwich Village recently put a large sign in his window that said: "Help us celebrate surviving our thirteenth year."

Many hostesses forbid thirteen at a dinner table, which seems to commemorate the thirteen celebrants at the Last Supper: the twelve apostles and Christ. One of the men (sometimes called the thirteenth man) was the treacherous Judas Iscariot, who betrayed his leader. At a legendary feast of the Nordic gods, only twelve were invited, but the mischievous fire god Loki intruded, making thirteen. During the party, Loki slew Baldur, a peaceful and beloved hero. Thus in at least two historic precedents, the thirteenth guest brings death.

For this reason, perhaps, the thirteenth Tarot card is called Death, symbolized by a scythe-bearing skeleton. The digits of the number thirteen add up to four $(1 + 3 = 4)$, and from Numerology we know that four is a weak, divisive number; people born with a four in their date or name, it is said, often have enemies plotting against them. The association with death of the Number 13, coupled with the fact that Jesus died on a Friday, makes Friday the thirteenth particularly ominous.

The fear of thirteen is not universal or consistent. In the Indian pantheon there are thirteen Buddhas, and the number thirteen was sacred to the pre-Columbian Mexicans. Even in the United States, thirteen often has a wholesome and pleasant association: the thirteen original colonies, the thirteen feathers in each wing of the American Eagle, thirteen stripes in the flag. In Judaism a boy reaches religious maturity at age thirteen.

Talismans and Amulets

A talisman is a good luck charm that may be worn on the person as a ring or medallion, carried, or merely kept as a possession. An amulet is identical to the talisman except that it is exclusively worn.

The earliest cultures used talismans and amulets for both decorative and propitiatory purposes. Certain items found in Neanderthal graves, such as animal's teeth, may have served for protection. The practice flourished in ancient Egypt and Mesopotamia. The sacred Scarab, or beetle, of the Pharaoh, inscribed against harm, was so popular in its time that literally thousands of these antiquities are still extant and are still used for talisman purposes.

In the Middle Ages, the use of protective devices was rampant. There were amulets to banish incubi and succubi (the fearful yet attractive sexual demons of witchcraft) and dozens of items to ward off the devil—everything from a sprig of garlic to the snout of a wolf nailed to the front door. Words, numbers, anagrams, and signs were likewise effective, especially if they involved a Christian or Jewish symbol, such as a cross or the Star of David; demons despise such remembrances of monotheism.

Perhaps no anachronism persists so steadily as does the use of and faith in amulets and talismans. Modern hippies often sport the Ankh cross of ancient Egypt, a symbol of life; beads, teeth, and the runic Peace symbol are also commonplace in the 1970s. More orthodox individuals, who would never dream of associating with the occult, nevertheless wear religious medals and crosses, Stars of David, or other similar items, all of which were originally intended to bring good fortune and to ward off disaster. The lucky rabbit's foot and four-leaf clover are still relatively popular. Each became a talisman for opposite reasons: the abundance of rabbits indicates fertility and prosperity, while the rarity of four-leaf clovers suggests divine favor and privilege.

Jewelry was first worn as amulets. The decorative aspect was probably incidental. Today those who wear pearls, gems, shells, and glass beads may not realize that they are really sporting amulets, especially when the ornament combines gold and the appropriate astrological stone (diamond for Libra, topaz for Scorpio, etc.). Pictures on the wall, though an integral part of today's decor, began as talismans, or icons, of saints and gods whose graphic presence protected the hearth.

Some examples of unusual talismans of former times are noted here: for good luck—a little bag containing the eye of a woodpecker, a penny with a hole in it, a fragment of a stone fallen from the sky; against slander—heliotrope and a wolf's tooth wrapped in a laurel leaf; against lawsuits—celandine carried on the person together with a mole's heart; against stomach trouble—a buttercup; against toothache—a cinquefoil; against halitosis—wear (or eat) verbena; to ward off demons—a lizard's tooth, freshly picked mandrake root, part of the rope used in a hanging, or a murderer's tooth; against nightmares—a piece of paper inscribed with sacred symbols and anagrams, which is then crushed into a wad and swallowed whole. Do the above and all the other numerous talismans actually work? Yes, in some cases they do, not because of any supernatural power or magnetism, but as a result of self-fulfilling aspirations. A superstitious actress, for example, is likely to fluff her lines or stumble on stage if she forgets to wear her lucky amulet. Yet if the same actress should leave the item behind without knowing it, she is likely to perform as usual without the damaging intervention of subconscious obstacles. Clearly the self-fulfilling goal is essential to the efficacy of talismans and all similar occultic paraphernalia.

Vampires and Werewolves

To the gullible, monsters are believed to be of occultic origin because they are the offspring of demons or other unnatural (ergo supernatural) parentage. This is particularly true of vampires and werewolves, who have reportedly been seen throughout history by terrified eyewitnesses.

In supernatural terms, a vampire is a ghoul unable to die because of his lust for blood. Instead, he sleeps by day in a coffin containing a layer of his native soil. As the sun sets, he stirs. The canine teeth begin to protrude, and an unholy thirst for blood wells up in his impious breast. Assuming the form of a huge bat, he then flies away to seek his victims; these he will drain of their life's blood by injecting his needle-sharp teeth into their jugular veins. Bloated, the monster finally slinks back to his coffin as dawn approaches. Only a wooden stake driven into his heart at the junction of three roads can dispel his evil presence.

Oddly enough this melodramatic description of the human vampire in large part applies to a tiny South American bat called *desmodus rotundus.* Three inches long and covered with rust-colored fur, this gliding rodent can actually siphon blood from a sleeping victim (usually an animal) with its needle-sharp teeth. The existence of these South American animals—which have counterparts in Europe—no doubt evoked the association of a hideous bat with the vampire fiend in transformation.

More to the point was the undoubted presence in history of individuals afflicted with hemothymia, an unnatural but real craving for blood that manifests itself in several forms. Studies in abnormal psychology report numerous cases of this psychosis in which murders are apparently committed not for the usual motive, but solely for the thrill of seeing blood gushing from a wound, usually in the throat. Havelock Ellis reveals several histories of sexual arousal accompanied by the sight of blood. Furthermore, blood drinking cults have been reported in Africa, where certain tribes in the past believed that consuming an enemy's blood emboldened the victor.

Blood mania is part of the modern trend as well. In 1970, artist Neke Carson exhibited soft plastic crosses reportedly filled with blood in veneration of the "new Christ who is Satan." One of his objets d'arts is a transparent vinyl chair that pulses with blood (or its facsimile) when someone sits on it.

It can be seen how the existence of a deranged hemothymiac and the knowledge of the *desmodus rotundus* combined to enforce the vampire legend in Europe. Unfortunately, old stories of vampires are still regarded by some as proof of the occult, whereas they are more probably evidence of pathological psychology.

Much of the same pertains to werewolves. In the popular imagination, these were men who, under the baleful influence of the full moon, suddenly sprouted a coat of shaggy hair and a set of claws and fangs and rushed off on the kill like any ravenous wolf.

Actual werewolves are in fact affected not by the moon (unless psychologically) but rather by hormone disorder. A disease called Cushing's Syndrome is known in medical science. In some versions, it produces rapid and copious hair growth on the face, acute emotional agitation, and often enlargement of the face and hands.

Individuals afflicted with this disease, either because of ostracism or because of the psychotic ramifications of their illness, were, in the past, forced to live apart from society. In conjunction with the "real life" werewolves, European folklore had, by the Middle Ages, established the age-old myth of man-into-beast; wolves are a favorite European form of such metamorphoses. (In India bewitched men become tigers; the choice is apparently dependant on what type of beast is deemed most dangerous in any given locale.)

Werewolves figured in the witch trials of the fifteenth and sixteenth centuries. At Poligny in the early 1500s, three men were tried for transforming themselves into *loups garous* (werewolves) and attacking and killing sheep. The accused were found guilty and duly burned. Greater leniency was shown to Frenchman Jean Grenier in 1603. Apparently Grenier suffered more from the delusion of being a werewolf (lycanthropy) than from the medical aspects of Cushing's Syndrome, since the symptoms he displayed were those of self-induced psychosis. Often he boasted of werewolf practices, admitting to the eating of babies and to mingling with wolf packs. When overcome fully by his delusion, Grenier would don a wolfskin cape and run about in a frenzy, performing harmless but bizarre antics. Doctors examining the suspect wisely decided that he was the victim of "a malady called lycanthropy," induced, they believed, by a demon. As a result of their relatively sober judgment, the judges sentenced Grenier to life imprisonment in a local monastery. Even there, the poor fellow continued to insist that he was a werewolf and a devourer of children.

In modern times, the werewolf supposedly restricts his hauntings to the outskirts of Haitian villages, left to the mercy of voodoo magic. He also frequently appears, along with the vampire, on late-night television, where horror movies are a specialty. In these presentations he is rarely shown for what he is, a diseased and pitiful psychotic, but rather he emerges in the typical twentieth century glorification of evil and terror.

Voodoo

The rituals of voodoo fit in with other aspects of this investigation because any reputed magic or supernatural power they entail can be shown to be merely manifestations of subconscious suggestibility and illusion.

Today voodoo flourishes in Haiti, where it blends aspects of the old snake cults of Dahomey, West Africa, with something resembling Roman Catholic ritual. In this sense, voodoo may be a living form of the heretical cults that plagued the Roman Catholic Church in the first millennium, cults that venerated the saints but at the same time flirted with demons.

In voodoo, the saints, who are in some cases also demons, are called loa; they are invoked through a trance, in much the same way as a spiritualist medium invokes his control. The ritual is elaborate and colorful, overseen by a hungan (priest) and a mamba (priestess), who usually act also as the mediums. After appropriate chanting, dancing, and the sacrifice of a chicken or goat, either the mamba or the hungan begins the transmogrification into the particular loa whose visit is desired by the celebrants. Should the celebrants wish to communicate with the frightful Baron Samedi (master of death), for instance, the hungan will, as he deepens his trance, don the elegant top hat and tails that characterize Baron Samedi. At a given point, when the hungan is fully possessed, he becomes the cheval (the horse) of the loa and figuratively carries the invisible god around on his back while the celebrants crowd around asking him for prophecies and divine protection.

The possession is temporary; in due time the loa returns to his realm and the hungan, to his. The celebrants likewise go their separate ways; after the Saturday night ritual, many attend the Roman Catholic Mass on Sunday morning.

Other aspects of equal psychiatric importance are conducted by voodoo advocates. Enemies are presumably destroyed by use of surrogate wax or rag figures upon which some personal aspect of the victim is attached—a lock of his hair, a nail paring, or an article of his personal attire. Pins and knives may be stuck into the figure's heart, or the item may be burned, twisted, or dismembered, depending on the desired effect. In most cases the intended victim finds the figure in his house or is told of its existence. If he is a believer, the evil spirits soon take hold, not in any supernatural form but as the result of psychosomatic suggestion. Consequently, the man's arm may go numb, his legs may double under him, pain may sear his temples or chest. In some extreme cases death occurs as surely as if the victim had been stabbed or strangled by human hands.

Medieval Europeans who believed they were cursed by witches often became ill and wasted away. Modern men, suffering guilt or repression, also progressively weaken, plagued by psychosomatic maladies that eventually become organically real.

The voodoo dependence on possession is indicative of the psychiatric as opposed to the supernatural basis of the cult. Self-hypnosis, self-fulfilling prophecy, and often catalepsy mingle in an expression of devotion that invariably produces the anticipated visitation of the loa or the destruction of specified enemies.

The cataleptic status achieved by some of the celebrants in voodoo sometimes becomes so severe as to be permanent; such unfortunates are known as zombis. To the Haitians, they are the "living dead" who have emerged from their graves to function as drones.

Drug use has not been verified as essential to voodoo rites, although incense is burned, and certain hard narcotics are known and used in the area. Whether by drugs or by self-induction, the voodoo practitioner manages to achieve a level of detachment and possession unrivaled by any similar cult in the past or by any current mediums.

The temporary transformation of the man into the loa's horse (the god himself) has nothing to do with bewitchment or the occult, nor are the rituals effective without the corresponding susceptibility of the victim. Even so, in many minds, voodoo remains one of the few living proofs of witchcraft, magic, and sorcery.

8

True Magic: An Epilogue

Toward the end of 1970, scientists in Buffalo, New York, synthesized a living cell, an achievement that, according to the *New York Times,* "opens up a new era for artificial life synthesis . . ." At the same time in Great Britain, researchers demonstrated that the nucleus of a skin cell of a fully grown frog transplanted into an unfertilized frog egg from which the nucleus had been removed can (and did) produce a living tadpole and eventually a living frog.

This truly magical and wonderful experiment and the one achieved in Buffalo are just two of hundreds that in any former time would have been considered beyond all possibility: a sorcerer's dream. Indeed, one of the fondest ambitions of medieval sorcerers was to produce, by magic, the homunculus, or "little man," which would one day become a robot-like slave, or *golem.*

No more effective magic wands have ever been waved by any sorcerer, witch, magician, or seer than those employed by the scientist. And yet, when Aldous Huxley described the test-tube babies of *Brave New World,* he did so scornfully, ill at ease with science's conquest of mystery and superstition. He perceived the misuse of knowledge, not its constructive utilization. But the frog experiment just described does not portend the monsters of a mad-scientist movie; it proves that the usual laborious and risky means of reproduction can be, one day, bypassed, thereby increasing our food supply by creating unlimited "test-tube" cattle, fish, poultry, and life forms essential to man.

Experiments in duplicative reproduction, or cloning, give rise to the eventual possibility of recreating, exactly, a given organism, whether it be a carrot, a thoroughbred bull, or a brilliant doctor, pianist, or legislator.

A form of humanoid drone could similarly be produced by cloning or by other genetic revolutions. By such developments, man would be liberated once and for all from slavish labor and drudgery, all of which would be undertaken exclusively by the drones. And lest this eventuality give cause for alarm, in terms of legal or libertarian principles, it should be remembered that such creatures in fact would be less alive than the horses or oxen that now labor in the fields. In a sense they would be merely humanoid extensions of machines.

The progressive causes of today, formulated in agony and causing grave unrest and turbulence, will yield one day to the "true magic" of chemical, biological, and technological science. Cloning is only one example. Another possibility is embryonic surgery, surgery that can remove major defects and psychoses from a fetus prior to birth. Such prenatal rehabilitation or similar chemical rehabilitation for the mentally ill and pathological criminals could one day make mental hospitals and prisons extinct. Even now, experiments with sodium lactate and other body chemicals are leading to the conquest of schizophrenia and appeasement of simple neurosis and anxiety.

There will come a time when barren women will give birth through an intermediary by formulas developed from the frog experiment cited above. The horrors of overpopulation will also yield to simple contraceptive devices breathed in the air. Diseases of every sort will be almost totally overcome by transplants, organ regeneration, and immunology, allowing for the prolonging of a vigorous life by means of artificial parts, some of which will be made of synthetics that can endure for centuries (the false teeth concept extended to every organ). There is also the possibility of providing man with extra hands or detachable "amplifiers" for certain dexterous or seemingly impossible labors.

Death itself may one day be overcome by means of hibernation, suspended animation, transplantation, and the introduction of protein and other elements that would replenish life and retard the currently ineluctable demise of brain cells (100,000 die every day and are not replaced). At such a point in time men could schedule themselves to die, to hibernate, or to live on as each may choose in a world no longer plagued by excess population.

In this new world, a rich long life would truly be worth living. It would be an existence of peace, plenty, and progress, limited not to the planet Earth but extended by means of space technology to the moon and nearby planets. In such a life, conflicts and war would disappear in the wake of mood-controlling chemistry that would diminish aggressiveness, greed, and all anti-social behavior. Knowledge in all areas would be a matter of introducing a cassette-like tape into a brain-connected instrument that would then impart to the individual any information he might require. There would be libraries or funds of such devices from which any man could learn what Einstein knew or what Shakespeare imagined.

Pain would vanish; electronic components would signal deficiencies in the system, and a similar device, probably of a push-button variety, would be available for correction and rehabilitation of body disorders.

The area of human genetics would be opened to undreamed-of forms of improvement by means of algeny (genetic engineering), which, despite the astrologic sign of one's birth, could arrange the hereditary factors in human cells (DNA) so that a baby at birth would be pre-programmed for health, intelligence, endurance, and productivity. As it is now, we do all these things by means of education, medical procedures and psychiatric therapy *after* the birth; even then it takes decades to produce a healthy, intelligent, and productive individual, and in many cases the years are wasted.

These are not idle fantasies. The future is already upon us. Scientists—not precogs—predict that by 1975 medicine will be utilizing extensive transplants, test-tube fertilization of human eggs, implantation of fertilized eggs in the human womb, extensive computerization, mind- and mood-modifying drugs on a widespread basis, and memory erasures, by which traumas are removed from human psychology, therefore removing neurosis and possibly psychosis.

By the year 2000, scientists predict personality and mental reconstruction by algeny, memory and intelligence funds, agronomic cloning, hibernation to extend life, prolongation of youthful vigor, test-tube human life, and organ regeneration.

Beyond the year 2000 the wonders increase: galaxy exploration and civilization, life without aging, cloned creatures for every labor, amplified human parts, and the postponement of death.

Without doubt these amazing but realistic developments must be carefully introduced, carefully controlled for the benefit of society, and utilized with the utmost care and concern for human dignity and development.

But how can these wonders become acceptable and thereby functional in an age that, even partially, subscribes to horoscopes, Tarot cards, witch cults and precogs? How pale and foolish these occult delusions seem against the wonders of science; how much greater hope and dignity the promise of these wonders affords than the semantic fantasies of astrology, numerology, palmistry, the archaic incantations of witchcraft, and the dubious attributes of psychic research.

For those who need faith in a faithless time, there are ample realities; for those who crave magic and mystery, there are myriad wonderments in everyday life that have nothing to do with the occult.

"The mystery of the world is in the visible, not the invisible," Oscar Wilde so wisely said. Nor is it science alone that can give us the required strength and comfort in this admittedly difficult time. Religion and philosophy, unburdened by psychological and spiritual perversions, can surely help those who take the time and have the strength to pursue them. As ever, the individual must "gird up his loins" to face the future—the real future, not one defined by the precog's crystal ball or the mystic's mumbo jumbo.

Bibliography

ADAMS, EVANGELINE. *Astrology: Your Place among the Stars.* New York: Dodd and Mead, 1930.

BELL, ERIC TEMPLE. *The Magic of Numbers.* New York: McGraw-Hill, 1946.

CAVENDISH, RICHARD. *The Black Arts.* New York: Putnam, 1967.

CONSTANT, ALPHONSE LOUIS (ELIPHAS LEVI). *The Key of the Mysteries.* London: Rider, 1969.

CROWLEY, ALEISTER. *Magick in Theory and Practice.* New York: Castle Books, 1929.

CUMONT, FRANZ. *Astrology and Religion among the Greeks and Romans.* New York: Dover, 1960.

EBON, MARTIN, comp. *The Psychic Reader.* New York: World Pub., 1969.

FODOR, NANDOR. *The Haunted Mind: A Psychoanalyst Looks at the Supernatural.* New York: Signet, 1963.

FREUD, SIGMUND. *Collected Papers.* New York: Basic Books, 1959.

GARDNER, GERALD B.   *Witchcraft Today.* London: Jarrods, 1968.

GARRETT, EILEEN J.   *The Sense and Nonsense of Prophecy.* New York: Berkley, 1968.

GRANT, ROBERT M.   *Gnosticism and Early Christianity.* New York: Columbia University Press, 1966.

GRAY, EDEN.   *The Tarot Revealed: A Modern Guide to Reading the Tarot Cards.* New York: Signet, 1969.

HAMON, LOUIS (CHEIRO).   *Palmistry for All.* New York: Arc Books, 1964.

HAMON, LOUIS (CHEIRO).   *When Were You Born?* New York: Arc Books, 1964.

HUGHES, PENNETHORNE.   *Witchcraft.* Baltimore: Penguin, 1965.

HUNT, DOUGLAS and KARI HUNT.   *The Art of Magic.* New York: Atheneum, 1967.

JAMES, EDWIN O.   *Prehistoric Religion: A Study in Prehistoric Archaeology.* New York: Barnes and Noble, 1961.

LA VEY, ANTON S.   *The Satanic Bible.* New York: Avon, 1969.

LEA, HENRY C., comp.   *Materials Toward a History of Witchcraft.* New York: T. Yoseloff, 1957.

LEEK, SYBIL.   *Diary of a Witch.* Englewood Cliffs, New Jersey: Prentice-Hall, 1968.

MACNEICE, LOUIS.   *Astrology.* Garden City, New York: Doubleday, 1954.

MASTERS, R. E. L. and JEAN HOUSTON.   *The Varieties of Psychedelic Experience.* New York: Holt, Rinehart, and Winston, 1966.

MURPHY, GARDNER.   *The Challenge of Psychical Research: A Primer of Parapsychology.* New York: Harper and Row, 1961.

MURRAY, MARGARET A.   *The Witch-Cult in Western Europe: A Study in Anthropology.* Oxford: Clarendon Press, 1962.

POINSOT, M. C.   Introduction to *The Encyclopedia of Occult Sciences.* New York: Tudor, 1939 (1968).

RHINE, JOSEPH B. and J. G. PRATT. *Parapsychology.* Springfield, Illinois: C. C. Thomas, 1957.

ROBBINS, ROSSELL H. *Encyclopedia of Witchcraft and Demonology.* New York: Crown Pub., 1959.

SMITH, SUSY. *Understanding ESP.* New York: Grosset and Dunlap, 1968.

SUMMERS, MONTAGUE. *The History of Witchcraft and Demonology.* New Hyde Park, New York: University Books, 1956.

WAITE, A. E. *Lamps of Western Mysticism.* New York: A. A. Knopf, 1923.

WEDECK, HARRY. *Treasury of Witchcraft.* New York: Philosophical Library, 1961.

Index

Adams, Evangeline, 36, 37
Adare, Lord, Earl of Dunraven, 193, 194
Aeschylus, xiv
Afterlife, 124, 128, 203–209
Ahriman, 72
Air signs, 14
Alchemy, 90, 91
Alexander, Shana, 39
Alexander the Great, 30, 52
Alphabet, numerical equivalents, 43–45
Amulets, 74, 75, 212–214
Apparitions, 177–179
    ectoplasmic appearances, 127, 129, 132, 134
    poltergeists, 198–201
Aquarius, 12
Aquarius, Age of, 38
Aries, 9, 55
Ascendant, 13, 14
Astral projections, 184–186

Astroflash, 2, 24–28
Astrology
    ages, 37, 38
    Chinese, 21, 22
    fallacies of, xv
    fundamentals, 6–9
    history, 2–6
    horary, 32–35
    horoscope, 22–32
    houses of the sky, 17–20
    Mesopotamian, 75–77
    numerology and, 45–48
    palmistry and, 52, 54, 55
    Zodiac, 9–17

Babylon. *See* Mesopotamia
Bajour (swindle), 172, 173, 176
Baptism, Satanic, 115
Bible
    numerical connotations, 41, 42
    prophets, 136, 153.
    See also Christianity

229

Birth Numbers, 44, 45, 49
Black cats, 67
Black magic, 72, 77, 78.
    See also Satanism
Black Mass, 91–95, 110, 115
Black witch. *See* Black magic,
    Satanism
Blood mania, 214, 215
Bonaparte, Napoleon
    numerology, 47, 49–51
    palmistry, 56, 57
    zodiac, 10, 30, 31
Buckland, Raymond, 119

Cabala, 90, 91
    numerical connotations in, 42
    sorcery, 90
    Tarot cards and, 63–65
Caesar, Julius, 10, 30, 31
Cancer, 10
Capricorn, 12
Cards, divination by.
    See Tarotology
Carington, W., 159
Cartomancy. *See* Tarotology
Cayce, Edgar, 144, 145, 196
Cellini, Benvenuto, 178, 179
Chaldea. *See* Mesopotamia
Charms, 212–214
Cheiro, 44–51
Chiromancy. *See* Palmistry
Christianity
    dualism of, 72, 79–81
    Satanism and, 103, 104
    seers, 152, 153
    thirteen, fear of, 211
Circle, use in conjuring, 85, 86
Clairvoyance, 154, 155
    déjà vu, 186–188
Communion, Satanic 110, 115
Conjuring
    procedure, 82–90
    voodoo, 217, 218
Corvo, André, 58, 59

Crandon, Mina (Margery),
    130–132, 179
Criswell, 142
Crookes, Sir William, 192–194
Cross, protection given by,
    86, 212, 213
Crowley, Aleister, 85, 87, 90,
    102, 206
Cults, 71–73, 99–101, 103–105,
    115–121
    Black Mass, 91–95, 110, 115
    devil, 106–109
    sabbats, 109–112
    voodoo, 217, 218
Cushing's Syndrome, 215, 216
Cusps, 13
Déjà vu, 185–188
    Freud, 149, 150

Delphic Oracle, 137
Demons,
    conjuring of, 82–90
    magic and, 71, 72, 77, 78
    offspring, 214–216
    protection from, 212, 213
    voodoo, 217, 218
De Sade, Marquis, 93, 94
Devi, Shanti, 207, 208
Devil. *See* Satan
Devil's mark, 108
Dildos, 117
Dixon, Jeane, 139, 143, 144, 152
Dolls, ritual. *See* Images
Doppelgänger, 184
Doyle, Sir Arthur Conan, 127, 130
Dreams, apparitions in, 183
Drugs
    astral projections, 185
    Delphic Oracle, 137
    hallucinations, 179, 180
    occult, place in, 86, 87, 92
    voodoo, 218
    witches and, 112–114
Dualism, in Christianity, 71–73,
    77–81

Earth signs, 14
Ectoplasmic appearances. *See*
  Apparitions
Edmunds, Simeon, 195
Egypt
  "evil eye," 188
  magic in, 73–75
  talismans and amulets, 212, 213
Elements, influence of, 14
Elixirs, 91, 204, 205
Ellis, Havelock, 179, 180
Ephemerides, 6
Esbats, 110
ESP. *See* Extrasensory perception
Evil eye, 188, 189
Exorcism, Mesopotamian, 76
Extrasensory perception (ESP),
  124, 153–163.
  See also Premonitions

Fascinatio. See Evil eye
Ferenczi, S., 187
Fertility ritual, 111, 112, 116, 117
Fire signs, 14
Fith faths. See Images
Fletcher, 133, 134
Fodor, Nandor, 182, 199
Ford, Arthur, 128, 132–134
Fortune telling, 66–68, 165–176.
  See also Astrology; Palmistry;
    Tarotology
Four-leaf clover, 213
Fox, Kate and Margaret, 126–128
Freud, Sigmund
  on extrasensory perception,
    154, 161–163
  on hallucinations, 180, 181
  on self-hypnosis, 149, 150
Friday the thirteenth, 212
Fuscus, Arellius, 39
Future, divination of,
  ancient, 66–68
  precognition, 124, 135–153
  reader-advisors and, 165–176
  scientific, 222, 223

Gall, Franz Josef 60, 61
Gardner, Gerald B., 118
Gardner, Jeanne, 135, 136, 152, 153
Garrett, Eileen J., 125, 134, 185,
  204
Gebelin, Count de, 65
Gematria, 42
Gemini, 10
Gerard, Maurice, 94, 95
Ghosts. *See* apparitions
Gnosticism, 79, 80
Gods,
  magic, 70–72
  planets named for, 7, 20, 21
Gowdie, Isobel, 105–109, 112, 116
Greece
  astrology, origins in, 3, 4, 7, 20,
    21
  Delphic Oracle, 137
  magic in, 77–79
  numerical philosophy in, 42
Greene, Daniel St. Albin, 120
Grenier, Jean, 216
Grimoires, 82–90
Guthrie Series, 157

Halloween, 189–191
Hallucination, 179–184
Haunted houses, 198–201
Hawthorne, Nathaniel, 182
Hemothymia, 214, 215
Herrmann, James M., 198–200
Hitler, Adolf, 10, 31, 32, 35
Home, Daniel Dunglas, 191–196
Hoover, Herbert, 51
Horary astrology, 32–35
Horoscope, 6, 22–28.
  See also Astrology
Houdini, Harry, 129–134
Houses of the sky, 17–20
Huebner, Louise, 73, 74
Hunt, Douglas, xiii, 158, 159
Hypnosis
  "evil eye" and, 188, 189

Hypnosis *(continued)*
  illusion, 193–196
  psychic's use, 148, 149
  self-hypnosis, 149, 150

Illusions, 162, 182–184, 195, 196.
  See also Apparitions
Images
  Rome, 78
  voodoo, 217, 218
  witchcraft, 106, 119, 120
Incantations
  demon conjuring, 87–89
  Mesopotamia, 75–77
  origins, 73–75
Isis, 73, 188

Jack o' lantern, 190
Jewelry, protective, 213
Joseph, Saint, 191
Jupiter, 7
  numerology, 46
  palmistry, 55
  Tarot card, 64, 65

Kreskin, 146

Ladder, walking under, 209
Lanza, Mario, 206
La Vey, Anton Szandor, 87, 91, 94, 95
Leek, Sybil, 5, 102, 103, 119
Le Normand, Mlle., 56, 57
Leo, 10, 30
Levi, Eliphas, 85, 206
Levitation, 130, 191–196
Libra, 11
Loa, 217
Loups garous. See Werewolves
Lunar year, Chinese, 21, 22
  21, 22
Lycanthropy. *See* Werewolves

Magic, 69–95
  appeal of, 100, 101
  "evil eye," 188
  fallacy of, xvi
  predictions, 219–223
  sorcerer's mass, 91–95
  sorcery, 81–90
  voodoo, 216–218
  witchcraft, 99
Manicheanism, 79, 80
Manson cult, 101, 103, 113, 115
Marcuse, Herbert, 206
Margery. *See* Crandon, Mina
Mars, 7
  numerology, 48
  palmistry, 55
Maskim, 76
Mass. *See* Black Mass
Mathers, Samuel, 102
Medicine
  astrology and, 15, 16
  Mesopotamian, 76, 77
  prophecies, 141, 142
  talismans, 213
Mercury, 7
  numerology, 47
  palmistry, 55
Mesopotamia, 75–77
  astrology in, 2–4, 20, 21
  medicine in, 15, 16
  talismans and amulets, 212, 213
Metoposcopy, 59
Michel de Nostre-Dame, 138, 139
Mind-over-matter, *See*
  Psychokinesis
Mind-reading, 146, 147, 150
Mirror, breaking of, 67, 209, 210
Moon
  astrology, 7–9
  "moon children," 10
  numerology, 46
  palmistry, 55, 56.
  See also Lunar year
Mummy, Egyptian, 74
Murphy, Bridey, 204, 205

Murray, Margaret, A., 106, 107, 110, 116
Mussolini, Benito, 10, 30, 31

Name Numbers, 43–51
Napoleon. *See* Bonaparte, Napoleon
Neptune, 4, 7
  numerology, 47
Nicol, J. Fraser, 156
Nostradamus, 138, 139
Numbers, occult meanings, 44–51
Numerology, 41–51
  thirteen, 211, 212

Occultism, x–xv, 2, 165–176, 219–223
  afterlife, 186
  laws against, 171–173, 176
  superstitions, 209–212
Omens, 67, 68
Orgy, 111, 112, 116, 117
Osiris, 73, 188
Ouija board, 196–198

Paganism
  cults, 71, 72
  halloween and, 190
  magic and, 79
  wood demons, 210, 211
Palladino, Eusapia, 132
Palmistry, 51–59
  interpretation of, 54–56
Paramnesia, 186
Parapsychology, 125, 126.
    See also Extrasensory percep-
      tion; Precognition;
      Psychokinesis; Spiritualism
Patton, George, 205, 206
Perception, tricks of, 183, 184
Phantoms. *See* Apparitions
Philosopher's Stone, 90

Phrenology, 52, 60, 61
Physiognomy, 59, 60
Pictures, protective aspect, 213
Pike, James A., 128
Pisces, 12, 13, 37
PK. *See* Psychokinesis
Planets
  astrology, 5–9
  numerology, 45–48
  palmistry, 54, 55
Pluto, 4, 7
Poltergeist, 198–201
Pont-Saint Esprit, 114
Pratt, J. Gaither, 125, 154, 199, 200
"Pratt, Reverend Mrs. Edna," 168–171
Precognition, 124, 135–154
  déjà vu effect, 187
Premonitions, 161, 162, 201–203
Prentice, Gordon, 143, 144
Prevision. *See* Precognition
Prophecy, xvi
  Biblical, 136
  "God-chosen" prophets, 151–153
  precognition, 124, 135–153
Protection, charms for, 84–86, 212, 213
Psychical research. *See* Extra-
      sensory perception;
      Precognition; Psychokinesis;
      Spiritualism
Psychokinesis, 124, 154, 199
Ptolemaic zodiac, 17–20
Pythagoras, 42

Rabbit's foot, 213
Regression, psychological, 204, 207
Reincarnation, 203–209
  déjà vu effect, 186–188
Religion,
  Christianity, 72, 79–81, 103, 104, 152, 153, 211

Religion *(continued)*
    Satanic. *See* Witchcraft;
        Satanism
    spiritualist churches, 128
Rem, Henri, 58
Rhine, Joseph B., xvi, 125, 154,
    199
Righter, Carroll, 38
Robbins, Rossell H. 92, 104, 106,
    198
Rome
    astrology in, 7, 20, 21
    Fuscus, Arellius, 39
    magic in, 77–79
Rosma, Charles B., 126–128

Sabbats, 109–112, 115–117
Sacrifice, in sorcery, 87
Sagittarius, 11, 12
St. Germain, Count of, 204–206
Salerno, Seigneur of, 20, 21
Samedi, Baron, 217
Satan
    attraction of, 99–101
    charms against, 212, 213
    description, 106–109
    history of, 72, 79, 80
Satanism, 97, 99–101
    activities of, 115–117
    Black Mass, 91–95, 110, 115
    halloween and, 190
    history of, 72, 80, 81, 103–105
    sabbats, 109–112
Saturn, 7
    numerology, 48
    palmistry, 55
Schmeidler, Gertrude R., 198, 199
Schrenck-Notzing, Dr. Albert von,
    193, 194
Science, "magic" of, 219–223
Scorpio, 11
Seances
    ectoplasmic appearances,
        177–179
Fox sisters, 126–128

tricks in, 129–132
Selenians, 8
Sex rites (cults), 70, 111, 112, 116,
    117
Shanti Devi of Delhi, 207, 208
Sinclair, Upton, 157
Solarians, 8
Soleil, Mme., 34
Sorcery. *See* magic
Spells (magic), 73, 74, 78, 188
Spirits. *See* Apparitions;
        Spiritualism
Spiritualism, 123, 124, 126–135
Star of David 86, 212, 213
Stern, Jess, 151
Stevenson, Ian, 207–209
Subconscious, role of, 159, 182,
    187, 205–209, 216–218
Sun
    astrology, 7–9
    numerology, 45
    palmistry, 55
Superstitions, 67, 68, 209–212
Sympathetic magic, 70, 71, 74, 88

Talismans, 212–214
Talmudists, 42
Tarotology, 61–66, 211
Taurus, 10
Telekinesis, 198
Telepathy, 154, 158–161, 195, 196
Thebes, Madame de, 16, 17
Thirteen, fear of, 211, 212
Transvection (flight), 98, 109,
    112–114
Trevor-Roper, Hugh, 104
Tripp, Peter, 181
Trisadixaphobia, 211, 212
Twain, Mark, 183
Tyrrell G., 159

Uranus, 4, 7
    numerology, 47

Vampires, 210, 214–216
Vasilyev, Leonid, 159, 160
Venus
  astrology, 7
  numerology, 47
  palmistry, 55, 56
Vera, Madame, 165–168
Virgo, 10, 11
  palmistry, 55
Voodoo, 216–218

Water signs, 14
Werewolves, 214–216
White magic, 72
Wicca, 97–101

Witchcraft, 81, 97–121
  attraction to, 99–101
  Black Mass, 91–95, 110, 115
  cults, 71–73, 103–105, 118–121
  flight, 112–114
  sabbats, 109–112,
  white, 97–101
Witch's mark, 108
Wood, knocking on, 210, 211
Woodruff, Maurice, 142, 143

Zener card test, 155, 156
Zodiac, 3, 4, 9–20, 37, 38
Zombis, 218
Zoroaster, 72, 80